First World War
and Army of Occupation
War Diary
France, Belgium and Germany

55 DIVISION
164 Infantry Brigade
King's (Liverpool Regiment)
8th Battalion
1 January 1916 - 31 January 1918

WO95/2923/1

The Naval & Military Press Ltd
www.nmarchive.com
Published in association with The National Archives

Published by

The Naval & Military Press Ltd

Unit 10 Ridgewood Industrial Park,

Uckfield, East Sussex,

TN22 5QE England

Tel: +44 (0) 1825 749494

www.naval-military-press.com

www.nmarchive.com

This diary has been reprinted in facsimile from the original. Any imperfections are inevitably reproduced and the quality may fall short of modern type and cartographic standards.

© Crown Copyright
Images reproduced by permission of The National Archives, London, England, 2015.

Contents

Document type	Place/Title	Date From	Date To
Heading	WO95/2923/1 1/8 Battalion Kings Liverpool Reg		
Heading	55th Division 164th Infy Bde 1-8th Bn King's Liverpool Regt Jan 1916-Jan 1918 From 51 Div 154 Bde To171 Bde 57 Div.		
Heading	War Diary Of 1/8th (Irish) Battalion The King's (L'pool Regt.) From January 1st 1916 To January 31st 1916.		
War Diary	Authuile	01/01/1916	02/01/1916
War Diary	Millencourt	03/01/1916	03/01/1916
War Diary	Beaucourt Sur L' Hallue	04/01/1916	04/01/1916
War Diary	Cardonnette	05/01/1916	05/01/1916
War Diary	Picquigny	06/01/1916	06/01/1916
War Diary	Airaines	07/01/1916	31/01/1916
Heading	War Diary Of 1/8 (Irish) Batt. "The Kings" (L'Pool Regt.) From February 1st 1916 To February 29th 1916 Vol X		
War Diary	Airennes	01/02/1916	02/02/1916
War Diary	Candas	03/02/1916	11/02/1916
War Diary	Berneuil	12/02/1916	15/02/1916
War Diary	Amplier	16/02/1916	16/02/1916
War Diary	Saulty	17/02/1916	25/02/1916
Miscellaneous	Bavincourt	26/02/1916	26/02/1916
Miscellaneous	Monchiet	27/02/1916	29/02/1916
Heading	War Diary Of 1/8th (Irish) Bn. "The King's (L'pool Regt.) From March 1st 1916 To March 31st 1916 Vol XI		
War Diary	Monchiet	01/03/1916	02/03/1916
War Diary	Trenches	03/03/1916	08/03/1916
War Diary	Bretencourt	09/03/1916	15/03/1916
War Diary	Bretencourt To Trench	15/03/1916	15/03/1916
War Diary	Trenches	16/03/1916	21/03/1916
War Diary	Monchiet	22/03/1916	27/03/1916
War Diary	Trenches	28/03/1916	31/03/1916
Heading	War Diary Of 1/8 (Irish) Battalion "The Kings" (Liverpool Regt.) From 1st April 1916 To 30th April 1916 Vol 12		
Miscellaneous	O. i/c, Terr. Infy. Records, G.H.Q. 3td Echelon.	26/05/1916	26/05/1916
War Diary	Trenches	01/04/1916	02/04/1916
War Diary	Bretencourt	03/04/1916	09/04/1916
War Diary	Trenches	10/04/1916	18/04/1916
War Diary	Monchiet	19/04/1916	25/04/1916
War Diary	Trenches	26/04/1916	30/04/1916
War Diary	Monchiet	18/04/1916	25/04/1916
War Diary	Trenches	27/04/1916	27/04/1916
War Diary	War Diary Of 1/8 (Irish) Batt. "Kings" (Liverpool Regt.) From May 1st 1916. To 1May 31st 1916. Vol 13		
War Diary	Trenches	01/05/1916	04/05/1916
War Diary	Bretencourt	05/05/1916	12/05/1916
War Diary	Trenches.	12/05/1916	20/05/1916
War Diary	Simencourt	21/05/1916	30/05/1916
War Diary	Simencourt.	30/05/1916	31/05/1916

Miscellaneous	D.A.G. Base.	02/07/1916	02/07/1916
Heading	War Diary 1/8th (Irish) Battalion The King's (L'pool Regt.) From 1st June 1916 To 30th June 1916		
War Diary	Trenches	04/06/1916	20/06/1916
War Diary	Agny	21/06/1916	30/06/1916
Heading	164th Brigade. 55th Division. 1/8th Battalion The King's Liverpool Regiment July 1916		
Heading	War Diary Of The 1/8th Liverpool Regiment. 164th Infantry Brigade. 55th (West Lancashire) Division For The Period 1st July, 1916 To 31st July, 1916		
War Diary	Agny	01/07/1916	03/07/1916
War Diary	Trenches	04/07/1916	13/07/1916
War Diary	Fosseux	14/07/1916	17/07/1916
War Diary	Avesnes	18/07/1916	20/07/1916
War Diary	Ivergny	21/07/1916	21/07/1916
War Diary	Gezaincourt.	22/07/1916	22/07/1916
War Diary	Fienvillers	23/07/1916	25/07/1916
War Diary	Meaulte	25/07/1916	26/07/1916
War Diary	Happy Valley	27/07/1916	30/07/1916
War Diary	Trenches	31/07/1916	31/07/1916
Heading	164th Brigade. 55th Division. 1/8th (Irish) Battalion The King's Liverpool Regiment August 1916		
War Diary	Trenches	01/08/1916	04/08/1916
War Diary	Trenches	31/07/1916	03/08/1916
War Diary	Bronfay Farm	05/08/1916	07/08/1916
War Diary	Trenches	08/08/1916	09/08/1916
War Diary	Bronfay Farm	10/08/1916	14/08/1916
War Diary	Mericourt	15/08/1916	19/08/1916
War Diary	Miannay	20/08/1916	30/08/1916
War Diary	D13 d 28	31/08/1916	31/08/1916
War Diary	D12d Central	31/08/1916	31/08/1916
Miscellaneous	Account Of Operation 8/9th August 1/8 L'pool R.	10/08/1916	10/08/1916
Miscellaneous	Brief Summary Of Messages Sent And Received During Operations.		
Heading	War Diary Of 1/8th (Irish) Bn. "The King's (L'pool Regt.) From 1st September 1916 To 30th Vol 17		
War Diary	D 12d Central	01/09/1916	06/09/1916
War Diary	F 13 A	07/09/1916	10/09/1916
War Diary	Trenches	11/09/1916	12/09/1916
War Diary	Ribemont	13/09/1916	15/09/1916
War Diary	Buire	16/09/1916	16/09/1916
War Diary	F.13. A	17/09/1916	17/09/1916
War Diary	Trenches	18/09/1916	18/09/1916
War Diary	Mametz.	19/09/1916	20/09/1916
War Diary	Trenches	21/09/1916	29/09/1916
War Diary	Dernacourt	30/09/1916	30/09/1916
Miscellaneous	Hd Qrs 164 Infy Bde.	01/10/1916	01/10/1916
Heading	War Diary Of 1/8 (Irish) Batt. King's (Liverpool Regt.) From 1st October 1916 To 31st October 1916 Vol 18		
War Diary		01/10/1916	03/10/1916
War Diary	G 6d 3.4	04/10/1916	14/10/1916
War Diary	I 7d. 33	15/10/1916	21/10/1916
War Diary	Ypres	22/10/1916	23/10/1916
War Diary	St.Jean	24/10/1916	27/10/1916
War Diary	Canal Bank	28/10/1916	30/10/1916
War Diary	B. Camp.	31/10/1916	31/10/1916

Heading	War Diary Of 1/8th (Irish) Battalion The King's (L'pool Regt.) From November 1st 1916 To November 30th 1916. Vol 19		
War Diary	Brandhoek	01/11/1916	07/11/1916
War Diary	Ypres	08/11/1916	08/11/1916
War Diary	Left. Sub Sector	09/11/1916	12/11/1916
War Diary	Ypres	13/11/1916	26/11/1916
War Diary	Elverdinghe	27/11/1916	29/11/1916
Heading	Brandhoek	30/11/1916	30/11/1916
Heading	War Diary Of The 1/8th Liverpool Regt. For The Period 1st December To 31st December 1916 Vol 20		
War Diary	B.Camp	01/12/1916	08/12/1916
War Diary	Ypres.	09/12/1916	13/12/1916
War Diary	Trenches	14/12/1916	18/12/1916
War Diary	Canal Bank Ypres.	19/12/1916	23/12/1916
War Diary	St. Jean.	24/12/1916	28/12/1916
War Diary	B.Camp.	29/12/1916	31/12/1916
Heading	War Diary Of The 1/8th Liverpool For The Period 1/1/17 To 31/1/17 Vol 21		
War Diary	Brandhoek	01/01/1917	07/01/1917
War Diary	Ypres	08/01/1917	12/01/1917
War Diary	Left Sub-Sector.	13/01/1917	16/01/1917
War Diary	Elverdinghe	17/01/1917	23/01/1917
War Diary	E Camp.	24/01/1917	31/01/1917
Heading	War Diary Of 1/8th (Irish) Battalion The King's (L'pool Regt.) From February 1st 1917 To February 28th 1917 Vol 22		
War Diary	E Camp	01/02/1917	03/02/1917
War Diary	Merckeghem	04/02/1917	15/02/1917
War Diary	B Camp	16/02/1917	17/02/1917
War Diary	Ypres	18/02/1917	21/02/1917
War Diary	Potijze	22/02/1917	24/02/1917
War Diary	Ypres	25/02/1917	28/02/1917
Heading	War Diary 1/8th (Irish) King's Liverpool Regt March 1917 Vol 23		
War Diary	Ypres.	01/03/1917	03/03/1917
War Diary	Wieltje-St. Jean Sector.	04/03/1917	09/03/1917
War Diary	Ypres	10/03/1917	13/03/1917
War Diary	Wieltje-St. Jean Sector.	14/03/1917	17/03/1917
War Diary	B Camp.	18/03/1917	28/03/1917
War Diary	Ypres	29/03/1917	31/03/1917
Heading	War Diary Of 1/8th (Irish) Battalion The King's (L'pool Regt.) From April 1st, 1917.to April 30th, 1917.		
War Diary	Ypres	01/04/1917	02/04/1917
War Diary	Wieltje St. Jean Sector.	03/04/1917	07/04/1917
War Diary	Ypres	08/04/1917	12/04/1917
War Diary	Wieltje St Jean Sector	13/04/1917	17/04/1917
War Diary	Y Camp Watou	18/04/1917	18/04/1917
War Diary	Houtkerque	19/04/1917	22/04/1917
War Diary	Arneke	23/04/1917	23/04/1917
War Diary	Eperlecques	24/04/1917	30/04/1917
Heading	War Diary Of 1/8th (Irish) Battalion The King's (L'pool Regt.) From May 1st 1917. To May 31st 1917. Vol 25		
War Diary	Eperlecques.	01/05/1917	06/05/1917
War Diary	Arneke.	07/05/1917	07/05/1917
War Diary	M Camp Poperinghe.	08/05/1917	08/05/1917

War Diary	A Camp Bramdhoek.	09/05/1917	13/05/1917
War Diary	A Camp.	14/05/1917	14/05/1917
War Diary	St-Jean Wieltje Sector.	15/05/1917	19/05/1917
War Diary	St. Jean	20/05/1917	20/05/1917
War Diary	Ypres.	21/05/1917	26/05/1917
War Diary	Wieltje Sector.	27/05/1917	31/05/1917
Heading	1/8th (Irish) Battalion The King's (L'pool Regt.) War Diary For The Month of June. Vol 26		
War Diary	Potijze Sector	01/06/1917	11/06/1917
War Diary	H.I.A.	12/06/1917	12/06/1917
War Diary	Merckeghem.	13/06/1917	16/06/1917
War Diary	Quercamp.	17/06/1917	30/06/1917
Miscellaneous	Report on a Raid Carried Out on the Night of the 5/8th June By the 1/8th (Irish) Battn. Kings Liverpool Regt.		
Heading	1/8th (Irish) Battalion The King's (Liverpool Regiment). War Diary For The Month Of July 1917, Vol 27		
War Diary	Quercamp	01/07/1917	02/07/1917
War Diary	Goldfish Chateau Ypres.	03/07/1917	05/07/1917
War Diary	Goldfish. Chateau.	06/07/1917	09/07/1917
War Diary	Potizje Sector.	10/07/1917	10/07/1917
War Diary	Potizje	11/07/1917	20/07/1917
War Diary	Red Rose Camp.	21/07/1917	21/07/1917
War Diary	Watou No 3 Area	22/07/1917	25/07/1917
War Diary	Concentraion Area H.8 B.	26/07/1917	31/07/1917
Miscellaneous	1/8 Irish/Offe/988.	29/07/1917	29/07/1917
Miscellaneous	To All Ranks On The 55th (West Lancashire) Division.	28/07/1917	28/07/1917
Miscellaneous	164th Inf. Bde. No. G.249.	28/07/1917	28/07/1917
Miscellaneous	Copy.	01/08/1917	01/08/1917
Miscellaneous	55th (West Lancashire) Division. Special Order OF The Day. 3rd August 1917.	03/08/1917	03/08/1917
Miscellaneous	1/8th (Irish) Batt. "King's" (L'pool Regt).	23/07/1917	23/07/1917
Miscellaneous	1/8 (Irish) Batt. "King's" (L'pool R).	26/07/1917	26/07/1917
Miscellaneous	1/8th (Irish) Batt." King's (Liverpool Regt). Operation Order No. 108.	27/07/1917	27/07/1917
Miscellaneous	Narrative Of Action. 31/7/17-1/8/17.		
Miscellaneous	Narrative Of Action. July 31st/Augt 1st/1917.		
Miscellaneous	Narrative Of Action, 31st July/ 1st Augt 1917.		
Miscellaneous	Narrative Of Action, 31st July/ 1st Aug. 1917.		
Miscellaneous	A Company.		
Miscellaneous	Narrative Of Action 31st July/1st Aug. 1917.		
Miscellaneous	Narrative Of Action, 31/7/17-1/8/17.		
Miscellaneous	Narrative of Action 31st July/1st August. 1918.		
Miscellaneous	Headquarters, 164th Infantry Brigade.	25/08/1917	25/08/1917
Miscellaneous	Ward B.6. High St Military Hosp. C-on-M. Manchester. 15/8/17.	15/08/1917	15/08/1917
Miscellaneous	Officers.		
Map	Frezenberg		
Heading	War Diary Of 1/8th (Irish) Battalion The King's (L'pool Regt.) From August 1st 1917 To August 31st 1917. Vol 20		
War Diary	E Of Ypres	31/07/1917	31/07/1917
War Diary	Ypres Original Front Line.	01/08/1917	02/08/1917
War Diary	Original Front Line Trench	02/08/1917	02/08/1917
War Diary	Watou Area (Billets-Camp)	03/08/1917	04/08/1917
War Diary	Bonningues	05/08/1917	31/08/1917

Miscellaneous	1/8th (Irish) Batt." King's" (Liverpool Regt). Narratives of Action 31/7/17-1/8/17.		
Miscellaneous	1/8th (Irish) Batt." King's" (Liverpool Regt).		
Miscellaneous	Copy Of Letter From Capt. J.F. Jones, Adjutant.To Lieut. Colonel E.C. Heath, Comdg. 1/8th L"pool R.		
Miscellaneous	Special Report On Capture Of Schuler Farm. 2nd Fighting Around Wurst. Farm.		
Miscellaneous	Narrative Of action 31st July/1st Augt 1st 1917		
Miscellaneous	Message Form.	31/07/1917	31/07/1917
Map	E.3		
Miscellaneous	Special Order.	06/08/1917	06/08/1917
Miscellaneous	Index To Map		
Miscellaneous	Ward B.6. High St Military Hosp. C-on-M. Manchester. 15/8/17	15/08/1917	15/08/1917
Miscellaneous	55th (West Lancashire) Division, Special Order Of The Day, 3rd August, 1917.	03/08/1917	03/08/1917
Miscellaneous	Address OF The Divisional Commander To 1/4th R. Lan., 1/8th L; Pool R, & 164th T.M. Battery.	08/08/1917	08/08/1917
Heading	D Company.		
Miscellaneous	Narrative of Action 31st July, /1st Aug. 1917.		
Map	E.3.		
Miscellaneous	Message Form.		
Miscellaneous	Narrative of Action 31st July/1st Aug. 1917.		
Miscellaneous	C Company.		
Miscellaneous	Narrative on Action 31st July/1st August. 1917.		
Miscellaneous	B Company.		
Heading	1/8th Liverpool Regt. Sep 1917		
Heading	Appendix No. 5		
Miscellaneous	War Diary of 1/8th (Irish) Battalion The King's (L"pool Regt.) From 1st Sept. 1917 to 30th Vol 29		
War Diary	Bonningues	01/09/1917	14/09/1917
War Diary	Goldfish Chateau Ypres	15/09/1917	18/09/1917
War Diary	Trenches	19/09/1917	23/09/1917
War Diary	Vlamertinghe No 2 Area	24/09/1917	24/09/1917
War Diary	Watou 3 Area	25/09/1917	26/09/1917
War Diary	Lechelle Area	27/09/1917	30/09/1917
Operation(al) Order(s)	1/8th (Irish) Battalion "Kings" (L'pool Regt). Operation Order No. 115.	13/09/1917	13/09/1917
Diagram etc	Order of Battle.		
Operation(al) Order(s)	1/8th (Irish) Batt, K.L.M, Operation Order No.119.	18/09/1917	18/09/1917
Operation(al) Order(s)	1/8th (Irish) Battalion "King's" (L'pool Regt). Operation Order No. 116.	17/09/1917	17/09/1917
Operation(al) Order(s)	1/8th (Irish) Battalion "King's" (L'pool Regt). Operation Order No. 117	17/09/1917	17/09/1917
Operation(al) Order(s)	1/8th (Irish) Battalion "King's" (L'pool Regt). Operation Order No. 118.	18/09/1917	18/09/1917
Operation(al) Order(s)	Operation Order No.119.		
Operation(al) Order(s)	1/8th (Irish) Battalion "King's" (L"pool Regt). Operation Order No113.	09/09/1917	09/09/1917
Miscellaneous	List of Officer, Warrant Officer, N.C. Os. and men Who received awards from the B.G.C. 164th Inf. Bde. on 9/9/17		
Miscellaneous	To all concerned.		
Miscellaneous	Narrative of Action. Sept. 19th to 23rd. 1917. 1/8th (Irish) Battalion "The King's (L"pool Regiment).	29/09/1917	29/09/1917
Miscellaneous	Amendment to Impose Operation Order No. 118.		

Type	Description	Date From	Date To
Operation(al) Order(s)	Addendum To 1/8th (Irish) Battalion K.L.R. Operation Order No. 118.	18/09/1917	18/09/1917
Operation(al) Order(s)	1/8th (Irish) Batt. K.L.R. Operation Order No. 119.	18/09/1917	18/09/1917
Diagram etc	Order d Batt		
Miscellaneous	Narrative Of Action 20/9/17. 23/9/17 by Cpl. Clare, Who Was the only N.C.O. Who Survived in "D" Company.		
Miscellaneous	Narrative Of Action 20/9/17-23/9/17. By 325025 CPl. James, No. 10 Platoon.		
Miscellaneous	Narrative Of Action 20/9/17-23/9/17. by 2/Lt. Cottier W.K. No. 9. Platoon.		
Miscellaneous	Narrative Of Action 20/9/17-23/9/17. by L/Cpl. Bowser, No. 7. Platoon.		
Miscellaneous	Narrative Of Action 20/9/17-23/9/17. by Cpl. Parry. No. 7. Platoon.		
Miscellaneous	Narrative Of Action 20/9/17. 23/9/17. by O.C. 6 Platoon.		
Miscellaneous	Narrative Of Action 20/9/17-23/9/17. by St. H. Cornall. No. 5. Platoon.		
Miscellaneous	Narrative Of Action 20/9/17-23/9/17. by O.C. No. 3. Platoon.		
Miscellaneous	Report on Capture of Schuler Farm, by O.C. No. 2. Platoon.		
Miscellaneous	Narrative of Action, 20/9/17-23/9/17. by O.C. No. 2 Platoon.		
Miscellaneous	Narrative Of Action. 20/9/17-23/9/17. by L/Cpl. Wood. No. 1. Platoon.		
Miscellaneous	L.35.		
Miscellaneous	1/8 Irish/Offe/988.	23/07/1917	23/07/1917
Miscellaneous	I.O.		
Miscellaneous	Operation Order, No. 120 By Lieut. Colonel B.C. Heath. Commanding 1/8th (Irish) Battalion "King's" (L'pool R.)	23/08/1917	23/08/1917
Operation(al) Order(s)	1/8th (Irish) Battalion K.L.R. Operation Order No. 121	25/09/1917	25/09/1917
Operation(al) Order(s)	1/8th (Irish) Battalion K.L.R. Administrative Instructions With reference to Operation Order No.121.	25/09/1917	25/09/1917
Miscellaneous	List of Casualities Sustainers in Operation from 19th to 23 Sept.		
Operation(al) Order(s)	1/8th (Irish) Battalion K.L.R. Administrative Instructions with reference to Operation Order No. 121.	25/09/1917	25/09/1917
Miscellaneous	Narrative Of Action. 20/9/17-23/9/17. By O.C. "A" Coy.		
Miscellaneous	E.3.		
Miscellaneous	Message Form.		
Map	E.3.		
Miscellaneous	Message Form.		
Miscellaneous	55th (West Lancashire) Division Order Of The Day.	23/09/1917	23/09/1917
Miscellaneous	55th (West Lancashire) Division Order Of The Day.	21/09/1917	21/09/1917
Miscellaneous	55th (West Lancashire) Division Order Of The Day.	27/09/1917	27/09/1917
Miscellaneous	55th West Lancashire Division Order Of The Day.	24/09/1917	24/09/1917
Miscellaneous	Ref Division of enemy Counter Attached		
Miscellaneous	Narrative of Action 31st July/1st August. 1917.		
Heading	War Diary 1/8th L'Pool R Oct.1917 Vol 30		
War Diary	Lechelle	01/10/1917	03/10/1917
War Diary	Villers Faucon	04/10/1917	12/10/1917
War Diary	Lempire	13/10/1917	13/10/1917

War Diary	Trenches Lempire Sector (Left)	14/10/1917	18/10/1917
War Diary	Support, Lempire.	19/10/1917	23/10/1917
War Diary	Trenches Left Sector Lempire	24/10/1917	29/10/1917
War Diary	Centre Sector	30/10/1917	31/10/1917
Operation(al) Order(s)	1/8th (Irish) Batt. "The King's" (L'Pool. R) Operation Order No.123.	12/10/1917	12/10/1917
Operation(al) Order(s)	1/8th (Irish) Batt. "The King's" (L'pool Regt) Operation Order No. 124	12/10/1917	12/10/1917
Operation(al) Order(s)	1/8th (Irish) Batt. "The King's" (L'pool Regt). Operation Order No. 126	18/10/1917	18/10/1917
Operation(al) Order(s)	1/8th (Irish) Batt. "The King's" (L'pool Regt). Operation Order No.126.	22/10/1917	22/10/1917
Heading	War Diary 1/8th Lpool R for November 1917 Vol 31		
War Diary	Trenches Centre Sector Lempire.	01/11/1917	02/11/1917
War Diary	Villers Faucon	03/11/1917	16/11/1917
War Diary	Trenches Centre Sector. Lempire.	17/11/1917	22/11/1917
War Diary	Hamel	22/11/1917	30/11/1917
Operation(al) Order(s)	1/8th (Irish) Batt."The King's" (L'pool Regt). Operation Order No. 128.	01/11/1917	01/11/1917
Miscellaneous	1/8th (Irish) Batt."The King's" (L'pool Regt). Administrative Instructions With reference to Operation Order No. 128	02/11/1917	02/11/1917
Operation(al) Order(s)	1/8th (Irish) Battalion "The King's" (L'pool Regt). Operation Order No. 130	15/11/1917	15/11/1917
Operation(al) Order(s)	1/8th (Irish) Battalion "The King's" (L'pool Regt). Administrative Instructions With reference to Operation Order No. 130	15/11/1917	15/11/1917
Miscellaneous	1/8th (Irish) Batt. "The King's" (L'pool Regt). Administrative Instruction No.	17/11/1917	17/11/1917
Miscellaneous	1/8th (Irish) Batt. "The King's" (L'pool Regt).	18/11/1917	18/11/1917
Operation(al) Order(s)	1/8th (Irish) Batt. "The King's" (L"pool Regt). Operation Order No. 131.	18/11/1917	18/11/1917
Operation(al) Order(s)	1/8th (Irish) Battalion "The King's" (L'pool Regt). General Instructions No. 1.With reference to Operation Order No. 131.	18/11/1917	18/11/1917
Operation(al) Order(s)	1/8th (Irish) Battalion "The King's" (L'Pool Regt). Operation Order No. 132	22/11/1917	22/11/1917
Operation(al) Order(s)	1/8th (Irish) Batt. "The King's" (L'pool Regiment). Administrative Instructions With reference to Operation Order No.132.	22/11/1917	22/11/1917
Miscellaneous	A Form Messages And Signals.		
Miscellaneous	1/8th (Irish) Battalion"The King's" (L"pool Regiment). Narrative of Operation East of Lempire-o-20/11/17.	27/11/1917	27/11/1917
Heading	War Diary for December 1917 1/8th (Irish) Bn K.L.R. Vol 32		
War Diary	Bn. In Trenches N.E. Epehy.	01/12/1917	21/12/1917
War Diary	Dennebroeucq	22/12/1917	31/12/1917
Heading	War Diary of The 1/8th Liverpool R For the period 1st to 31st January 1918 Vol 33		
War Diary	Dennebrouq	01/01/1918	31/01/1918
Miscellaneous	B.O.O.1		
Operation(al) Order(s)	1/8th (Irish) Bn. K.L.R. Operation Order No.A	06/12/1917	06/12/1917
Operation(al) Order(s)	1/8th (Irish) Batt. "The King's" (L'pool Regiment). Operation Order No.144		
Operation(al) Order(s)	1/8th (Irish) Batt. "The King's" (Liverpool Ret). Operation Order No.135.	10/12/1917	10/12/1917

Operation(al) Order(s)	1/8th (Irish) Batt. "The King's" (L'pool Regiment). Operation Order No.136	10/12/1917	10/12/1917
Operation(al) Order(s)	1/8th (Irish) Batt. "The King's" (L'pool Regiment). Operation Order No.137.	11/12/1917	11/12/1917
Operation(al) Order(s)	1/8th (Irish) Batt. "The King's" (L'pool Regiment). Operation Order No.138.	12/12/1917	12/12/1917
Miscellaneous	Special Order, To All Of The 1/8th (Irish) Battalion "The King's" (L'pool R).	24/12/1917	24/12/1917
Miscellaneous	Special Order Of The Day, by Lieut. Colonel E.C. Heath D.S.O., Commanding 1/8th (Irish) Batt. King's" (Liverpool Regiment).	16/11/1917	16/11/1917

WO 95
2923/1

1/8 Battalion Kings
Liverpool Reg

55TH DIVISION
164TH INFY BDE

1-8TH BN KING'S LIVERPOOL REGT
JAN 1916 - DEC ~~1917~~ JAN 1918

From 51 Div 154 Bde

To 171 Bde
57 Div.

Absorbing 2/8 Kings L'pool

Box 2923

Confidential.

War Diary.

of

1/8TH (IRISH) BATTALION THE KING'S (L'POOL REGT.)

From January 1st 1916
to January 31st 1916.

WAR DIARY
INTELLIGENCE SUMMARY

Army Form C. 2118.

Place	Date	Hour	Summary of Events and Information	Remarks and references to Appendices
	January 1916			
AUTHUILE	1	-	2nd Lincolns Capt. A.H. MEADOWS assumed command 31/12/15 and 2nd Lincolns gave duty in trenches 1/1/16	
AUTHUILE	2	-	Relieved by 2nd ROYAL INNISKILLING FUSILIERS and 16th LANCASHIRE FUSILIERS (who took over line as far as the Sy. killed)	
			154th INFANTRY BRIGADE relieved by 96th INFANTRY BRIGADE. Battalion marched to MILLENCOURT and there billeted. Casualties - midday to midday Nil.	
MILLENCOURT	3	10.30	Batt. leaves by motor transport. Brigade via HENENCOURT and proceeds to Brigade HQ at D.12/B.04 and BEHENCOURT on L'HALLUE met the BEHENCOURT and 1/6 SCOTTISH RIFLES. Billet and 1/6 SCOTTISH RIFLES. Casualties midday to midday Nil.	
BEAUCOURT sur L'HALLUE	4	10 am	Batt. proceeds route march to CARDONNETTE and then billets with 1/6 SCOTTISH RIFLES. Casualties midday to midday Nil.	
CARDONNETTE	5	-	L'HALLUE - clear up. Brigade at MENTONVILLERS. 51st Division at FLESSELLES. Division now in 13th Corps, left of IVth CORPS, 3/	

Army Form C. 2118.

WAR DIARY
INTELLIGENCE SUMMARY.
(Erase heading not required.)

Place	Date	Hour	Summary of Events and Information	Remarks and references to Appendices
PICQIGNY	6	1-45 p.m.	Batt. proceeds by Brigade route march to PICQUIGNY & there billets for night. 6-1-16. Brigade H.Q. at ARGOEUVES. Batt. now attached to 164th Infantry Brigade, 55th West Lancs. Division. Casualties midday to midday NIL.	JM.
AIRAINES	7	1-30 p.m.	Batt. proceeds by route march to AIRAINES & there billets. Brigade H.Q. at LONGPRE, Division H.Q. at HALLENCOURT. 2/Lt. N.N. LEVENE arrived as reinforcement 7-1-16. Casualties midday to midday NIL.	JM.
AIRAINES	8	-	Batt. rested. General cleaning up of clothing, equipment, &c.	JM.
"	9	-	Church Parade.	JM.
"	10	-	Batt. commenced a course of elementary training as per scheme formulated by the Division.	JM.

Army Form C. 2118.

WAR DIARY
or
INTELLIGENCE SUMMARY.
(Erase heading not required.)

Instructions regarding War Diaries and Intelligence Summaries are contained in F. S. Regs., Part II. and the Staff Manual respectively. Title pages will be prepared in manuscript.

Place	Date	Hour	Summary of Events and Information	Remarks and references to Appendices
AIRAINES	11	-	Training. Specialists under their respective commanders.	JM.
"	12	-	Training. Machine gun section went to BETTENCOURT, to join Bde M.G. Coy.	JM.
"	13	-	Training. All horses were ordered to be kept out of AIRAINES, on account of disease. Transport went to BETTENCOURT.	JM.
"	14	-	Training. 2/Lt. COLLISON, C.B.J., 2/Lt. BAXTER, E.F., 2/Lt. LAMOTHE, G.A. arrived as reinforcements. A serious fire occurred in a stable which we had occupied 2 nights before & several French horses were burnt to death. Our troops assisted largely in the matter & No. 2346 Pte. J. HOLLIS was badly burnt in attempting to rescue the horses. 2/Lt. WOODS, F.P. went to ROUEN as instructor.	JM.
"	15	-	Brigadier's Inspection S.W. of BETTENCOURT. Football now in full swing.	JM.

1577 Wt. W10791/1773 500,000 1/15 D. D. & L. A.D.S.S./Forms/C. 2118.

WAR DIARY
INTELLIGENCE SUMMARY.
(Erase heading not required.)

Army Form C. 2118.

Place	Date	Hour	Summary of Events and Information	Remarks and references to Appendices
AIRAINES	16	—	Church Parade. Capt. CHAMBERLAIN, G.H. went to 3rd Army School on a course. 2/Lt. MOUNTFIELD, R.N.H. evacuated to Field Ambulance	J.M.
"	17	—	Training under Weekly Scheme.	J.M.
"	18	—	Training. Major of AIRAINES thanked the C.O. for the assistance rendered by the inhabitants in putting out the fire on the 14th	J.M.
"	19	—	Batt. Route march scheme (attack on hills EAST of BETTENCOURT)	J.M.
"	20	—	Training.	J.M.
"	21	—	Training in the morning. Afternoon Batt. v 1/4 L.N.L Soccer. No.6 O. 2305 Pte. J Maddox slightly wounded by dummy bomb whilst throwing.	J.M.
"	22	—	Brigadier's Inspection & march past. General EAST of BETTENCOURT.	J.M.

WAR DIARY
or
INTELLIGENCE SUMMARY.
(Erase heading not required.)

Army Form C. 2118.

Place	Date	Hour	Summary of Events and Information	Remarks and references to Appendices
HARPINES	23	—	Church Parade. Practical Lecture on Gas & the use of Tube Smoke Helmet by Capt. HARTLEY, Chemical Adviser to the 3rd Army. All Officers & other rank's went through a gas laden area.	AM
"	24	—	Training. All Specialists (Bombers, Snipers, Scouts, Signallers) actively engaged. 30 & 200 yards Rifle range opened.	AM
"	25	—	Training. Batt. attended the Divisional Baths at BETTENCOURT. 2/Lt. LEVENE, N.N. & 2/Lt. La MOTHE, G.A. to Divisional School of Instruction.	AM
"	26	—	Batt. route march & scheme of attack EAST of BETTENCOURT. 2/Lt. La MOTHE, G.A. evacuated to Hospital.	AM
"	27	—	Training.	AM

Army Form C. 2118.

WAR DIARY
or
INTELLIGENCE SUMMARY.
(Erase heading not required.)

Instructions regarding War Diaries and Intelligence Summaries are contained in F. S. Regs., Part II. and the Staff Manual respectively. Title pages will be prepared in manuscript.

Place	Date	Hour	Summary of Events and Information	Remarks and references to Appendices
AIRAINES	28	—	Training.	JM.
"	29	—	Divisional concentration march & Inspection by 14th Army Corps Commander (Earl of Cavan, K.C.B., M.V.O.), NORTH of HALLENCOURT.	JM.
"	30	—	Church Parade. Lecture at LONGPRÉ by Commandant, 3rd Army Training School, to Officers & Platoon Commanders of Brigade, subject "Esprit de Corps", &c, &c.	JM.
"	31	—	Training. The weekly scheme of training is progressive & inclusive. Boxing Tournament at night. Regiment entry successful, winning 6 events out of 8. Coy "A" marched to CANAPLES relieved one Company 11th Inniskilling Fusiliers. Total Casualties for month 2.	JM.

L A Fagan Lt Col
Comdg 1/8th (Irish) Bn. "The King's" (L'pool Regt)

CONFIDENTIAL

WAR DIARY

of

1/8 (IRISH) BATT. "THE KINGS" (L'POOL REGT.)

from February 1st 1916

to February 29th 1916

Vol X

WAR DIARY
or
INTELLIGENCE SUMMARY.

Army Form C. 2118.

Place	Date	Hour	Summary of Events and Information	Remarks and references to Appendices
AIRENNES	Feb 1		(1st A Coy) Battalion moved into billets for night at BERTEAUCOURT.	J.M.
	2		A & C Coy proceeded to billets at GEZAINCOURT. D Coy to LONGUEVILLETTE. A Coy remained in billets at CANAPLES. Battn. headqrs, Quartrs, Transport, MG, Signallers etc etc to billets at CANDAS	J.M.
CANDAS	3		Company training. Small fatigue parties from each Coy daily	J.M.
"	4		ditto	J.M.
"	5		"	J.M.
"	6		"	J.M.
"	7		"	J.M.
"	8		"	J.M.
"	9		"	J.M.
"	10		"	J.M.
"	11		Whole Battalion moved to billets at BERNEUIL	J.M.
BERNEUIL	12		Company training.	J.M.
"	13		Church Parade. Cleaning up.	J.M.

WAR DIARY
or
INTELLIGENCE SUMMARY.
(Erase heading not required.)

Army Form C. 2118.

Instructions regarding War Diaries and Intelligence Summaries are contained in F.S. Regs., Part II. and the Staff Manual respectively. Title pages will be prepared in manuscript.

Place	Date	Hour	Summary of Events and Information	Remarks and references to Appendices
BERNEUIL	14	—	Company Training.	JMM
"	15		Whole Battalion moved to billets (huts) at AMPLIER (via HEM & DOULLENS). Distance about 11 miles.	JMM
AMPLIER	16		Whole Battalion moved to billets at SAULTY. Distance about 9 miles. Very heavy rain & strong wind made the march seem much further. 2/Lt. F.E. BODEL went on Trench Mortar Course	JMM
SAULTY	17		Companies cleaned up generally.	JMM
"	18		Company training. Received our 4 Lewis Machine Guns.	JMM
"	19		— do — Working party of 60 other ranks.	JMM
"	20		Church Parade. — do — 500 — do — (Corps Line)	JMM
"	21		Company training. Bombing, &c. Heavy snow.	JMM
"	22		— Do. — Working party of 320 other ranks.	JMM
"	23		— Do. — — Do — 200 — do —	JMM
"	24		— Do. — — Do — 160 — do —	JMM
"	25		Concert at Regimental Canteen in the evening. Whole Battalion moved to billets at BAVINCOURT. Distance about 3 miles. Heavy snowstorm.	JMM

WAR DIARY
or
INTELLIGENCE SUMMARY.

(Erase heading not required.)

Army Form C. 2118.

Place	Date	Hour	Summary of Events and Information	Remarks and references to Appendices
BAVINCOURT	26	-	Whole Battalion moved to MONCHIET. Distance about 4½ miles. Billetted in huts built by the French.	
MONCHIET	27	-	Working party of 500 other ranks on Corps Line.	
"	28	-	Company training. Patrols, snipers, Bombers, Lewis Guns, &c.	
"	29	-	- Do -	

90 Fagan Lt. Col.
Comm 1/8th (Irish) Bn. "The King's" (L'pool Regt.)

Confidential.

War Diary
of
1/8th (Irish) Bn. "The King's" (L'pool Regt.)

From March 1st 1916
to March 31st 1916.

Army Form C. 2118.

WAR DIARY
or
INTELLIGENCE SUMMARY.
(Erase heading not required.)

Instructions regarding War Diaries and Intelligence Summaries are contained in F. S. Regs., Part II. and the Staff Manual respectively. Title pages will be prepared in manuscript.

Place	Date	Hour	Summary of Events and Information	Remarks and references to Appendices
MONCHIET	1	—	Company Training. Working party of 200 clearing snow + ice from road. MONCHIET-GOUY.	
"	2	—	Batt. relieved the 1/4. R. LANC. R. in the Right Sub Sector, Centre Section "E" Lines. BRETENCOURT. Four Coys. in the firing line but each Coy. left a Platoon in support. Casualties - NIL.	
TRENCHES	3	—	Very quiet. Casualties - NIL.	
"	4	—	do. Casualties - NIL. 1 Officer (2/Lt. C.J HOWARTH) + 2 O.R's arrived as reinforcements	
"	5	—	Slight shelling. Casualties - NIL.	
"	6	—	do. Casualties - NIL.	
"	7	—	Do. A. Coy. Patrol bombed a German Sap. Casualties NIL. 3 cases of Trench feet reported	

1577 Wt. W10791/1773 500,000 1/15 D. D. & L. A.D.S.S./Forms/C. 2118.

Army Form C. 2118.

(2)

WAR DIARY
INTELLIGENCE SUMMARY.
(Erase heading not required.)

Place	Date	Hour	Summary of Events and Information	Remarks and references to Appendices
	1916 March			
TRENCHES	8	—	Batt. relieved by 1/4 R.LANC.R. Batt. (less 2 Platoons of A Coy left in support) & 1 Platoon in support at SUGAR FACTORY) went into billets at BRETENCOURT.	
BRETENCOURT	9	—	Working parties. 6 Officers & 360 O.Rs. Casualties – 1 O.R. Accidental injury.	
BRETENCOURT	10	—	A Coy at reserve. Working parties. Casualties nil.	
BRETENCOURT	11	—	B Coy at reserve. Working parties. Casualties nil. Valley – accidentally killed (but had always been)	
BRETENCOURT	12	—	C Coy at reserve. Working parties. Casualties nil.	
BRETENCOURT	13	—	D Coy at reserve. Working parties. Casualties nil.	
BRETENCOURT	14	—	A Coy at reserve. Working parties. Casualties – one O.R. wounded.	
BRETENCOURT	15	2 p.m.	B Coy went into trenches. Relieve 1/4 R. LANC R. Regt. on E line – right subsect. by signal. Effect every. Line at BLAIREVILLE. Relief complete 3.35 p.m. [over]	

WAR DIARY

INTELLIGENCE SUMMARY
(Erase heading not required.)

Army Form C. 2118.

Place	Date	Hour	Summary of Events and Information	Remarks and references to Appendices
	March 1916			
BRETENCOURT to Trenches	15th (contd)	—	Dugouts in trench. E1-E2 held by B Co. with one platoon A Co. E3-E4, D Co. Supports C Co. — 2 platoons A Co. in support of Left sub sect and 1 platoon A Co. at SUGAR FACTORY in support of left subsect. Casualties Nil.	
TRENCHES 16	—	B Co. Left a/s LANCS Fus. & Right. C Co. Right a/s 1/5 R. LANC REGT of 166 Brigade.	
TRENCHES	17th	—	Enemy artillery active on BRETENCOURT. Casualties. Nil.	R2
Trenches	18th	—	Quiet. 2/LIEUT COULTHARD and 2/LIEUT PRESCOTT joined Battalion in trenches. Casualties. Nil.	R2
TRENCHES	19th	—	Quiet Day with little activity on either side. Casualties Nil.	R2
Trenches	20th	—	Quiet Day. Shells on Bn sector 41 of 77mm. Casualties. 1 Pte SANDELL B?. Sniper killed while trying to locate enemy sniper. A patrol under Capt A.H. MEADOWS returned with some German wire.	R2
Trenches	21st	—	Bnt was relieved about 5pm by other units of Brigade and marched to MONCHIET. Casualties. Nil	R2

Army Form C. 2118.

WAR DIARY
or
INTELLIGENCE SUMMARY.
(Erase heading not required.)

Instructions regarding War Diaries and Intelligence Summaries are contained in F. S. Regs., Part II. and the Staff Manual respectively. Title pages will be prepared in manuscript.

Place	Date	Hour	Summary of Events and Information	Remarks and references to Appendices
MONCHIET	22nd		A quiet day employed in general cleaning up and small working parties.	B
MONCHIET	23rd		Training in wiring, musketry, Bayonet fighting and Grenade work carried on by companies.	B
MONCHIET	24th		Battalion Training continued. About 4 inches of Snow fell during the night.	B
MONCHIET	25th		Training proceeded with.	
MONCHIET	26th		C of E Church parade cancelled owing to rain. In a football match the Battalion beat the 4th W.L. (Howitzer) Bgde R.F.A. by 6 goals to 1.	B
MONCHIET	27th	2.30 p	A draft of 2/Lt TUNBRIDGE and 2/Lt CLOTHIER and 122 O.R.'s arrived at LARBRET from base and marched to MONCHIET	R
		6.30 p	Battalion (less new draft) marched to trenches by platoons at 200 yards interval the leading platoon crossing DOULLENS—ARRAS road at 6.45 pm, to relieve the 1/4 K.O. Royal Lancaster. R. and 1 Coy 2/5 L.F in support. Relief was complete by 10 pm. The line was held by 2 platoons of each company with two platoons in support near Bn Headquarters. Lunt on right 1/5 K.O.R.L of 166th Bgde on left 2/5 Lancs F. of this brigade.	R
TRENCHES	28th		Very Quiet day. Draft marched to BRETENCOURT to be used for working parties	

WAR DIARY
~~INTELLIGENCE~~ SUMMARY.
(Erase heading not required)

Army Form C. 2118.

Place	Date	Hour	Summary of Events and Information	Remarks and references to Appendices
TRENCHES Continued	28th		2/Lt TONBRIDGE and 2/Lt CLOTHIER joined unit in trenches. 2/Lt PRESCOT [struck through] to hospital. Casualties Nil	
TRENCHES	29th		A quiet day. 36 shells on battalion sector all of 77mm. Casualties Nil. Capt A.H. MEADOWS to hospital. Bn on night 10th Scottish Bn KLR	
TRENCHES	30th		Our artillery was active on a house in BLAIREVILLE with good effect. The enemy replied with rather heavier shells than usual, blowing in a portion of BLAIRVINT trench. Casualties Nil.	
TRENCHES	31st		A quieter day. A sentry of a tenous of new aeroplanes brought down in the German lines. The SUGAR FACTORY was shelled by the enemy with some effect. Casualties Nil	

J.W. Fagan Lt Col
Comdg 1/8th (Irish) Bn. "The King's" (L'pool Regt.)

Vol 12

Confidential
War Diary
of
1/8 (Irish) Battalion "The King's" (Liverpool Regt.)

from 1st April 1916
to 30th April 1916

O. i/c,
 Terr. Infy. Records,
  G.H.Q. 3td Echelon.

Could following addition kindly be inserted in War Diary for April.
"A German prisoner who gave himself up on 21/4/16 to the Battalion on our Left reported that the Germans xuffered 57 casualties - the result of our raid."

26/5/16.

Ireland Capt. & Actg/Adjt.
for O.C. 1/8 Liverpool Regt.

WAR DIARY
or
INTELLIGENCE SUMMARY.
(Erase heading not required.)

Army Form C. 2118.

Place	Date	Hour	Summary of Events and Information	Remarks and references to Appendices
TRENCHES	1/4/16		Quiet day with little shelling. Casualties NIL. Capt. E.H. Murphy to 3rd Army School.	R2
TRENCHES	2/4/16		Bn was relieved less B Coy and marched to BRETENCOURT in Brigade reserve. Relieving unit 1/14 K.O.R.L. B company was left in outpost at QUARRY POST. Casualties NIL	R2
BRETENCOURT	3/4/16		2/Lt SELDON arrived from base. Casualties - NIL. 2/Lt TONBRIDGE to T.M. School	R2
"	4/4/16		Working parties. Casualties NIL	R2
"	5/4/16		Company in QUARRY Post slightly shelled. Casualties NIL	R2
"	6/4/16		Fairly heavy artillery fire on front by own artillery. Casualties NIL	R2
"	7/4/16		Quiet day. Usual working parties. Casualties NIL	R2
"	8/4/16		Capt. A.H. MEADOWS and Lt L.J. DENNIS rejoined unit from hospital and joined B company at QUARRY POST. Casualties NIL	R2
"	9/4/16		Quiet day. Casualties NIL. 2/Lt TOMS arrived from base.	R2
TRENCHES	10/4/16		Bn relieved 1/14 K.O.R.L. during the afternoon. Relief completed by 6.30 p.m. Bn on R. 15 KORL on left 2/5 L.F. Casualties 1 OR wounded	R2
TRENCHES	11/4/16		A wet day. All quiet. Casualties NIL	R2
"	12/4/16		2/Lt L J DENNIS left for T.M. SCHOOL. Casualties NIL	R2

WAR DIARY
INTELLIGENCE SUMMARY

Army Form C. 2118.

Place	Date	Hour	Summary of Events and Information	Remarks and references to Appendices
TRENCHES	13/4/16	—	Much artillery activity by our guns. Leave stopped. Casualties Nil	P2
"	14/4/16	—	Our artillery shelled the BARRIER. Casualties Nil	P2
"	15/4/16	—	T.A.C. given at 10 p.m. (intense artillery bombardment). Casualties Nil	P2
"	16/4/16 and 17/4/16	—	Quiet day. A raiding party of CAPT J.H. MAHON 2/LT P.O. LIMRICH and 2/LT E.F. BAXTER and 43 O.R. went out. The wirecutting party sent out cut through 13 rows of wire but had to return at 3.30 AM with the approach of dawn, leaving their work unfinished. Casualties Nil	P2
"	17/4/16 to 18/4/16	9.6 P. -11.30	A patrol went out to ascertain if the wire cut the previous night had been mended and found it untouched	
"	18/4/16	12 and night	The patrol went out and a wirecutting party of 2 officers and 2 NCO's went out. Commencing to cut wire at 12.30 AM. All the wire except a little triangle was cut by 2.15 AM and an NCO sent back to bring up the storming party of 1 officer and 23 men. The party entered the trench at 2.25 AM. A cable was immediately cut and the parties proceeded along the trench. The left party killed 4 men and bombed dugouts 174 and 176 the right 3 men and bombed a dugout 171. Cries and groans where heard from all the dugouts. No prisoners were obtained. In regaining our trench 2/LT BAXTER was missing and a patrol which went out at	

WAR DIARY
INTELLIGENCE SUMMARY.
(Erase heading not required.)

Army Form C. 2118.

Place	Date	Hour	Summary of Events and Information	Remarks and references to Appendices
TRENCHES	18/4/16	4 AM	ove failed to get any trace of him. Two German helmets were brought in as trophies by the raiding party. Machine guns and artillery supported the raiding party. Casualties 1 Officer (2/Lt E. F. BAXTER) missing. Bn relieved at 6.30 p.m. and marched to MONCHIET but was relieved by 1/4 K.O. Royal Lancaster R.	R2 R2 R2 R2
MONCHIET	19/4/16		Day spent in cleaning up. Casualties Nil.	R2
"	20/4/16		Bn training. Casualties Nil.	R2
"	21/4/16		A and B Coys Inoculated. Casualties Nil	R2
"	22/4/16		C & D Coys and Details Inoculated. Casualties Nil. Draft of 40 O.R. arrived.	R2
"	23/4/16		Easter Sunday. Casualties Nil. Commanding Officer to 3rd Army Conference.	R2
"	24/4/16		An enemy aeroplane dropped a bomb about 110 yds from hutments and killed 13 horses. The Bn team beat team of 2/5 Lancs Fusiliers by 5 – 3.	R2
	25/4/16		Bn training. Casualties Nil	W.D.
TRENCHES	26/4/16		Decorations for N.C.O's. Men who took part in the raid on the 17th & 18th April announced; one D.C.M., three Military Medals. Bn relieved 1/4 K.O.R.L. during the evening. Relief completed 6/10.30 p.m. 2nd unit on R.1/5 K.O.R.L. left 2/5 L.F. Casualties Nil.	W.D.

WAR DIARY
or
INTELLIGENCE SUMMARY.

Army Form C. 2118.

Place	Date	Hour	Summary of Events and Information	Remarks and references to Appendices
TRENCHES	27/4/16		Quiet day. Casualties 1 O.R. wounded	W.D.
"	28/4/16		A patrol under Major Leech went out at dawn and remained between the lines all day, returning at dusk. Casualties NiL 2Lt COLLISON TO DIV. SCHOOL. W.D.	
"	29/4/16		Enemy shelled BLAMONT in afternoon. Several great Casualties 2 O.R. wounded. Commanding Officer returned from 3rd Army Conf Bergevesne. W.D.	
"	30/4/16		Quiet day. Casualties NiL. CAPT. E.M. MURPHY returned from THIRD ARMY SCHOOL W.D.	
			Lieut. Col. The Earl of Lanesborough M.V.O. 2/10th Battalion London Regiment was in trenches with unit for instruction from 11th to 13th April.	

E.G. Tayon Lt. Col.
Comm¹ 1/8th (Irish) Bn. "The King's" (L'pool Regt)

WAR DIARY

INTELLIGENCE SUMMARY

Army Form C. 2118.

Place	Date	Hour	Summary of Events and Information	Remarks and references to Appendices
MONCHIET	18/4/16	7-0 p.m	Regimental bombing raid carried out on night 17/18th April the following telegrams and letters have been received from 164th Infantry Brigade. APPENDIX. "55th Div. wire from AAfollowing from 7th Corps AAA The Corps Commander congratulates General Edwards and the officers and men of the Liverpool Regt on last nights successful raid AAA He considers it was skillfully planned and that its execution reflects great credit on all concerned including the Artillery whose co-operation appears to have been admirable AAA Ends. A and so follows:-	
"	24/4/16		55th (West Lancashire) Division. "The name of ———— 1/8 Liverpool Regt has been brought to my notice for gallant conduct on the night of 17/18th April 1916 at BLAIRVILLE and a record has been made." (Signed) I. MacKenzie. Brigadier General Comm'g 55th (West Lancs) Div." 23rd April 1916 was received for each of the following Officers, N.C.O.'s and men. 2/Lt. (T/Capt) J.H.MAHON. 2/Lt. E.F.BAXTER. 2/Lt. P.O.LIMRICK. Cpl. T.MAHON. Cpl. W.H.DAVIES. Pte. J.McEVOY. Cpl. F.BROPHY.	

WAR DIARY
or
INTELLIGENCE SUMMARY.

Army Form C. 2118.

Place	Date	Hour	Summary of Events and Information	Remarks and references to Appendices
MONCHIET	24/4/16		Pte. P.W. FUSSELL. Pte. T. MUNNERLEY. Sgt. W. McCLELLAND. Pte. W.F. CROWE. Sgt. A.J. BURKE.	
"	25/4/16	4-30 p.m.	"Commander in Chief awards Distinguished Medal to 4474 Sgt. McCLELLAND Military Medals to 4570 Pte. FUSSELL 4565 Pte. CROWE 2248 Sgt. BURKE. AAA Please convey Army - Corps - Division - and Brigade Commanders congratulations."	
TRENCHES	27/4/16		"The Army Commander has read with interest and pleasure the account of the daring and successful raid carried out in the 55th Division by the 1/8th (Irish) Batt. K.L.R. of the 164th Infantry Brigade. Please convey the Army Commanders congratulations to Lieut. Colonel E.A. FAGAN and to the Officers and men who so ably carried out the operation. (Signed) L.E. Bols, Major Gen., General Staff, 3rd Army." 26th April 1916.	

E A Fagan Lt Col
Comm of 1/8th (Irish) Bn. "The King's" (L'pool Regt.)

CONFIDENTIAL.

War Diary
of
1/8 (Irish) Batt. "KING'S" (Liverpool Regt.)

From May 1st 1916.
To May 31st 1916.

WAR DIARY
or
INTELLIGENCE SUMMARY.
(Erase heading not required.)

Army Form C. 2118.

Place	Date	Hour	Summary of Events and Information	Remarks and references to Appendices
TRENCHES	1/5/16		Quiet day. Casualties NIL	W.D.
"	2/5/16		Quiet day. Casualties NIL. MAJOR M. CHARLESWORTH 2/7 DUKE OF WELLINGTONS Regt ordered for instruction	W.D.
"	3/5/16		Line re-adjusted. The BATTALION handed over to 2/5" LAN FUS. the portion of the line left of BLAIRVILLE STREET, and took over from the 10" (SCOTTISH) Bn. K.L.R. (166 BDE) the portion of the front line of G WILLOW STREET and of the support line G DYKE STREET. D. Company moved from left to right of Battalions line to complete this move. Quiet day. Casualties. NIL.	W.D.
	4/5/16		T.A.C. given as 4 A.M. Artillery activity in the afternoon. Bn were relieved less C. Coy and marched to BRETENCOURT in BDE RESERVE. Relieving unit 1/4 K.O.R.L. C. Coy were left in support at QUARRY POST. Casualties, 10.R wounded. LIEUT. J.P. CASTLE and 1 O.R. to THIRD ARMY SCHOOL	W.D.
BRETENCOURT	5/5/16		2Lt. J.S. SHARPE arrived for duty. 2Lt. G.A. LA MOTHE returned from ROUEN. MAJOR M. CHARLESWORTH 2/7 DUKE of WELLINGTONS REGT left. Casualties 1 O.R. died	W.D.
	6/5/16		Training and working parties. 2Lt E.B. PALMER from 17" BN CHESHIRE REGT and 2Lt. R BURROWS from 14" BN CHESHIRE REGT arrived for duty. Casualties 1 O.R. killed	W.D.

WAR DIARY
or
INTELLIGENCE SUMMARY.
(Erase heading not required.)

Army Form C. 2118.

Place	Date	Hour	Summary of Events and Information	Remarks and references to Appendices
BRIENCOURT	7th		Quiet Day. Batt furnished usual working parties. Casualties Nil	
	8th		Slight Shelling. Usual working parties. Casualties Nil	
	9th		Quiet Day. Casualties Nil	
	10th		C coy in BEAUMONT supports shelled with 5.9" shells. Casualties 1 OR severely wounded	B2
	11th		Quiet Day. A.T.A.C. was given to Brigade Reserve. CAPT HEWSON YORKS & LANCS R arrived for duty functions	B2 B2 B2
	12th		All Quiet. Usual working parties. 53rd Division transferred from VII to VI Corps	B2
			Battalion relieved 9th K.O.R.L. in trenches, taking over the new line. A coy held the line temporarily held by D coy when last in the Trenches. The line was held by all 4 Coys with 2 platoons A. 1 platoon B. 1 platoon C and 2 platoons D coy in support. Units on right 16th Scottish R.L.R. to left 9/5 lines Fusiliers. Casualties Nil	B2
TRENCHES	13th		Quiet in Trenches. Each coy furnished standing patrols outside the wire. Casualties Nil	B2
"	14th		Quiet Day. 18th R BED raided by night. Casualties Nil	
	15th		Quiet Day. Our artillery was fairly active without response. Casualties Nil	B
	16th		Quiet Day. A standing patrol came in contact with hostile patrol who were driven off. Casualties 1 OR killed 1 OR wounded.	B2 B2
	17th		Very little activity. 1 OR wounded.	B2

WAR DIARY
or
INTELLIGENCE SUMMARY.
(Erase heading not required.)

Army Form C. 2118.

Place	Date	Hour	Summary of Events and Information	Remarks and references to Appendices
TRENCHES.	18th		Little activity during daylight. A patrol of 1 NCO & 8 OR was driven out of OSIER BED and suffered 4 casualties. The OSIER BED was then reached with MG fire. Casualties 4 OR wounded	A2
	19th		Bn on left 1/5 K.O.R.L. Enemy snipers increased slightly. Casualties 1 OR killed 2 OR wounded.	A2
	20th		Bn was relieved by 1/4 K.O.R.L. and marched to SIMENCOURT to Divisional Reserve Relief was complete by 5 pm. Casualties 1 OR Killed	A2
SIMENCOURT	21st		Day devoted to Church parades and cleaning up. Casualties Nil	A2
"	22nd		Battalion training and working parties. Casualties Nil	A2
"	23rd		Battalion Training and working Parties. Casualties Nil	A2
"	24th		Battalion training, working parties. Casualties Nil	ERP
"	25th		Battalion training, working parties. Casualties Nil	ERP
"	26		Battalion training, working parties. Casualties Nil	ERP
"	27		Battalion training, working parties. Casualties Nil	ERP
"	28		Battalion training, working parties. Casualties Nil	ERP
"	29		Battalion training working parties. Casualties Nil	ERP
"	30		Battalion training, working parties. Casualties Nil	ERP

WAR DIARY
or
INTELLIGENCE SUMMARY.

(Erase heading not required.)

Army Form C. 2118.

Place	Date	Hour	Summary of Events and Information	Remarks and references to Appendices
Suncoin	30/5/16		Battalion having working parties Crawshawbut	E.R.P.
" " "	30/5/16		The following Officers reported for Duty. W.D.G.B. M^cCABE 2/Lt WHITESIDE	E.R.P.
			2/Lt W.G. LOFTHOUSE 2/Lt J.A. SISSON 2/Lt W.H. SPARGO 2/Lt A.O. HORNER 2/Lt W.D.H. LILLEY	
			2/Lt E.P. LOUP from 3/8 (Irish) K.L.R.	E.R.P
			E.W. Fagan Lt. Col.	
			Commdg. 1/8th (Irish) Bn. "The King's" (L'pool Regt.)	
	31/5/16		The following wire was received from 164 Infantry Brigade:—	
			"55th Div Wire begins. AAA Please give my hearty congratulations to	
			Liverpool Irish on being one of the 6 Territorial Battalion specially mentioned	
			in the Commander in Chief's last dispatch published to-day having done good	
			work in repelling or carrying out raids. AAA."	

D.A.G.
　　Base.

　　　　Herewith War Diary of this unit for
the month of June, 1916.

2/7/16.

　　　　　　　　　　　E.H. Fagan
　　　　　　　Commdg. 1/8 Liverpool Regt.　　　　Lt. Col.

WAR DIARY

1/8TH (IRISH) BATTALION THE KING'S (L'POOL REGT.)

from 1st June 1916
to 30th June 1916

WAR DIARY or INTELLIGENCE SUMMARY.

Army Form C. 2118.

Place	Date	Hour	Summary of Events and Information	Remarks and references to Appendices
TRENCHES	4.6.16	10.45pm	Battalion relieved 7th K.O.R.L. Companies taking over the same part of the line as before. Between 1½ & ½ AM a heavy bombardment towards the S.W. of RANSART. Casualties 1 wounded.	ERP
"	5.6.16		Quiet day. Casualties nil. Patrols were sent out, but they did not come into contact with enemy patrols.	ERP
"	6.6.16		Artillery fairly active on both sides. No much damage caused. Casualties nil.	ERP
"	7.6.16		Line quiet. Casualties Nil.	ERP
"	8.6.16		Quiet day. Moving patrols at night. Casualties 1 wounded (accidentally)	ERP
"	9.6.16		Quiet day. Standing patrols at night. Casualties nil.	ERP
"	10.6.16		Quiet day. 2/Lt J.B. McCABE attached Lieut. 8th Liverpool Scottish Artillery very quiet	ERP
"	11.6.16		Frontage quiet. 2/Lt W.F. ELLIS report for duty from 2/K (York) K.L.R. Casualties Nil.	ERP
"	12.6.16		Frontage quiet. Casualties Nil.	ERP
"	13.6.16		Enemy artillery sent about 30 shell round BEAUMONT doing no damage. Casualties Nil. 1st A.S. reinforcement.	ERP
"	14.6.16		Quiet day. Casualties Nil.	ERP

Army Form C. 2118.

WAR DIARY
or
INTELLIGENCE SUMMARY.
(Erase heading not required.)

Instructions regarding War Diaries and Intelligence Summaries are contained in F.S. Regs., Part II. and the Staff Manual respectively. Title pages will be prepared in manuscript.

Place	Date	Hour	Summary of Events and Information	Remarks and references to Appendices
TRENCHES	15/6/16		Enemy machine guns very active on BLANCOURT Casualties 1 O.R. wounded	ERP
"	16/6/16		Quiet day Casualties NIL	ERP
"	17/6/16		Enemy artillery fairly active but no damage done Casualties Nil	ERP
"	18/6/16		Amendment the following Officers were mentioned in Sir DOUGLAS HAIG'S dispatch dated 16.6.16 Lt Col E.A FAGAN MAJOR H.LEECH CAPT G.S. BRIGHTEN CAPT E.M MURPHY Lt J.P. CASTLE LT E.F OVCHAVD.	
"	18/6/16		Quiet day 2/Lt D.J.B. McCABE returns from sick leave Casualties Nil 4 O.R. on reinforcement.	ERP
"	19/6/16		Quiet day Casualties Nil	ERP
"	20/6/16	9.30 pm	"23" Battalion relieved by 1/10 "Liverpool Scottish" proceed to BRETENCOURT Battalion moved to AGNY A"D" Co's going into Reserve A"B"C going in Reserve Casualties NIL.	ERP
AGNY	21/6/16		Battalion training working parties A"D" Coys went into supports to 1/4 Kings Own; Casualties Nil	ERP
"	22/6/16		Battalion training working parties Casualties N.L. The following N.C.O awarded the Military Medal 2702 L/Cpl (now Sergt) Thompson. W. per B"" Orders N° 141 d. 22.6.16	ERP

WAR DIARY
or
INTELLIGENCE SUMMARY.
(Erase heading not required.)

Army Form C. 2118.

Place	Date	Hour	Summary of Events and Information	Remarks and references to Appendices
Agny	23/6/16		Quiet day. Battalion training & working parties "B" Coy moved into Reserve. Casualties Nil	ERP
"	24/6/16		Battalion training working parties. Heavy bombardment in progress all day at BLAIREVILLE. Casualties 2 O.R. wounded (gassed shell). 6 D.R. gassed in trenches.	ERP
"	25/6/16		Battalion training working parties. Heavy bombardment in progress between 2pm & 3pm at BLAIREVILLE. Casualties Nil	ERP
"	26.6.16		Battalion training working parties. Heavy bombardment at BLAIREVILLE. Casualties Nil.	ERP
"	27.6.16		Battalion training working parties. "D" Coy relieved from support by "A" Coy 9 1/4th King's numerous into village about 2 AM.	
		3.10 - 3.30	AGNY shelled to damage done. Series of bombardments at BLAIREVILLE. Casualties 2 O.R. wounded	ERP
"	28.6.16		Battalion training working parties. Casualties Nil.	
		3pm-5pm	Heavy bombardment. Two Sad over at Blairville. Mobile artillery replying weakly.	ERP
"	29.6.16		Battalion training working parties. Agny shelled between 3 AM & 4 AM	ERP

WAR DIARY
or
INTELLIGENCE SUMMARY.

(Erase heading not required.)

Army Form C. 2118.

Place	Date	Hour	Summary of Events and Information	Remarks and references to Appendices
ASNY	29/6/16		Again between 3pm & 6pm doing considerable damage. Casualties 4. OR wounded. Major SMITH goes to take command of SALVAGE VI Corps.	EAP EAP
—	30/6/16		Battalion training, working parties. Casualties Nil.	

E W Ryan Lt. Col.
Comm'dg 1/8th (Irish) Bn. "The King's" (L'pool Regt.)

164th Brigade.

55th Division.

1/8th BATTALION

THE KING'S LIVERPOOL REGIMENT

JULY 1 9 1 6

War Diary,

of the

1/8th Liverpool Regiment,

164th Infantry Brigade.

55th (West Lancashire) Division

for the period

1st July, 1916 to 31st July, 1916.

Place	Date	Hour	Summary of Events and Information	Remarks and references to Appendices
AGNY	1/7/16		Battalion training, working parties. About 12 shells fired into village causing casualties 2 killed 6 wounded.	RAP
"	2/7/16		Battalion training, working parties. D Coy moves into support to 1/4 Kings Own Casualties Nil	RAP
"	3/7/16		Battalion training working parties. Casualties Nil	RAP
TRENCHES	4/7/16	6 pm	Battalion relieves 1/4 King Own Trenches extend from 9,1 to 9,12 from R1, R2 to left D@ (B) A Coy Bn platoon each company in support. Casualties N.2. Enemy active with trench mortars. Casualties N.2	RAP
"	5/7/16		Quiet day Casualties 3 wounded (one self inflicted)	RAP
"	6/7/16		Quiet day Casualties 1 killed, 4 (Green + N.C.O.) & (S) Bn ?	
"	7/7/16		Heavy bombardment in progress on our R.T.O. probably at Albert. Casualties 1 killed 1 wounded (self inflicted) two of our aeroplanes brought down on enemies field and German over other came down under control W/ely O & in which	RAP
"	8/7/16		Quiet day. Casualties 1 wounded Casualties N.L.	RAP
"	9/7/16		2/Lynch E.F. reported for duty Lt Lockhart L.A.R. 2/Tipping W	RAP
"	10/7/16		Quiet day 2 k. 4 Green & N.C.O ? '(S) Bn ? Wellingtons return W/Cu 6nd ?	RAP

INTELLIGENCE SUMMARY.
(Erase heading not required.)

and the Staff Manual respectively. Title pages will be prepared in manuscript.

Place	Date	Hour	Summary of Events and Information	Remarks and references to Appendices
Trenches	11.7.16		Casualties 3 other wounded on Machine gun duty	S&P.
"	12.7.16		Quiet day Casualties Nil.	S&P.
"	13.7.16	12.30AM	Battalion is relieved by 1/5 South Lancs R.f.K. Relief complete at 2.30 AM Companies march independently to FOSSEUX. Casualties 6 other wounded	S&P.
FOSSEUX	14.7.16		Battalion training new practice trenches generally training Casualties Nil	S&P.
"	15.7.16		Battalion training over practice trenches Casualties Nil	S&P.
"	16.7.16		Battalion training on practice track Casualties Nil	S&P.
"	17.7.16		Battalion training. Battalion marched into billets at AVESNES-LE-COMTE	S&P.
AVESNES	18.7.16		Battalion training into practice trench training Casualties Nil	S&P.
"	19.7.16		Battalion training in preparation trenches Casualties N.L.	S&P.
"	20.7.16	7AM	Battalion parades at 7 AM march to IVERGNY arriving at 10AM Casualties Nil	S&P.
IVERGNY	21.7.16	7AM	Battalion parades at 7AM march to SEZAINCOURT Casualties Nil	S&P.
SEZAINCOURT	22.7.16	7AM	Battalion parades at 7AM march to FIENVILLERS Casualties Nil	S&P.
FIENVILLERS	23.7.16		Church parades Casualties Nil.	S&P.
"	24.7.16		Battalion training Casualties Nil	S&P.
"	25.7.16	8.30AM	Battalion parades at 8.30 AM march to Candas Station entrain thereon at MERÉCOURT	

INTELLIGENCE SUMMARY.

(Erase heading not required.)

Summaries are contained in F.S. Regs., Part II. and the Staff Manual respectively. Title pages will be prepared in manuscript.

Place	Date	Hour	Summary of Events and Information	Remarks and references to Appendices
MÉAULTE	25.7.16		March to MÉAULTE	
" "	26.7.16		Battalion parade at 3.45 pm march to HAPPY VALLEY Casualties NIL EAP;	
HAPPY VALLEY	27.7.16		Battalion training Casualties NIL	EAP
" "	28.7.16		Battalion training Casualties NIL	EAP
" "	29.7.16		Battalion training Casualties NIL	EAP
" "	30.7.16		Battalion parade at 8 pm moves to trenches EAST of TRONES WOOD Casualties NIL EAP	
Trenches	31.7.16		Relief complete at 4 AM Battalion relieves 'Battalions of 30' Division. Two (C.D) Companies in front line A. B Coys in 2nd line 2/S LANC Fusiliers being in support. 2/LT C.W. TOMS + 2/LT C.J. HOWARTH wounded Casualties 1 OR KILLED 16 wounded BEP	

J A Forsyth
Lt Col.
Comm. 1/8th (Irish) Bn. "The King's" (L'pool Regt.)

164th Brigade.
55th Division.

1/8th (Irish) BATTALION

THE KING'S LIVERPOOL REGIMENT

AUGUST 1 9 1 6

Account of operations attached.

Army Form C. 2118.

WAR DIARY
or
INTELLIGENCE SUMMARY.
(Erase heading not required.)

Instructions regarding War Diaries and Intelligence Summaries are contained in F.S. Regs., Part II. and the Staff Manual respectively. Title pages will be prepared in manuscript.

Place	Date	Hour	Summary of Events and Information	Remarks and references to Appendices
TRENCHES	1/8/16		Batt Battalion consolidated line. Reliever up trenches. Several wounded & unwounded men of 16th & 18th Manchester Regt brought in. Casualties Officers wounded CAPT J.A. ROCHE, 2/LT A.D. HORNER, 2/LT A PRESCOT, 2/LT B CLOTHIER, 6 OR KILLED 35 wounded	
"	2/8/16		Battalion continues cleaning [trenches?] reconstructing trenches 10 OR Reinforcement. Reference operation see [shop] separate sheet.	
"	3/8/16		Casualties 4 OR Killed 32 OR wounded. Battalion relieved by 1/5 Lancs Fusiliers commencing 6.30PM. Relief complete by 2AM Battalion moves into support. Casualties 2/LT J. SELDON wounded 6 killed 15 OR wounded 2 missing. Copy of wire received from GENERAL JEUDWINE "Have just received your report of last nights fighting AAA I was [good] work & I congratulate you & [illegible] 1/4 R LANCS Regt 1/8 Kings LIVERPOOL Regt on the useful result clearly of their	

WAR DIARY
or
INTELLIGENCE SUMMARY
(Erase heading not required.)

Army Form C. 2118

Place	Date	Hour	Summary of Events and Information	Remarks and references to Appendices
Trenches	2.8.16		The enemy appears to be recovering from its abject attitude & has arrived lately men trying to occur points on the Crest line East, S.E. of the Sunken road which runs from GUILLEMONT to the right of our Batt. in the trenches. I therefore decided to establish a post on the crest about S.30.B.50.70. I ordered my company on the right to find a platoon up the Sunken road to carry out the operation. The platoon was under the command of CAPT WARD & LT DUNCAN remained of 2/H.S.R. The operation commenced at 6.0 PM on the platoon emerged from the trenches about 20 of the enemy bolted down the Sunken road towards GUILLEMONT were disposed of by the M.G. at ARROW HEAD COPSE. The platoon then advanced towards the Crest Line about 60 or 70 Germans then emerged from a trench unseen of the Batt. on my right & advanced to attack the platoon. LT FISHER the M.G. Officer informs me that at the same time other Germans emerged from the cliff been with the Corps on our East & the enemy's side of the crest. The platoon formed along the bank of the road, took a good toll of the advancing Germans. G.H.Q. came into the zunch however commenced I believe by CAPT BODIE opened fire most opportunely. The Germans broke down never fired at by M.G. i L.G. who believe they accounted for 50 or 60. The Germans then sent up their S.O.S. and a severe barrage was laid on the EASTERN EDGE of TRONES WOOD for about an hour.	

WAR DIARY or INTELLIGENCE SUMMARY

Army Form C. 2118.

Place	Date	Hour	Summary of Events and Information	Remarks and references to Appendices
TRENCHES	2.8.16		CAPT WARD as Coy. on the Turcoman Trench established himself on the Turcoman road & connected up a shallow trench to our front line, then making both his flanks secure.	
			The first was Passed over to the 2/5" LAN. Fus. who were relieved about 11.20 PM 3/8/16. The Company of LAN. Fus. Bgd. had arrived at 7.30 pm. relieving one of my support companies. Our own Artillery of their own accord put up an H.O. a most effective barrage. We did not send up any S.O.S signal as we did not think it necessary. Our casualties were slight about 14 killed & 40 wounded (returns sent up in war diary ENP)	
			The bombing posts of my left company say they saw some Turcoman advancing and if SAILGHONT towards the Civil Line at S30 to 50-70	
			E.A. FAGAN LT-COL	
			6 E.A. FAGAN LT-COL	
			A ration party in the valley had 15 casualties by a shell down the right. Refs: 5th Div L° 117/1 (G) Am. Trees 4" 127" I.P. 27 Bde. Staten that 2 hr 124 L.R. 27 Bde. had heavily in an attack on the right of the 2/5 Regt.	BBP

WAR DIARY or INTELLIGENCE SUMMARY

Army Form C. 2118.

Place	Date	Hour	Summary of Events and Information	Remarks and references to Appendices
TRENCHES	3/8/16		Spirit shown by all ranks of the Battalion "AAA" Following wire received from 164 Inf Bde "Brigadier wishes to express his congratulations to 1/1st R.Lanc Regt 1/8 King Liverpool Regt they Royal Lancs he appreciates the good work they did last night".	CRP
"	4/8/16		Battalion relieved by 1/9 King Liverpool Regt. Commencing at 9.30pm Relief complete by 12 midnight. 4/5.8.16. Casualties 2/Lt L.A.R. LOCKHART wounded 1 O.R. wounded	CRP
"	3/8/16 - 5/8/16		Total prisoners taken = 8. 4 wounded 4 unwounded	CRP
BRONFAY FARM	5.8.16		Battalion training Casualties Nil	CRP
"	6.8.16		Battalion training Casualties Nil	CRP
"	7.8.16		Battalion march to the trenches relieving 1/9 Kings, Liverpool Regt relief complete by 10.30 p.m. Lt J.P. CASTLE WOUNDED.	
TRENCHES	8.8.16		Battalion attack styled to commence on far side of valley of GUILLEMONT 4.'14AM. Battalion commences to follow up barrage. The battalion appears to have advanced over 1st line trenches without much loss and into the village. Owing to the battle on Right + Left not being able	

WAR DIARY or INTELLIGENCE SUMMARY

Army Form C. 2118.

Place	Date	Hour	Summary of Events and Information	Remarks and references to Appendices
TRENCHES	8.9.16.	a.m.	To the President home the enemy were able to make a strong attack on the NORTH LANE Ry. forcing the German front line trench. The attack was so strong that the NORTH LANE Ry. led broken from the trenches & the Battn were thus left in position in the village with Resources on their front, flank & Rear. Communications were cut by retaliatory barrage, M.G. fire had on the ground between our security trench, the German front line & by the enemy from information received from 3 men of "D" Coy who came in early the morning. "D" & "B" Coys who formed the left reached their objective & announced to by in the enemy they found a heavy M.G. fire on them from all sides & they were given the order to withdraw by Capt Murphy OC "D" Coy. "A" & "B" Coys who were on the right, no information received would not be seen owing to the mist & smoke. Your barrage thrusts trenches of the enemy. German reinforcements appeared to come from GINCHY. The trench appears to have suffered a certain amount of fire on the Germans by bombing dug-outs, they L.G. fire on reinforcements coming from GINCHY. You then shells were used by the Germans. CASUALTIES WOUNDED Capt G.H. CHAMBERLAIN Missing Capt A.H. MEADOWS (reported killed) 2nt M.N. KEVENS Lt R.H. GORDON (reported wounded) Lt J.S. SHARPE (reported wounded) Capt E.N. MURPHY (reported wounded) Lt W. DUNCAN (reported gassed) "Lt C.B.G. COLLISON 2nt H. WHITESIDE 2/t R. BURROW "2nt W.D.H. LILLEY 2nt J.A. SISSON 2nt W.W.H. SPARGO 2nt W.W. TIPPING 10 m KILLED	

WAR DIARY
or
INTELLIGENCE SUMMARY.
(Erase heading not required.)

Army Form C. 2118.

Place	Date	Hour	Summary of Events and Information	Remarks and references to Appendices
TRENCHES	8.8.16		Casualties wd 47 n Wounded 502 n Missing	EBP
"	9.8.16		Battalion relieved by 1/5 N.LANCS. REGT Casualties Nil Lt J. T SMITH 4th G.A	EBP
LA MOTHE			" repd for duty	EBP
BRUN FAY FARM	10.8.16		BATTALION inspected by MAJOR GENERAL JUDWINE Casualties Nil	EBP
"	11.8.16		Battalion training Casualties Nil	EBP
"	12.8.16		Battalion training Casualties Nil	EBP
"	13.8.16		Church parade Casualties Nil	EBP
"	14.8.16		Battalion training. Heard at 3.35pm heard to killed at HÉRICOURT Casualties Nil	EBP
HÉRICOURT	15.8.16		Battalion training Casualties Nil Billets inspected by BRIGADIER GEN EDWARDS	EBP
"	16.8.16		Battalion training Reinforcement Draft of 290 n Rank marched. Pvt. Casualties Nil	EBP
"	17.8.16		Battalion training Casualties Nil	EBP
"	18.8.16		Battalion training Casualties Nil	EBP
"	19.8.16		Battalion entrained at HÉRICOURT STATION at 6AM +detrain at PONT REMY + march to Billet. A+B Coy at BOULLINCOURT - C.D Coy at MIANNAY Casualties Nil	EBP
MIANNAY	20.8.16		Church Service Casualties Nil	EBP

Army Form C. 2118.

WAR DIARY
or
INTELLIGENCE SUMMARY.
(Erase heading not required.)

Instructions regarding War Diaries and Intelligence Summaries are contained in F. S. Regs., Part II. and the Staff Manual respectively. Title pages will be prepared in manuscript.

Place	Date	Hour	Summary of Events and Information	Remarks and references to Appendices
NIANNAY	21.8.16		Battalion known Casualties Nil Two R.E. Signal Service men attached for duty	E.R.P.
"	22.8.16		Battalion training Casualties Nil 10 Reinforcement	E.R.P.
"	23.8.16		Battalion training Casualties Nil	E.R.P.
"	24.8.16		Battalion training Casualties Nil 60 or Reinforcement	E.R.P.
"	25.8.16		Battalion training Casualties Nil	E.R.P.
"	26.8.16		Battalion training Casualties Nil	E.R.P.
"	27.8.16		Battalion training Lt.Col E.A. FAGAN relinquishes the command & He takes command	
"	"		of the 23rd Inf.Bde. Casualties Nil	E.R.P.
"	28.8.16		Battalion training Casualties N.k	E.R.P.
"	29.8.16		Battalion training Casualties Nil	E.R.P.
"	30.8.16		Battalion parades at 1AM marches entrains at ABBEVILLE detrains at HEREÉCOURT	E.R.P.
			marches & bivouacks at HQ NAP ALBERT 57000 D.13.d.2.6. M.W.7 DERNACOURT	
D.13.d.2.6	31.8.16		Battalion moves when 75 man ALBERT-AMIENS Rd about D.12.d Central	E.R.P.
D.12.d central	31.8.16		Lt C.W. RICHARDS reports for duty & 20 OR Reinforcement	E.R.P.

Meed Major
Commdg. 1/8th (Irish) Bn. "The King's" (L'pool Regt.)

Account of Operations 8/9th August.

1/8/ L'pool R.

My Battalion appears to have advanced over 1st line trenches without much loss and into the village.
Owing to the attacks of the battalions on the right and left not being able to be pushed home, the enemy were able to make a strong attack on the N. Lan. R. holding the German front line trench. The attack was so strong that the N. Lan. R. had to retire from the trenches and my men were thus left in position in the village with Germans on their front, flank and rear.
Communication was cut off and a heavy barrage of machine gun fire put on the ground between our assembly trenches and the German front line by the enemy.
From information received from two men of D. Coy. who came early this morning my D and B Coys. who formed the left half of the first and second waves appeared to have reached their objective and commenced to dig in. The enemy then opened a heavy machine gun fire on them from all sides and they were given the order to "retire slowly" by Capt. MURPHY, O.C. D Coy.
I can give no information as to what happendd to A and C Coys. who were the right Coys. of the first and second waves respectively. Owing to the mist, smoke of our barrage and smoke bombs of the enemy, the Coys. appear to have got considerable mixed up.
The two men of "D" Coy. above referred to state that when they began to retire machine guns fired at them from concealed positions, and the party of 18 they were with eventually dug themselves into a shell-hole on Western slope of Village. I have no doubt many more of the Battalion have done the same.
The Battalion appears to have inflicted a certain amount of loss on the Germans by bombing dug-outs and by Lewis Gun fire on reinforcements coming from GINCHY.
Gas and Tear shells appear to have been used by the Germans.

SD/ E.A. FAGAN,
Lt. Colonel,
Commdg. 1/8th Liverpool R.

10/8/16.

BRIEF SUMMARY OF MESSAGES SENT AND RECEIVED DURING OPERATIONS. 7/8/16 - 9/8/16.

7-8-16.

- 6-7 p.m. Brigade Operation Order 49 received.
- 8-0 p.m. Battalion marched off from F.23 A. to trenches.
- 11-30 p.m. (1) Received order in SUNKEN ROAD to send 2 orderlies to get connection with Brigade No.2 Relay Post. Sent 2 runners who returned after getting touch.

8-8-16.

- 12-18 a.m. (2) Reported relief complete (3) Reported 1/Lieut Castle wounded.
- 1-45 a.m. Received following from Brigade Headquarters (4) Note as to relay system (5) 8 copies of GUILLEMONT sketch map and note (6) as to changes of Battalion Headquarters.
  (7) Reported location to Brigade of Battalion Hdqrs.
- 1-12 a.m. (8) Sent 2 copies of GUILLEMONT sketch map to each Company.
- 1-27 a.m. (9) Sent note as to position of dumps to each Company.
- 1-57 a.m. (10) Plans of barrage and note as to Zero hour received from Brigade.
- 1-58 a.m. (11) Received note from Brigade reference troublesome Machine Guns in GUILLEMONT.
- 3-45 a.m. Men formed up out of trenches ready to attack.
- 4-0 a.m.   Our barrage fire commences intense.
- 4-8 a.m.   Enemy Machine Guns commence. Enemy send up Red rockets.
- 4-14 a.m. Our men commence following up barrage.
- 4-20 a.m. Zero hour.
- 4-25 a.m. (12) Second notice re Zero from Brigade
- 5-55 a.m. 25009 Pte. W. HEATON "B" Coy. 1st King's stated his Company had retired and thought his Battalion was cut up.
- 5-58 a.m. (13) Sent message to any Officer of Battalion warning them as to 4th King's Own being held up on right and to assist right flank. This message sent in duplicate, by 2 orderlies. No reply received.
- 6-3 a.m. (14) Reported to Brigade, 4th King's Own hung up, Irish in village and we were watching right flank.
- 6-12 a.m. (15) Message to 4th King's Own. "Irish reported in village" Asked them for information and could they push forward.
- 6-45 a.m. (16) Message from Brigade to help 4th King's Own.
- 7-22 a.m. (17) Message to Brigade. "Irish in village. 4th King's Own and 1st King's fallen back. Very heavy enemy barrage and Machine Gun fire". Gave supposed location of Machine Guns.
- 7-37 a.m. (18) Message from Brigade Signals with French lamp, which was not received.
  (This was the 2nd message received stating lamp herewith but lamp was never received).
- 8 a.m.   Intelligence Officer having tried to get touch with 1st King's found subaltern with 2 platoons. He stated he thought 2 companies of his Battalion and probably more had been cut up and thought they had been surrounded by enemy on left of cattle trucks on railway.
- 8-15 a.m. (19) Message from 4th King's Own received They were held up and trying to bomb Machine Guns.
- 8-20 a.m. Intelligence Officer of 4th King's Own arrived. Reported they were hung up. Capt. Sartorious of 164th Machine Gun Coy. in command.
- 8-25 a.m. (20) Message from brigade. No information from Companies. Can see men in village. 1st King's reported badly cut up.
- 8-30 a.m. (21) Message from Brigade. Would be new artillery barrage. Parties dealing with strong points.
- 9-50 a.m. Message to Brigade. No news of Battalion. Fear very heavy casualties.
  (22) Message from 4th North Lancs. R. to Major Leech as to situation and asked as to King's Own. (23) Message to 4th North Lancs. No information.

9-50 a.m. Message from Brigade. Attempt being organised on enemy strong points. To OOE. No news of Batt- [illegible] very heavy casualties
10 a.m. Message from Brigade as to keeping in touch with Signal Office and for situation.
10-12 a.m. Reply to Brigade. Signallers were at Signal Office. No news. Big casualties. Battalion apparently cut off. Very heavy mist at commencement of operations.
11-45 a.m. Telephone message from Capt. Brocklebank, Adjutant, 4th King's Own. They were going to attack again. C.O. gave him full information as to position.
1-0 p.m. Received message. 4th King's Own going to attack midday. Message to King's Own. Out of touch with Companies - cannot help. Received their message 1 p.m.
1-45 p.m. Message from Brigade as to position giving aeroplane news. Could we get in touch visual signalling and information as to R.E.s accompanying our Battalion.
1-55 a.m. Replied to Brigade on all these points. Informed them these messages timed between 9 a.m. and 11-30 a.m. reached us 1-45 p.m.
2-30 p.m. Message from Officer 4th North Lancs Regt. He had 40 men in our advanced trench.
2-55 p.m. Reported to Brigade number of garrison in trenches.
3-10 p.m. 2 companies 5th North Lancs. commenced occupying our trenches.
4-30 p.m. Message from Brigade with instructions reference 5th North Lancs and asking position.
Replied. No information.
6-22 p.m. Message from Brigade through 2/5th Lancs Fusiliers as to number of rifles. Replied about 30.
6-55 p.m. Message from Brigade Further aeroplane report and asking for estimated casualties.
7-5 p.m. Replied to Brigade.
7-57 p.m. Message from Brigade as to further supplies of water
9-30 p.m. Note from 2/5th Lancs Fusiliers as to instructions they had to relieve us. Replied to Lancs Fusiliers.
9-55 p.m. Note from Brigade. Lt.Col. Fagan to proceed to Sunken Road telephone and take over Brigade forward area.
Note from brigade to have guides ready if required.
11-20 p.m. Sent note from Lt.Col. Fagan to all units to collect in areas allotted.

9-8-16.

2-30 a.m. Operation Order 50 and order for guides received.
3-52 a.m. Message to Brigade asking as to relief.
3-45 a.m. Left trenches.
6 a.m. Reported this unit at Transport.

2.

Confidential

WAR DIARY

of

1/8th (Irish) Bn. "The King's" (L'pool Regt.)

from 1st September 1916
to 30th "   "

WAR DIARY or INTELLIGENCE SUMMARY

Army Form C. 2118

11821/1st R.

SEPTEMBER

Place	Date	Hour	Summary of Events and Information	Remarks and references to Appendices
D 12 d central	1.9.16		Battalion goes into Corps line trenches for construction from 2 pm till 12 midnight. Casualties Nil. 44 on Reinforcement.	BP
"	2.9.16		12 midnight Battalion is relieved by 1/4 N Lanc Rgt. Casualties Nil.	BP
"	3.9.16		Battalion training tpts in Copseline trenches at 12.30 pm relieving 1/4 N.Lancs. Regl Casualties Nil. 2/Lt R.B. Hodson reports for duty.	BP
"	4.9.16		Battalion comes out of Copseline trenches at 10 pm. Casualties Nil.	BP
"	5.9.16		Battalion training. 25 on Reinforcement. Casualties Nil.	BP
"	6.9.16	8.0 AM	Batt. come to camp at F 13 A area.	
F 13 A	7.9.16		Batt. training.	
"	8.9.16	8.15 PM	Batt. proceeded to Montauban defences.	
"	9.9.16		Moved into York trench in support 2/5 Lancs Fus. & North Lancs. Moved up to support 2/5 Lancs. Fus. & North Lancs. & B & C Coys. took part in the attack on Hop & Ale Alley near Delville Wood.	w.e.k. w.e.k. w.e.k.
"	10.9.16		D Coy & Stout Trench. H. Casualties 2/Lt W.F. Ellis killed, 2/Lt T. Boultard wounded 2/Lt J.F. Smith wounded & 2/Lt N.G. Loft-House wounded 19 O.R. killed & 64 wounded 2 missing. Batt. succeeded in getting into communication with Guards Div. on right who had captured Ginchy. Casualties 2/Lt Galamothe 10 killed, 48 wounded & 2 missing (Lajourdale).	w.e.k.

WAR DIARY
or
INTELLIGENCE SUMMARY

Army Form C. 2118

Place	Date	Hour	Summary of Events and Information	Remarks and references to Appendices
TRENCHES.	11-9-16		BATT in trenches. Casualties ORs 14 killed, 46 wounded + 4 missing	wek
	12.9.16		BATT in trenches. Relieved by - BATT RIFLE BDE 41ST DIV. Casualties 2/Lt POLIMRICK, Capt J.H.MAHON. (wounded) ORs 31 wounded, 9 missing	wek
RIBEMONT	13.9.16		Batt proceeded to billets at RIBEMONT. Reinforcements ÷ Capt. L.A.M. MURPHY. 2/Lt H.S DUDER 2/Lt C.A.BEAN, 2/Lt A.B TICKLE, 2/Lt S.B. POOLE 2/Lt K.E.J.SMITH, 2/Lt F.E. GILBERT. 2/Lt R.B THORPE, 2/Lt A.T. ALLEN, 2/Lt H.S.L TOLHURST. 2/Lt B MALLINSON. 2/Lt A.W WATKINS 2/Lt D.S. O'RIORDAN + 49 ORs Casualties (NIL)	wek
"	14.9.16		BATT TRAINING Casualties nil	wek
	15.9.16		BATT " 195 OR's Reinforcements arrived Casualties NIL	wek
BUIRE	16.9.16		Batt. proceeded to Camp at BUIRE at 2.15PM " "	wek
F.13.A	17.9.16		BATT proceeded to Camp at F.13.A at 2PM. 30 other ranks reinforcements arrived Casualties NIL.	wek
TRENCHES	18.9.16		LEFT Camp at 4.30AM + proceeded to YORK TRENCH + relieved 15th HAMPSHIRE REG in Div. reserve. Casualties NIL.	wek
HAMETZ.	19.9.16		BATT left SAVOY TRENCH at 2.45PM + proceeded to Camp near HAMETZ. Casualties NIL	wek

Army Form C. 2118

WAR DIARY
or
INTELLIGENCE SUMMARY
(Erase heading not required.)

Instructions regarding War Diaries and Intelligence Summaries are contained in F. S. Regs., Part II. and the Staff Manual respectively. Title Pages will be prepared in manuscript.

Place	Date	Hour	Summary of Events and Information	Remarks and references to Appendices
MAMETZ	20.9.16		Batt. Training. Casualties Nil.	WeK
TRENCHES	21-9.16		Batt. proceeded from Camp at 6 P.M. to Savoy & Carleton Trenches & relieved 7th Kings (165 Bde) Casualties Nil	WeK
"	22.9.16		Batt. in trenches Casualties Nil	WeK
"	23.9.16		"	WeK
"	24.9.16		Casualties O.R. 1 killed 4 wounded	WeK
"	25.9.16		Left Savoy & Carleton trenches at 8 P.M. & proceeded to support of 165 Bde in front line. Casualties O.R. 1 missing	WeK
"	26.9.16		165 Bde withdrawn from trenches & 164 Inf. Bde take over. Batt. in front line Casualties 2/Lt D.S. O'Riordan O.R. 1 killed 4 wounded, 1 missing (2/Lt O'Riordan wounded)	WeK
"	26.9	1(am) 10 P.M.	Orders received from 164 I.B. to attack enemy position in conjunction with New Zealanders on left & capture Gird Trench & Gird Support. Our objective from Flers-Ligny Thilloy Road on left to junction of Gird & Gird Support Trench with Factory Corner — Gueudecourt Road on right. Length of objective 800 yds. from left to right	WeK

1875 Wt. W593/826 1,000,000 4/15 J.B.C. & A. A.D.S.S./Forms/C. 2118.

WAR DIARY
or
INTELLIGENCE SUMMARY
(Erase heading not required.)

Army Form C. 2118

Place	Date	Hour	Summary of Events and Information	Remarks and references to Appendices
TRENCHES	27-9-16	2.15 PM	Zero-hour. Heavy barrage commenced & attack launched. Weather ideal. Our men carry enemy position & attain objective. Several prisoners taken. Casualties light. Heavy loss inflicted on enemy who appeared very demoralised. Captured trenches contained many German dead. Enemy machine gun captured. NEW ZEALANDERS attain objective. 5.0 PM The following message was received. "Following was received from Divisional Commander begins AAA. Please convey hearty congratulations to Major Leech & Liverpool Irish on their success & accept the same myself. Ends AAA Brig. Genl Commanding adds his heartiest congratulations. Casualties. 2/Lt C.W. Richards (killed). 2/Lt E.C. Gilbert, 2/Lt Cabern, 2/Lt K.J. Smith, 2/Lt E.J. Palmer, (wounded) O.R's 12 killed, 130 wounded, 34 missing, 8 shell shock.	W.E.K
	28.9.16	2.0 AM	Battn relieved by 1/4 "Kings Own" & proceed to support trenches & relieved 2/5 Lancs. Fus. men Casualties 1 O.R. killed. Durham Light Infy (41st Div) 11 PM Left support trenches relieved by 20th Durham Light Infty (41st Div) & proceeded to Camp near HAMETZ	
	29.9.16	2.30 PM	Battn proceeded to DERNACOURT. Casualties NIL	W.E.K

Army Form C. 2118

WAR DIARY
or
INTELLIGENCE SUMMARY
(Erase heading not required.)

Instructions regarding War Diaries and Intelligence Summaries are contained in F. S. Regs., Part II. and the Staff Manual respectively. Title Pages will be prepared in manuscript.

Place	Date	Hour	Summary of Events and Information	Remarks and references to Appendices
DERNACOURT	30-9-16		BATT training Bawaltie N 11.	WEK

J Keech. Lt Col.
Comdg 1/8th (Irish) Bn. "The King's" (L'pool Regt.)

(Type)

Hdqrs.
164 Infy. Bde.

I beg to report that in the attack of 27th inst. a small body of men of this Battalion pursuing the enemy, advanced beyond their final objective (GIRD SUPPORT trench) along EAST edge of FLERS - L'THILLOY Road until close up to RED HOUSE. N.13.D.6.7.

They report that many retreating Germans took cover in this House and that it may be strongly fortified. No M.G. was observed to fire from it at the time. They also noticed many retreating Germans making for village LIGNY-THILLOY along this road. There were no dug-outs observed in the bank of the road but many small rifle pits capable of holding 1 or 2 men who would be able to command the approach to RED HOUSE. The road seemed to be in good condition and no attempt at mining or barricade could be seen. They got into trench approximately N.19.B.75.95. which runs from Road EAST into Valley N.14.C.7.1. This they found to be about 4' feet deep unoccupied and in poor condition and containing about 10 dead Germans.

The ground over which they advanced was soft soil pitted with shell holes. No long grass or crops of any kind and no obstacles were encountered. They were not fired upon, nor could they locate any organised enemy position.

S. Kuch.
Major.
1/10/16. Commdg. 1/8 Liverpool Regt.

Vol 18

Confidential.

WAR DIARY.
of
1/8 (Irish) Batt. "KING'S" (Liverpool Regt.)

from 1st October 1916
to 31st " "

WAR DIARY
or
INTELLIGENCE SUMMARY
(Erase heading not required.)

Army Form C. 2118

1/8 L'pool R

Place	Date	Hour	Summary of Events and Information	Remarks and references to Appendices
	Oct 1st/16		Batt. left DERNACOURT & entrained at EDGEHILL at 2.30PM Batt arrived at LONGPRE at 12 MN & proceeded to billets at L'ETOILE. Casualties NIL	WBK
	2/10/16		Batt left L'ETOILE at 10.45AM & proceeded to LONGPRE to entrain for POPERINGHE. Casualties NIL	WBK
	3/10/16		1.30AM Batt arrived HOPOUTRE STATION & proceeded through POPERINGHE to C CAMP on the POPERINGHE – YPRES ROAD. arriving 4.30AM Casualties NIL	WBK
G 6 d 3 4	4/10/16		BATT moved to B CAMP at 12.30PM Casualties NIL	WBK
"	5/10/16		BATT. training. Working party of 200 was found for work on corps line at YPRES. from 6PM to 12MN. Casualties NIL	WBK
"	6/10/16		BATT. training. Casualties NIL	WBK
"	7/10/16		BATT. training. Working party of 200 was found for work on corps line at YPRES. from 6PM to 12MN. Casualties NIL	WBK
"	8/10/16		BATT. training. Casualties NIL	WBK
	9/10/16		BATT. training. Working party of 400 was found for work on corps line at YPRES from 6PM to 12MN. Casualties NIL. 2/Lt T H HILL reported for duty	WBK
	10/10/16		BATT. training. Reinforcements OR's 4. Casualties NIL.	WBK

WAR DIARY or INTELLIGENCE SUMMARY

Army Form C. 2118

(Erase heading not required.)

Instructions regarding War Diaries and Intelligence Summaries are contained in F.S. Regs., Part II. and the Staff Manual respectively. Title Pages will be prepared in manuscript.

Place	Date	Hour	Summary of Events and Information	Remarks and references to Appendices
G 6 d 3 4	11-10-16		BATT. Training. Working party of 400 was found for work on books line at YPRES. 6 PM to 12 MN. Casualties NIL	WBK
"	12.10.16		BATT. Training. 2/LT JOHN JOHN. 1st BRECKNOCKSHIRE REG ~ 2/LT H.T.H.S. GRIFFITH.S. 1st BRECKNOCKS REG. 2/LT H.S.L TOLLHURST accidentally wounded at 2nd ARMY Grenade Sch reported for duty. Casualties	WBK
"	13.10.16		BATT. Training. Inspection of Batt by Brig-Gen STOCKWELL at 10.30 a.m. Working party of 400 was found for work on Corps Line at YPRES from 6 P.M. to 12 M.N Casualties NIL	Army
"	14-10-16		BATT. Training. B. Camp taken over from BATT at 5.30 PM by 2/5 LANC. FUS BATT entrained at BRANDHOEK SIDING at 6.30 PM and arrived at YPRES at 8.30 P.M and proceeded to billets at YPRES taking same over from 1/9 K.L.R BATT. in Brigade Reserve from 8.30 PM. Casualties NIL	Army
In L 23	15.10.16		BATT left Brigade Reserve at YPRES at 5.30 PM and took over from 1/9 K.L.R. line. from I.5.8 to I.11.5 C+D Companies in front line A+B Coys in support on left of BATT 2/5 K.O.L.R. on right of Batt 2/4 K.O.L.R. Casualties NIL	Army Army Army
	16.10.16		BATT holding line as on 15-10-16 Casualties nil	
	17.10.16		BATT holding line as on 15-10-16 Casualties NIL 18 O.R Reinforcement arrived	
	18.10.16		BATT holding line as on 15.10.16 Casualties ONE O.R Killed CAPTS N WILKINSON J E HERRNE J E JONES Lt B M BARNES 2/Lt S HESKETH C S WHITEHEAD	

Army Form C. 2118

WAR DIARY
or
INTELLIGENCE SUMMARY
(Erase heading not required.)

Instructions regarding War Diaries and Intelligence Summaries are contained in F.S. Regs., Part II. and the Staff Manual respectively. Title Pages will be prepared in manuscript.

Place	Date	Hour	Summary of Events and Information	Remarks and references to Appendices
#	19.10.16		A B CARBERRY G SURTEES F G FRANKLIN C H BOOTS F H HART M J BROWNE all of the 8th MANCHESTER REG' reported for duty	June
	20.10.16		BATT relieved by 2/5 Lanc Fus and moved into Brigade Reserve at YPRES taking over billets from 2/5 Lanc Fus. Casualties NIL	June
	21.10.16		BATT in Brigade reserve at YPRES. Working party of 3 Officers and 100 O.Rs left at 5.15 P.M. to work on new trench near CAMBRIDGE ROAD. 11 O.Rs reinforcements reported for duty. Casualties NIL	June
YPRES	22.10.16		BATT in Brigade Reserve at YPRES.	
			BATT in Brigade reserve at YPRES. At 5.0PM BATT relieved 1/10th K.L.R. on CANAL BANK. 2/LT A J ALLEN to hospital sick. Casualties O.R. 1 killed 14 wounded	100M
	23.10.16		BATT relieved by 2/5 Lancs Fus at 5PM + moved up + relieved 1/5 NORTH LANCS REGT in Left Sub-Sector WIELTJE. A+B Coys in front line C.C Coy in support + D Coy in reserve. Casualties NIL	WM
ST JEAN	24.10.16		Batt in trenches 2/Lt E MICHAELLS reported for duty. Casualties OR 1 wounded	WM
"	25.10.16		BATT in trenches. Casualties O.R. 1 wounded	WM
"	26.10.16		BATT in trenches. Casualties NIL	WM
"	27.10.16		BATT in trenches. BATT relieved by 2/5 Lancs Fus + moved to CANAL BANK DUG OUTS in Brigade support. Casualties OR 1 wounded. Reinforcements 9 ORs	WM

Army Form C. 2118

WAR DIARY
or
INTELLIGENCE SUMMARY
(Erase heading not required.)

Place	Date	Hour	Summary of Events and Information	Remarks and references to Appendices
CANAL BANK	28.10.16		Batt. in Brigade support. CANAL BANK. Casualties Nil	w.e.k
"	29.10.16		Batt. in Brigade support. CANAL BANK.	w.e.k
"	30.10.16		Batt. in Brigade support. CANAL BANK. 6.0 P.M. Batt relieved by 1/5th North Lancs. & proceeded by train to B. Camp. BRANDHOEK. Casualties Nil	w.e.k
B. CAMP.	31.10.16		Batt. in training. Casualties Nil	w.e.k

Willard Capt.
Comm. Offr. 1/8 L'pool Regt.

Confidential.

WAR DIARY

of

1/8TH (IRISH) BATTALION THE KING'S
(L'POOL REGT.)

from November 1st 1916.
to   November 30th 1916.

WAR DIARY or INTELLIGENCE SUMMARY

Army Form C. 2118

Place	Date	Hour	Summary of Events and Information	Remarks and references to Appendices
BRANDHOEK	1.11.16		BATT in training. Casualties NIL	A.A.6
"	2.11.16		BATT in training Casualties NIL	A.A.6
"	3.11.16		BATT in training. CAPT L.A.M. MURPHY proceeded to ENGLAND Casualties NIL	A.A.6
"	4.11.16		BATT in training Casualties NIL	A.A.6
"	5.11.16		BATT in training. The Divisional Reserve comprised the 164th BRIGADE Casualties NIL	A.A.6
"	6.11.16		BATT in training. 12 O.Rs arrived from Reinforcements Casualties 1 O.R wounded	A.A.6
"	7.11.16		BATT in training. BATT moved into Brigade Reserve at YPRES taking over Billets from 1/9 K.L.R. took over 'B' CAMP from BATT. Casualties NIL	A.A.6
YPRES	8.11.16		BATT moved out of Brigade Reserve at YPRES being relieved by 2/5 LANC FUS and took over LEFT SUB-SECTOR from 1/7 K.L.R. C and D companies in front line. A. B. companies in Support Casualties NIL	A.A.6

WAR DIARY or INTELLIGENCE SUMMARY

Army Form C. 2118

Place	Date	Hour	Summary of Events and Information	Remarks and references to Appendices
LEFT SUB SECTOR	9.11.16		BATT in trenches. Casualties 1 OR killed 4 ORs wounded	A&L
"	10.11.16		BATT in trenches. Casualties NIL	A&L
"	11.11.16		BATT in trenches. Casualties 2 ORs wounded	A&L
"	12.11.16		BATT in trenches. BATT relieved by 2/5 Lancs FUS and moved into Brigade Reserve at YPRES taking over billets from 2/5 Lancs FUS. Working parties supplied. Casualties NIL	A&L
YPRES	13.11.16		BATT in Brigade Reserve at YPRES. Working parties supplied for work in CAMBRIDGE ROAD. Casualties NIL	A&L
"	14.11.16		BATT in Brigade Reserve at YPRES. The whole BATT out on working parties. J MONKS 1/4 S LANCS, 2 Lt W AISTON 4th Res S LANCS, 2 Lt H WORMALD 4 RES S LANCS, 2 Lt S ROTHWELL 4th Res S LANCS arrived from reinforcements and reported for duty. Casualties NIL. Capt 'A'	A&L
"	15.11.16		BATT in Brigade Reserve at YPRES. The whole BATT out on working parties. Casualties NIL	A&L
"	16.11.16		BATT in Brigade Reserve at YPRES. The whole BATT out on working parties. Casualties NIL	A&L

WAR DIARY or INTELLIGENCE SUMMARY

Army Form C. 2118

(Erase heading not required.)

Instructions regarding War Diaries and Intelligence Summaries are contained in F. S. Regs., Part II. and the Staff Manual respectively. Title Pages will be prepared in manuscript.

Place	Date	Hour	Summary of Events and Information	Remarks and references to Appendices
YPRES	17.11.16		Batt in Brigade Reserve relieved by 1/5 NORTH LANCS. Regt. 166 Inf Brigade @ CANAL BANK. Casualties NIL	Appx
	18.11.16		Batt moved out of Brigade Reserve at YPRES being relieved by 1/10 SCOTTISH An. & L.I. 166 Inf Bde in WIELTJE Sector. A. & B. Coy Front Line. C. Coy support, D. Coy Reserve. Casualties NIL	Appx
	19.11.16		Batt in trenches. 4 other ranks accd. as Reinforcements. Casualties NIL	Appx
	20.11.16		Batt in trenches. Casualties NIL	Appx Appx
	21.11.16		Batt in trenches " 1 other rank missing	Appx
	22.11.16		Batt in trenches " NIL	Appx
	23.11.16		Batt in trenches " 1 other rank killed and 1 other rank wounded	Appx
	24.11.16		Batt relieved by 2/5 LANC.S. FUS. and moved to Brigade Reserve at CANAL BANK, YPRES. taking over from 2/5 LANCS FUS. Casualties NIL	Appx
	25.11.16		@ CANAL BANK. working parties 2/Lt F.H. HART to ENGLAND Echelons Gun trams both to Scotland 1 other rank serious Reinforcement Casualties NIL	Appx
	26.11.16		Batt relieved @ CANAL BANK by 1/5 N LANC. Regt. and marched to ELVERDINGHE and to St James. Help. @ 15 Camp in ELVERDINGHE CHATEAU A Coy + E B Coy + 13 Cs 1.4 Casualties	A.A.L.

Army Form C. 2118

WAR DIARY
or
INTELLIGENCE SUMMARY
(Erase heading not required.)

Instructions regarding War Diaries and Intelligence Summaries are contained in F.S. Regs., Part II. and the Staff Manual respectively. Title Pages will be prepared in manuscript.

Place	Date	Hour	Summary of Events and Information	Remarks and references to Appendices
ELVERDINGHE	27.11.16		Batt at ELVERDINGHE & Ldefences. Batt training Casualties 1 other rank wounded.	a.d.
"	28.11.16		Batt at ELVERDINGHE & Ldefences. Batt training Casualties NIL.	O.d.
"	29.11.16		Batt returned at ELVERDINGHE & Ldefences by 1/1 CAMBS Regt 118thy Bgde and proceeded to "B" Camp BRANDHOEK. Casualties 1 other rank wounded	O.d.
BRANDHOEK	30.11.16		Batt at "B" Camp. Inspection by G.O.C. 164th Infty Bgde. Batt not wounded. C Camp. Batt training Casualties NIL	a.d.

Wheeler Major
Comm'dg 1/8th (Irish) Bn. "The King's" (L'pool Regt.)

Vol 20

War Diary
of the
1/8th Liverpool Regt.
for the period
1st December to 31st December, 1916.

20 W
2 sheets.

WAR DIARY
or
INTELLIGENCE SUMMARY

Army Form C. 2118

1/8 1/Pool R

Place	Date	Hour	Summary of Events and Information	Remarks and references to Appendices
B.C. CAMP.	1/12/16		Batt. training. Casualties Nil.	WEK
"	2/12/16		Batt. training. Casualties Nil.	WEK
"	3/12/16		Batt. training. Casualties Nil.	WEK
"	4/12/16		Batt. training. Brigade practice turn-out. Reinforcements 4 O.Rs. Casualties Nil.	WEK
"	5/12/16		Batt. training. Casualties Nil.	WEK
"	6/12/16		Batt. training. Inspection by Corps. Comm order. Casualties Nil.	WEK
"	7/12/16		Batt. training. Casualties Nil.	WEK
"	8/12/16		Batt. training. Batt. moved to Billets in YPRES. 9 relieved 2/5th Lancs. Fus. Casualties Nil.	WEK
YPRES.	9/12/16		Batt. training & supplying working parties. Casualties wounded 1 O.R.	WEK
"	10/12/16		Batt. training & supplying working parties. Casualties wounded 1 O.Rs	WEK
"	11/12/16		Batt. training & supplying working parties. Casualties Nil	WEK
"	12/12/16		Batt. training & supplying working parties. Casualties wounded 1 O.R.	WEK
"	13/12/16		Batt. training. At 5.0 P.M Batt moved up into trenches on Left Sub-sector Railway Wood & relieved 2/5th Roy. Lancs Fus. Right: B Coy. Left D Coy. Supports: Right A Coy. Left B Coy. 1 Platoon D Coy. POTIJZE DEFENCES. Casualties wounded 1 O.R	WEK
TRENCHES	14/12/16		Batt. in trenches. Casualties Nil. Reinforcements Major P.E. ROBATHAN. 21st R.W.F. reported for duty.	WEK
			instruction. 56 O.Rs.	
"	15/12/16		Batt. in trenches. Casualties killed 1 O.R. & wounded 1 O.R.	WEK
"	16/12/16		Batt. in trenches. Casualties killed 1 O.R. & wounded 2 O.Rs. Lt/Col R.P.KEATING reported for duty.	WEK
"	17/12/16		Batt. in trenches. Casualties killed 2 O.Rs & wounded 1 O.R.	WEK
"	18/12/16		Batt. in trenches. Reinforcements 2/Lt J. HODGE reported for duty. Batt relieved by 1/9th N.L.R	WEK
"	19/12/16		& took over dugouts on CANAL BANK, YPRES from 2/5th Lancs. Fus. Casualties Nil.	WEK

WAR DIARY or INTELLIGENCE SUMMARY

Army Form C. 2118

(Erase heading not required.)

Place	Date	Hour	Summary of Events and Information	Remarks and references to Appendices
CANAL BANK YPRES.	19/12/16		Batt. in Brigade Reserve. Casualties Nil. 1. O.R.	UBR
"	20/12/16		LT. W.A. LOGAN & LT. B.M. BARNES transferred to 12th Batt. Manchester Reg. Casualties Nil.	UBR
"	21/12/16		Batt. in training. Casualties Nil.	UBR
"	22/12/16		Batt. in training. Casualties Nil.	UBR
"	23/12/16		Batt. in training. Batt relieved 2/5th Lancs Fus. in Left Sub-Sector ST JEAN. Front line C. Coy in right & "D" Coy on left. "B" Coy in support & "A" Coy in reserve in ST JEAN. Batt. H.Qs ST JEAN. Casualties Nil.	UBR
ST. JEAN.	24/12/16		Batt in trenches. Casualties Nil.	UBR
"	25/12/16		Batt in trenches. 2/Lt J. HODGE transferred 4th Batt. K.L.R. & 2/Lt A.J. ALLEN to R.F.C. Casualties Nil.	UBR
"	26/12/16		Batt. in trenches. Lieut-Col. F.C. Heath assumed temporary command of 164 Brigade. Casualties Nil.	UBR
"	27/12/16		Batt. in trenches. Casualties Nil.	UBR
"	28/12/16		Batt. in trenches. Batt. relieved by Liverpool Scottish, & proceeded to B Camp. 2nd Lieut. C. Slew 2nd Lt. W.C. Keys transferred to X Corps Gas School. Casualties Nil.	C.Slew
B Camp.	29/12/16		Batt. in training. Casualties Nil.	C.Slew
"	30/12/16		Batt. in training. 3 bombs dropped by hostile aircraft. Casualties Nil.	C.Slew
"	31/12/16		Batt. in training. Casualties Nil.	C.Slew

P.S. Rathen A/Lyn
Commdg 1/8th (Irish) Battalion The King's
(L'pool Regt.)

Vol 21

164/55

21 W
3 sheets

War Diary
of the
1/8th Liverpool
for the period
1/1/17 to 31/1/17

1/8² West post R

Army Form C. 2118.

WAR DIARY
or
INTELLIGENCE SUMMARY. January 1917.
(Erase heading not required.)

Place	Date	Hour	Summary of Events and Information	Remarks and references to Appendices
Brand Hoek	1/1/17		Batt. in Training. Brigade Holiday. Maj. Leck to 2nd Army C.O.'s Course. Casualties Nil.	C.S.W.
"	2/1/17		Batt. in Training. Casualties Nil. Maj. Leck, Capt. Ward, Lt.S.F.G. Ireland, QMS Carr, B.M.S. Knatings mentioned in Despatches. Cdr.	C.S.W.
"	3/1/17		Batt. in Training. Draft of 71 O.R. from Div. Reinforcement Camp. Casualties Nil.	C.S.W.
"	4/1/17		Batt. in Training. Casualties Nil.	C.S.W.
"	5/1/17		Batt. in Training. Smoking Parties. Men's Xmas Dinner in Church Army Hut. Casualties Nil. C.S.W.	C.S.W.
"	6/1/17		Batt. in Training. Casualties Nil.	C.S.W.
"	7/1/17		Batt. in Training. Batt. moved to Ypres took over from 2/5th Lancs. Fus. Major G.S. Brighton rejoined from England. Major H Leech rejoined from 2nd Army C.O's Course. Casualties 1 O.R. wounded.	C.S.W.
Ypres	8/1/17		Batt. in Brigade Reserve. Ypres heavily shelled from 8.30 a.m. until 11.45 p.m. Casualties 2 killed, 15 wounded.	C.S.W.
"	9/1/17		Batt. in Brigade Reserve. Draft of 9 O.R. from Div. Reinforcement Camp. 2 O.R. to Cadet School, England. Casualties 1 O.R. died of wounds. Casualties Nil.	C.S.W.
"	10/1/17		Batt. in Brigade Reserve. Casualties Nil.	C.S.W.
"	11/1/17		Batt. in Brigade Reserve.	C.S.W.
"	12/1/17		Batt. in Brigade Reserve. Batt. relieved 2/5th Lancs. Fus. in Potijze Sector, 'A' Co. and 2 platoons 'B' Co. in Front Line; 'C' + 'D' Co. in support (Cambridge T, St James T. and Potijze Defences) Casualties Nil.	C.S.W.

Army Form C. 2118.

WAR DIARY
or
INTELLIGENCE SUMMARY.
(Erase heading not required.)

January 1917.

Instructions regarding War Diaries and Intelligence Summaries are contained in F.S. Regs., Part II. and the Staff Manual respectively. Title pages will be prepared in manuscript.

Place	Date	Hour	Summary of Events and Information	Remarks and references to Appendices
Left Sub Sector.	13/1/17		Batt. in Trenches. Corps Commander (Gen. Sir Aylmer Hunter Weston) inspected Batt. front, and expressed himself pleased with what he saw. Casualties NIL	C.S.W.
"	14/1/17		Batt. in trenches. White Chateau & Bde HQrs shelled at noon. Casualties 1 killed 6 O.R. wounded.	C.S.W.
"	15/1/17		Batt. in trenches. Draft of 80 O.R. joined Batt. Casualties NIL.	C.S.W.
"	16/1/17		Batt. in Trenches. Lt.Col. E.C. Heath, having returned from 164 Inf. Bde, resumed command. Batt. relieved by 11th Royal Sussex Regt. and proceeded to billets in ELVERDINGE. Casualties NIL.	C.S.W.
ELVERDINGE	17/1/17		Batt. in Reserve to 38th (Welsh) Division. Training. Working parties. Casualties NIL.	C.S.W.
"	18/1/17		Batt. in Reserve to 38th (Welsh) Division. Training. Working parties (cable burying). Casualties NIL.	C.S.W.
"	19/1/17		Batt. in Reserve to 38th (Welsh) Division. Casualties 1 O.R. accidentally injured.	C.S.W.
"	20/1/17		Batt. in Reserve to 38th (Welsh) Division. Casualties NIL.	C.S.W.
"	21/1/17		Batt. in Reserve to 38th (Welsh) Division. Lt. E.F.G. Orchard rejoined from 164 Bde. Bombing School. Casualties NIL.	C.S.W.
"	22/1/17		Batt. in Reserve to 38th (Welsh) Division. Casualties NIL.	C.S.W.
"	23/1/17		" " Batt. relieved by 2/5th LANCS. FUS. and proceeded to 'E' Camp. Casualties NIL.	C.S.W.

Army Form C. 2118.

WAR DIARY
or
INTELLIGENCE SUMMARY.
(Erase heading not required.)

January 1917.

Place	Date	Hour	Summary of Events and Information	Remarks and references to Appendices
'E' Camp.	24/1/17		Batt. in Reserve to 38th (Welsh) Division. Training & working parties. Casualties Nil.	C.S.W.
"	25/1/17		Draft of 92 O.R. arrived from Div. Reinforcement Camp. Batt. in Reserve to 38th (Welsh) Division. 2nd Lt. W.B. Robinson & 1 O.R. arrived as reinforcements. Casualties Nil.	C.S.W.
"	26/1/17		Batt. in Reserve to 38th (Welsh) Division. 2nd Lt. G. Surtees proceed of Btn. Casualties Nil.	C.S.W.
"	27/1/17		Batt. in Reserve to 38th (Welsh) Division. Casualties Nil.	C.S.W.
"	28/1/17		" " " " 2nd Lt. J.S. Rimmer arrived as reinforcement. Casualties Nil.	C.S.W.
"	29/1/17		" " " " Casualties Nil.	C.S.W.
"	30/1/17		" " " " "	C.S.W.
"	31/1/17		" " " " "	C.S.W.

E.C. Heath
Lieut. Colonel
Commdg 1/8th (Irish) Battalion The King's
(L'pool Regt.)

CONFIDENTIAL.

WAR DIARY
OF
1/8th (IRISH) BATTALION THE KING'S
(L'POOL REGT.)

from February 1st 1917
to February 28th 1917

WAR DIARY or INTELLIGENCE SUMMARY.

Army Form C. 2118.

February 1917.

Place	Date	Hour	Summary of Events and Information	Remarks and references to Appendices
'E' Camp.	1/2/17		Battalion in reserve. Casualties Nil.	C.Sh.
"	2/2/17		Battalion in reserve. Hard frost continues. Yser Canal froze. Casualties Nil.	C.Sh.
"	3/2/17		Battalion in reserve. Bn. relieved by 1/1st South Lancs. Regt.; and proceeded to Bolzeele Area by train. Billeted in village of Merckeghem, in farm-buildings. Casualties Nil.	C.Sh.
Merckeghem.	4/2/17		Battalion in Divisional Rest. Lieut. Col. E.C. Heath assumed command of 164 Inf. Bde. pending arrival of Brig. Gen. Stockwell. At 11 a.m. urgent orders arrived for Brigade to concentrate immediately in Merckeghem, & proceed in direction of Herzeele. On arrival at Esquelbecq however, Brigade turned about & proceeded back to original billets.	C.Sh.
"	5/2/17		Battalion in Training. Platoon Company work. Casualties Nil.	C.Sh.
"	6/2/17		" " " Companies in the Attack.	C.Sh.
"	7/2/17		" " " Concentration March followed by Tactical Situation.	C.Sh.
"	8/2/17		" " " Attack on Strong Points; and Night Concentration.	C.Sh.
"	9/2/17		March by Company Beaving. Battalion in Training. Brigade Concentration March.	C.Sh.

Army Form C. 2118.

WAR DIARY
or
INTELLIGENCE SUMMARY.
(Erase heading not required.)

February 1917.

Place	Date	Hour	Summary of Events and Information	Remarks and references to Appendices
MERCKEGHEM	10/2/17		Battalion in Training. Company & Battalion Drill. Little enemy. Brigade held a Boxing Tournament in BOLEZEELE; the Battalion won two Finals, — Heavy Welter — and two Semi-Finals.	C.Slo.
"	11/2/17		Battalion in Training. Church Parade took place in a large barn.	C.Slo.
			Brigade held a Cross-Country run for teams consisting of 1 Officer + 30 men per Battalion, 9th Bn. third.	C.Slo.
"	12/2/17		Battalion in Training. Casualties NIL.	C.Slo.
	13/2/17		Battalion in Training. Brigade night operations. Draft of 46 O.R. arrived for duty.	C.Slo.
"	14/2/17		Battalion in Training. Attack on trenches, n. trenches, T.Ms. co-operating with Barrage fire.	C.Slo.
"	15/2/17		Battalion proceeded to 'B' Camp, Brandhock, and relieved 12th Battn. Royal Sussex Regt. Casualties NIL.	C.Slo.
'B' Camp	16/2/17		Battalion in Reserve. Reconnaissance carried out, with the object of finding suitable routes for the Battn. to move up to the support of the Right Left Division in case of necessity. Casualties NIL.	C.Slo.

1577 (Wt. W10791/1773 500,000 1/15 D. D. & L.   A.D.S.S./Forms/C. 2118.

WAR DIARY
INTELLIGENCE SUMMARY

Army Form C. 2118.

February 1917.

Place	Date	Hour	Summary of Events and Information	Remarks and references to Appendices
"B"Camp.	17/2/17		Batt. in Reserve. Batt. proceeded to Ypres & relieved 16th Bn. Rifle Bde.	C.S.W.
YPRES	18/2/17		Casualties NIL.	
	19/2/17		Batt. in Reserve. Casualties NIL.	C.S.W.
	20/2/17		Batt. in Reserve. Two O.Rs wounded.	C.S.W.
	21/2/17		" " " Casualties NIL.	C.S.W.
			" " " Batt. relieved 7th Bn. K.R.R. in POTIJZE Sector, taking the place of the 9th Bn. K.R.R. who were in Saunders.	C.S.W.
POTIJZE	22/2/17		Batt. in trenches. Capt. J.E. MILNE. D.S.O. R.A.M.C., the Medical Officer of the Unit, killed by a sniper. In the evening of same day, a reconnoitring patrol under 2nd Lt. MALLINSON failed to return, with the exception of 2nd Lt. A.E.B. SUTTON, who had accompanied patrol for instruction, & was wounded by bomb fragments. He stated that patrol reached Boche trenches, but was attacked & dispersed. 3 O.Rs were lost with 2nd Lt. Mallinson.	C.S.W.
	23/2/17		Batt. in Trenches. Reinforcements of 10 O.Rs from Base. Casualties NIL.	C.S.W.
	24/2/17		" " " Batt. relieved by 9th Bn. K.L.R. & proceeded to Ypres Prison. Casualties NIL.	C.S.W.

Army Form C. 2118.

WAR DIARY
or
INTELLIGENCE SUMMARY.
(Erase heading not required.)

Place	Date	Hour	Summary of Events and Information	Remarks and references to Appendices
YPRES	25/2/17		Bde. Batt. in Reserve. Lt. Col. E.C. Heath proceeded to England on leave, and Major N. Leech took over command of the Battalion. Chanoler M.C.	C.S.W.
"	26/2/17		Batt. in Bde. Reserve. Company Training & working parties. 2 O.R. wounded.	C.S.W.
"	27/2/17		Batt. in Bde. Reserve. 1 O.R. died.	C.S.W.
"	28/2/17		Batt. in Bde. Reserve. Deep concern & regret was expressed by the Major-General & Brigadier-General, commanding 55th Division & the Brigade respectively, at the death of Capt. Milne, & the loss of our patrol under 2nd Lt. Mallinson. At the same time, congratulations were offered to Capt. A.J. MONKS and 2nd LT. S. ROTHWELL upon the good work they performed after that loss, in an attempt to trace the patrol.	C.S.W.

H.Leech Major
Comm^{dg} 1/8th (Irish) Bn. "The King's" (L'pool Regt.)

vol 23

23.W
5 sheets

War Diary

1/8th (Irish) King's Liverpool Regt

March 1917

WAR DIARY
INTELLIGENCE SUMMARY

Army Form C. 2118

March 1917.

Place	Date	Hour	Summary of Events and Information	Remarks and references to Appendices
YPRES	1/3/17		Batt. in Bde. Reserve. Training carried on. Working parties provided. Bombing Cos. instructed. Casualties NIL.	C.S.W.
"	2/3/17		Batt. in Bde. Reserve. O.C. Cos. carried out preliminary reconnaissances of Cos. fronts. Casualties NIL.	C.S.W.
"	3/3/17		Batt. in Bde Reserve. Batt. relieved 2/5th Lancs. Fus. in WIELTJE Sector. Disposition as follows: Right front Co. – A Co.: Left front Co. – B Co.: Co. in Support – D Co.: in Reserve – C Co. Casualties NIL.	C.S.W.
WIELTJE - ST. JEAN Sector.	4/3/17		Batt. in Trenches. MAJOR G.S. BRIGHTEN took over temporary command of 2/5th Lancs. Fus. LIEUT. C.H.M. WILSON transferred to R.F.C. Casualties 2 O.R. killed in action; 4 O.R. wounded.	C.S.W.
"	5/3/17		Batt. in Trenches. Large wiring parties nightly at WIELTJE. Casualties NIL.	C.S.W.
"	6/3/17		Batt. in Trenches. Casualties NIL.	C.S.W.
"	7/3/17		Batt. in Trenches. Every working party and other snipers moving. Leopard Gun especially CAMBRAI and CAMEL TRENCH. He was Leopard Gun snipers shewing jund. Casualties NIL.	C.S.W.
"	8/3/17		Batt. in trenches. Batt. relieved by 2/5th Lancs. Fus, and proceeded to YPRES PRISON. Casualties 1 O.R. wounded.	C.S.W.
"	9/3/17		Batt. in Bde. Reserve. Company Kit Inspection & Bathing Parade. Casualties NIL.	C.S.W.

Army Form C. 2118

WAR DIARY
INTELLIGENCE SUMMARY
(Erase heading not required.)

March 1917.

Place	Date	Hour	Summary of Events and Information	Remarks and references to Appendices
YPRES.	10.3.17		Batt. in Bde. Reserve. Major P.E. Rubathan, between duties of Second in command of 1/4th R. Lancs. Regt. Vocal Training carried out. R.S.M. R.T. Simpson granted Commission, posted to "D" Coy. Casualties NIL.	C.S.W.
"	11.3.17		Batt. in Bde. Reserve. Church Parade held in main Corridor of Prison. Casualties NIL.	C.S.W.
"	12.3.17		Batt. in Bde. Reserve. Lieut.-Col. S.C. Neuth rejoined, took over command of Batt. Casualties NIL.	C.S.W.
"	13.3.17		Batt. in Bde. Reserve. Batt. relieved 2/5th Lancs. Fus. in WIELTJE Sector. Casualties NIL.	C.S.W.
WIELTJE – ST. JEAN Sector.	14.3.17		Batt. in Trenches. Usual work of building dug-outs, revetting, wiring carried on. Enemy very quiet; no patrols were made to encounter any enemy in No Man's Land. 6120 Pte. L/Cpl. Beresford D.C., and 3239 Pte. Riley T.R. awarded Italian Bronze Medal for Military Valour. Casualties 2.O.R. wounded	C.S.W.
"	15.3.17		Batt. in Trenches. Casualties 3 O.Rs. wounded, two remaining at duty.	C.S.W.
"	16.3.17		Batt. in Trenches. Casualties 3 O.Rs. wounded.	C.S.W.
"	17.3.17		Batt. in Trenches. St. Jean shelled intermittently during morning & afternoon. Batt. relieved by 1/10th Liverpool Scottish,	

Army Form C. 2118

WAR DIARY
INTELLIGENCE SUMMARY
(Erase heading not required.)

Instructions regarding War Diaries and Intelligence Summaries are contained in F.S. Regs., Part II. and the Staff Manual respectively. Title Pages will be prepared in manuscript.

Place	Date	Hour	Summary of Events and Information	Remarks and references to Appendices
B Camp.	18-3-17		and proceeded to YPRES, thence by train to 'B' Camp. Batt. in Divisional Reserve. Church Parade in Army Hut, Brandhoek.	C.S.W. Cronnelles M.L.
"	19-3-17		Batt. in Divisional Reserve. Capt. F.S. Fletcher. R.A.M.C. proceeded on leave to England. Lieut. W. ARNOTT reported for duty as M.O.	C.S.W. Cronnelles M.L.
"	20-3-17		Batt. in Divisional Reserve. Company & Battalion training. MAJOR H. Ruck proceeded to Aldershot Senior Officers' Course. on leave & detailed to attend	C.S.W. Cronnelles NIL
"	21-2-17		Batt. in Divisional Reserve. POPERINGHE shelled at dusk.	C.S.W. Cronnelles NIL
"	22-3-17		Batt. in Divisional Reserve. Brigadier-General emdg. 160 Inf. Bde. inspected the Battalion during the morning. 3.O.R. arrived as reinforcements.	C.S.W. Cronnelles NIL
"	23-3-17		BOPERINGHE shelled by H.V. gun at dusk. Batt. in Divisional Reserve. Brigadier-General emdg. 160 Inf. Bde. inspected Batt. Transport.	C.S.W. Cronnelles M.L.
"	24-3-17		Batt. in Divisional Reserve. 1 Officer & 29 O.R. returned to Batt. from Carpott Coy. R.E.	C.S.W. Cronnelles M.L.
"	25-3-17		Batt. in Divisional Reserve. Lieut.-Col. E.C. HEATH proceeded to C.O.'s course, 2nd Army School. Capt. F.S. WARD. took on command of the Batt. in the absence of Lieut.-Col. E.C. HEATH. 4 O.R. arrived as reinforcements. Church Parade in Church Army Hut, Brandhoek.	C.S.W. Cronnelles M.L.

1875 Wt. W593/826 1,000,000 4/15 J.B.C. & A. A.D.S.S./Forms/C.2118.

Army Form C. 2118

WAR DIARY
or
INTELLIGENCE SUMMARY
(Erase heading not required.)

Instructions regarding War Diaries and Intelligence Summaries are contained in F. S. Regs., Part II. and the Staff Manual respectively. Title Pages will be prepared in manuscript.

Place	Date	Hour	Summary of Events and Information	Remarks and references to Appendices
B Camp	26.3.17		Battn in Divisional Reserve. Company & Battalion Training. Casualties Nil.	P&R
B Camp	27.3.17		Battn in Divisional Reserve. Company & Battalion Training. Casualties Nil.	P&R
B Camp	28.3.17		Battn in Divisional Reserve. Batt relieved 2/5th Bn Lancs Yeols in Reserve. Casualties Nil	P&R
Ypres			Battn in Brigade Reserve. Usual training carried out. Bathing parade. Casualties Nil	B.R.
Ypres	29.3.17		Battn in Brigade Reserve. Usual inspections & training carried out. Casualties Nil	B.R.
	30.3.17		Bathing parade. Working parties provided.	
	31.3.17		Battn in Brigade Reserve. Usual inspection & training carried out. Bathing parade. Working parties provided. Casualties Nil.	P&R

Hulard Captain
Comm of 1/8th (Irish) Battalion The King's (L'pool Regt.)

CONFIDENTIAL.

WAR DIARY.

of

1/8TH (IRISH) BATTALION THE KING'S
(L'POOL REGT.)

from

APRIL 1st, 1917.

to

APRIL 30th, 1917.

-o-o-o-o-o-o-o-o-o-o-o-o-o-o-o-

WAR DIARY

INTELLIGENCE SUMMARY

(Erase heading not required.)

Army Form C. 2118

Place	Date	Hour	Summary of Events and Information	Remarks and references to Appendices
YPRES	Apl 1/17		Battalion in Brigade Reserve. Church Parade, working parties provided. Working parade. Lt Col. P.E. Heath returned from C.O. Course. Casualties 2. O.R. accidentally wounded.	Sd.
"	Apl 2/17		Battalion in Brigade Reserve. Battalion relieved 7/Lancs Fusiliers in the WIELTJE - ST JEAN sector. Dispositions:- RIGHT FRONT Coy. "A" Coy. LEFT FRONT Coy. "B" Coy. Support "D" Coy. Coy in Reserve "C" Coy. Casualties NIL.	Sd.
WIELTJE ST JEAN SECTOR	Apl 3/17		Battalion in the trenches. Large working parties in front line at night reclaiming same. Casualties NIL.	Sd.
"	Apl 4/17		Battalion in the trenches. Some working parties. Large fighting patrol sent out but did not encounter any enemy. Casualties NIL.	Sd.
"	Apl 5/17		Battalion in the trenches. Work in front line continued. Capt R. Roy, D.V. Jones returned from leave. Lieut W. Grant R.A.M.C. proceeded on leave & was relieved by Capt A.R. Turner R.A.M.C. Wire received informing us ranks that Lord Loms—bury has been appointed Colonel Commandant of the "Kings" (Liverpool) Regt. Casualties NIL.	Sd.

WAR DIARY
INTELLIGENCE SUMMARY
(Erase heading not required.)

Army Form C. 2118

Place	Date	Hour	Summary of Events and Information	Remarks and references to Appendices
WIELTJE ST JEAN SECTOR	Apl 6/17		Battalion in Reserve. Took to continue on front line. Large fighting patrol was sent out but again had no luck. The enemy were encountered. Casualties Nil.	S/L
"	Apl 7/17		Battalion in Reserve. Hurricane bombardment by right Brigade to which enemy replied with his SOS barrage. Our trenches suffered very little. Battalion relieved by 1/S Lancs Fusiliers and took over trenches in prison YPRES. Road to ST JEAN was eighty Shelled whilst the battalion was coming out. Casualties 8 O.R. wounded.	S/L
YPRES	Apl 8/17		Battalion in Brigade Reserve. Church parade. Working parties provided. 2/Lt F.J. WRIGHT (3rd K.L.R.) arrived for duty posted to 'B' Coy. Capt A.T. Monks returned from Corps Lewis Gun School. 2/Lt CM. TOMS. 2/Lt D.J.B. McCABE to Corps Lewis Gun School.	S/L
			Casualties nil.	S/L
"	Apl 9/17		Battalion in Brigade Reserve. Menu training carried out. Working parties provided. 2/Lt GAS SHAW (3rd K.L.R.) arrived for duty posted to D Coy.	S/L
			Casualties 3 O.R. wounded.	S/L

WAR DIARY
INTELLIGENCE SUMMARY

(Erase heading not required.)

Army Form C. 2118

Instructions regarding War Diaries and Intelligence Summaries are contained in F.S. Regs., Part II. and the Staff Manual respectively. Title Pages will be prepared in manuscript.

Place	Date	Hour	Summary of Events and Information	Remarks and references to Appendices
YPRES.	Apl. 10/17		Battalion in Brigade Reserve. Usual training carried out. Working parties provided. Bathing parade. Casualties nil.	Sd.
"	11/17		Battalion in Brigade Reserve. Usual training carried out. Working parties provided. Casualties nil.	Sd.
"	12/17		Battalion in Brigade Reserve. Battalion relieved 2/5 King's Liverpool in the WIELTJE - ST JEAN Sector. Dispositions:- Right front Coy. C Coy, Left front Coy D Coy, Coy in support B Coy. Coy in reserve A Coy. Casualties Nil.	Sd.
WIELTJE ST JEAN SECTOR	13/17		Battalion in the trenches. Large working parties widening front line. Casualties 3 (1 killed 2 wounded).	Sd.
"	14/17		Battalion in the trenches. Work continued in front line. Two working fighting patrols sent out but encountered no enemy, way wet rough. 20 % away to hospital sick. Casualties nil.	Sd.
"	15/17		Battalion in the trenches. Work continuing in front line. 2nd Lt D.J.B. McGill from R.G. course (VIII Corps) 2nd Lt E. Penn & 2nd Lt. C. Clarke arrived as reinforcement. Casualties 1 wounded.	Sd.
"	16/17		Battalion in the trenches. Work continues in front line. Casualties 3 wounded.	Sd.

WAR DIARY
INTELLIGENCE SUMMARY
(Erase heading not required.)

Army Form C. 2118.

Instructions regarding War Diaries and Intelligence Summaries are contained in F. S. Regs., Part II. and the Staff Manual respectively. Title pages will be prepared in manuscript.

Place	Date 1917	Hour	Summary of Events and Information	Remarks and references to Appendices
WIELTJE ST JEAN SECTOR Y Camp. WATOU	April 17		Battalion relieved by 1st (Canad) Bn. The Kings Liverpool Regt. and took over billets in Y Camp. Bavachie Hk.	S.I.
HOUTKERQUE	18.		Battalion on training. Marched HOUTKERQUE and took over billets. Capt. R.P. Keating appointed 2nd in Command of the Battalion vice Major Speed (to England) with effect from 27/4/17. 2nd Lieut. S.G. Franklin takes over Command and pay of "A" Coy vice Lieut. E.J.S. Oakes (to R Coy) with effect from 19/4/17. Bavachie Hk.	S.I.
"	19.		Battalion in training. Bearing parades two sections. to 2/Lt R.P.Keating assumed command of the Battalion Lieut Estcah having proceeded to C/ps School. Bavachie Hk.	S.I.
"	20.		Battalion in training. Canal having carried out. Bavachie Hk.	S.I.
"	21		Battalion in training. Douai having carried out. Lieut G.J. Scab resumes Command Vice Capt R.P.Keating (2nd in Command) Lieut H.B. Fickell from Reinforcement Camp Bavachie Hk.	S.I.
"	22.		Battalion in training. Marched HARYEKE taking over billets. Bavachie Hk.	S.I.
HARYEKE	23		Battalion in training. March to EPERLECQUES taking on. Heels Bavachie Hk. 2 Lieut JE Penn from Polkestone Course.	S.I.

WAR DIARY
INTELLIGENCE SUMMARY.
(Erase heading not required.)

Army Form C. 2118.

Place	Date 1917	Hour	Summary of Events and Information	Remarks and references to Appendices
EPERLECQUES	APRIL 24.		Battalion in training. Battalion Musketry parade. Training carried out. "A" Coy. on the range.	Sd. Bouacho M/L.
"	25.		Battalion in training. Platoon & Company training carried out. 2nd Lieut J. Skinner and 6.6. field from Bucquoas School. No. 305446 C.S.M. Cain W. appointed A/R.S.M. vice No. 308540 A/R.S.M. Simpson (absorbed 2/L) A/4/4/17. Bouacho M/L.	Sd.
"	26		Battalion in training. Platoon & Company training carried out. "B" Coy on the range. Lieut McArnott R.A.M.C. arrived for duty vice Capt H.M. Turner (to field Ambulance). Bouacho M/L. Battalion House having carried out. Bathing parade.	Sd. Bouacho M/L.
"	27.		Battalion in training. House having carried out. Range allotted to "D" Coy and Headquarters.	Sd. Bouacho M/L.
"	28.		Battalion in training. House having carried out. Platoon Range allotted to "D" Coy and Headquarters. Bouacho M/L.	Sd.
"	29.		Battalion in training. House having carried out. Football matches arranged in the afternoon (inter Company). 2nd Lieut R.A. May from hospital. Bouacho M/L.	Sd.

Army Form C. 2118.

WAR DIARY
or
INTELLIGENCE SUMMARY.

(Erase heading not required.)

Instructions regarding War Diaries and Intelligence Summaries are contained in F. S. Regs., Part II. and the Staff Manual respectively. Title pages will be prepared in manuscript.

Place	Date	Hour	Summary of Events and Information	Remarks and references to Appendices
EPERLECQUES	1917 April 30.		Battalion in training. Musketry carried out. Range allotted to "C" Coy and Headquarters Platoon. Cowards Pit.	Al.

E. J. Hoath
Lieut. Colonel
Comm'd'g 1/8th (Irish) Battalion The King's
(L'pool Regt.)

Confidential.

WAR DIARY
OF

1/8TH (IRISH) BATTALION THE KING'S
(L'POOL REGT.)

from May 1st 1917
to May 31st 1917.

Army Form C. 2118.

WAR DIARY
or
INTELLIGENCE SUMMARY.
(Erase heading not required.)

Instructions regarding War Diaries and Intelligence Summaries are contained in F. S. Regs., Part II. and the Staff Manual respectively. Title pages will be prepared in manuscript.

Place	Date	Hour	Summary of Events and Information	Remarks and references to Appendices
EPERLECQUES	1917 MAY. 1.		Battalion in training. Naval Company and Section having carried out Tactical Scheme. 2nd Lt. J.G. RIMMER to hospital (sick). Casualties Nil.	Sd.
"	2.		" Naval training. Brigade all night scheme, followed by attack at dawn carried out. Casualties Nil.	Sd.
"	3.		" No training owing to previous night's operations. Casualties Nil.	Sd.
"	4.		" Naval training carried out. Company schemes for attack on trenches. Casualties Nil.	Sd.
"	5.		" Naval training carried out. Brigade scheme. Casualties Nil.	Sd.
"	6.		" for attack (open warfare). Battalion marches to ARNEKE taking over lines here. 2nd C.M. Yeos from 2nd Army School. Casualties Nil.	Sd.
ARNEKE	7.		" Company Kit-inspections & cleaning parades. Battalion moves to "M" Camp POPERINGHE by Hawkins D and East C Coy who move to YPRES. Casualties Nil.	Sd.

Army Form C. 2118.

WAR DIARY
or
INTELLIGENCE SUMMARY.
(Erase heading not required.)

Instructions regarding War Diaries and Intelligence Summaries are contained in F. S. Regs., Part II. and the Staff Manual respectively. Title pages will be prepared in manuscript.

Place	Date 1917	Hour	Summary of Events and Information	Remarks and references to Appendices
"M" Camp POPERINGHE	May 8		Battalion in training. Company training. Move by march route to "A" Camp taking over huts from 1st King's Own Royal Lanc. Regt.	S.P.
"A" Camp BRANDHOEK	9		1st & 2nd Reinforcement Camps 1/5/17 Casualties Nil. Company training carried out.	S.R.
-DO-	10		Bayonet fighting, Lewis Gun instruction, Platoon in Attack.	C.S.W.
-DO-	11		Usual Company training. 'A' and 'B' Companies inoculated against Typhoid Fever.	C.S.W.
-DO-	"		Lieut. A.B. Tickle, 2nd Lt. R.C. Davis, 2nd Lt. A. Marsden, 2nd Lieut. E. Michaeli to Divisional School.	C.S.W.
-DO-	12		Company training carried out.	C.S.W.
			YPRES and neighbouring villages heavily bombarded every day. ST. JEAN received some 21 c.m. shells.	
-DO-	13		Church Parade in Canteen. Capt. H.S. Dudley to 2nd Army Central School.	C.S.W.

1577 Wt.W10791/1773 500,000 1/15 D.D. & L. A.D.S.S./Forms/C. 2118.

WAR DIARY
INTELLIGENCE SUMMARY.

Army Form C. 2118.

Place	Date	Hour	Summary of Events and Information	Remarks and references to Appendices
"A" Camp.	MAY 14		Batt. in training. Company parades and inspection during the morning. Batt. proceeded by train to YPRES, and relieved 2/1st Lnre. Bns. in WIELTJE Sector. 10 R. wounded.	C.S.W.
ST-JEAN – WIELTJE SECTOR.	15		Bn. in Trenches. SUPPORT LINES and ST. JEAN shelled intermittently. 3 O.R. wounded. BN. FRONT – C.29.4 (STRAND) to PRATT ST (exclusive).	C.S.W.
-do-	16		Bn. in Trenches. Quiet day. Casualties NIL.	C.S.W.
-do-	17		Bn. in Trenches. Great aerial activity. Enemy Zeppelin balloon brought down in flames. Casualties NIL.	C.S.W.
-do-	18		Bn. in Trenches. Enemy bombarded our trenches in whole front from 6 a.m. throughout the day, with 77m.m.s, 4.2s and medium heavy MINNENWERFER BOMBS. At 9.20 p.m., he put up an intense barrage, and under cover of same, raided our trenches at WARWICK FARM. He was quickly driven out. Casualties 5 wounded. 2 O.R.	C.S.W.
-do-	19		Bn in Trenches. 5 O.Rs arrived as reinforcements. 1 O.R. and 6 R.a.m. wounded till Casualties 2 O.R. wounded.	C.S.W.

WAR DIARY
or
INTELLIGENCE SUMMARY.
(Erase heading not required.)

Army Form C. 2118.

Place	Date	Hour	Summary of Events and Information	Remarks and references to Appendices
ST. JEAN	MAY 20		Bn in Trenches. Bn relieved by 2/5th Lancs Fus., and on relief proceeded to Prison, Ypres. Casualties NIL.	C.S.W.
YPRES.	21		Bn Bde Reserve. Neighbourhood of Prison heavily bombarded during the night, but little damage done. Casualties 1 O.R. wounded.	C.S.W.
do	22		Bn in YPRES. Company training carried out. Practically whole Bn. employed on night working parties. 10.R. to Troops Transportation Depot, Boulogne. Casualties NIL.	C.S.W.
do	23		Bn in YPRES. Company training carried out during the afternoon. 2nd Lt. P.G. FRANKLIN appointed Acting-Captain whilst commanding a Company; dated 12.5.17. Casualties 4 O.Rs. wounded.	C.S.W.
do	24		Bn in YPRES. Working party of approximately 300 found, to dig new Communication Trench – LONE TRENCH – from CONGREVE WALK to FRONT LINE at C.29.9. Work carried on until dawn. Casualties NIL.	C.S.W.

Army Form C. 2118.

WAR DIARY
or
INTELLIGENCE SUMMARY.
(Erase heading not required.)

Place	Date	Hour	Summary of Events and Information	Remarks and references to Appendices
YPRES.	MAY 25		Bn. in YPRES. Same parts of 300 men found for further work on LONE TRENCH. 1 O.R. wounded.	C.S.W.
do	26		Bn. in YPRES. Bn. relieved 2/5th 13th LANCS. FUS. in ST JULIEN Sector. New frontage: NEW JOHN ST (exclusive) to C.29.3, one Company. CONGREVE WALK – one Company. PROWSE TRENCH and GARDEN OF EDEN – one Company. POTIJZE DUGOUTS – one Company. BATTALION HEADQUARTERS – POTIJZE. 1 O.R. wounded.	C.S.W.
WIELTJE Sector.	27		Bn in Trenches. Enemy available men employed on new jumping-off trench behind front line from NEW JOHN ST. to WARWICK CROSSALLEE. 1 O.R. wounded.	C.S.W.
"	28		Bn. in Trenches. Working parties as yesterday. Our artillery bombarding enemy lines and wire. Gaps in wire reconnoitred nightly.	C.S.W.
"	29		Bn. in Trenches. Work proceeding on new trench. New C.T. being dug by 2/5th LANCS. FUS. from CONGREVE WALK to FRONT LINE. 2nd Lt. HILL wounded on patrol. 3 O.R's wounded.	C.S.W.
"	30		Bn. in Trenches. Enemy artillery reply ORS. (artillery) were active to our bombardment. CROSSALLEE 2 Rifled, 3 wounded.	C.S.W.

Army Form C. 2118.

WAR DIARY
or
INTELLIGENCE SUMMARY.
(Erase heading not required.)

Instructions regarding War Diaries and Intelligence Summaries are contained in F. S. Regs., Part II. and the Staff Manual respectively. Title pages will be prepared in manuscript.

Place	Date	Hour	Summary of Events and Information	Remarks and references to Appendices
WIELTJE SECTOR	MAY 31		Bn in TRENCHES. ST. JEAN and CONGREVE WALK shelled in the morning. Casualties 2 O.Rs killed 2 wounded.	C.L.L.

C. J. Oak
Lieut Colonel
Commd 1/8TH (IRISH) BATTALION THE KING'S
(L'POOL REGT.)

CONFIDENTIAL.

1/8th (IRISH) BATTALION THE KING'S (L'POOL REGT).

WAR DIARY for the

month of JUNE.

Army Form C. 2118.

WAR DIARY
INTELLIGENCE SUMMARY.
(Erase heading not required.)

Place	Date	Hour	Summary of Events and Information	Remarks and references to Appendices
POTIJZE SECTOR	1917			
	1/6/17	—	Battalion in the trenches. Usual work carried on at nights. WARWICK TRENCH proceeded with. 2nd D.I.B. 1st GDS. proceeded on leave. Casualties killed 3 wounded.	S.L.
	2/6/17	—	Work on WARWICK TRENCH proceeded with. Repairs carried on in front line. Casualties 4 wounded (one of wounds).	S.L.
	3/6/17	—	Work on WARWICK TRENCH finished. Casualties 2 killed 3 wounded.	S.L.
	4/6/17	—	Repairs carried out in front line. Casualties 2 wounded.	S.L.
	5/6/17	—	Successful raid carried out by 2nd/Lt. C.S. Whitehead, causing heavy casualties on the enemy. 2nd/Lt. Whitehead returned wounded. Casualties 1 wounded.	
	6/6/17	—	Lt. Col. B.C. Heath having proceeded on leave Capt. R.P. Geary assumed command.	S.L.

WAR DIARY

INTELLIGENCE SUMMARY
(Erase heading not required.)

Army Form C. 2118.

Instructions regarding War Diaries and Intelligence Summaries are contained in F. S. Regs., Part II. and the Staff Manual respectively. Title pages will be prepared in manuscript.

Place	Date	Hour	Summary of Events and Information	Remarks and references to Appendices
POTIJZE SECTOR	6/6/17	—	Battalion in trenches. Horse rescue carried out. Casualties 8 wounded. 1 missing.	Sd.
	7/6/17	—	Return to trenches. Casualties nil.	Sd.
	8/6/17	—	Horse Rescue. Capt A.J. Morris proceeds on leave to England. Casualties. Killed 1. Wounded 1.	Sd.
	9/6/17	—	Lieut E.F.G. Orchard proceeds on leave to England. Casualties nil. Reserve gunned.	Sd.
	10/6/17	—	Casualties 1 killed.	Sd.
	11/6/17	—	Battalion relieved by the 4th Batt. K.R.R. & moved by road to Camp in H.I.A. Casualties 3 wounded.	Sd.
H.I.A.	12/6/17	—	Battalion in training. Battalion moved to MERCKEGHEM. to-day. Train to ESQUELBECQ. hence by march route.	Sd.

Army Form C. 2118.

WAR DIARY
INTELLIGENCE SUMMARY.
(Erase heading not required.)

Instructions regarding War Diaries and Intelligence Summaries are contained in F. S. Regs., Part II. and the Staff Manual respectively. Title pages will be prepared in manuscript.

Place	Date	Hour	Summary of Events and Information	Remarks and references to Appendices
	1917			
H.1.A	11/6/17 cont.		Battalion on having to MERCKEGHEM taking up billets there.	SA.
MERCKEGHEM	12/6/17		Eisvalrie H.L.	L.
			Cleaning parades & inspections under Company Arrangements.	
			Casualties Nil.	
	14/6/17		Parades under Company Arrangements	SL.
			Lt. F.E.BODELL arrived for duty. Casualties Nil.	
	15/6/17		Parades under Company arrangements. Casualties Nil.	SL.
	16/6/17		Bathing parades. Battalion marched to billets at QUERCAMP, LOHATTRE. (BORBINGHEM AREA) Casualties Nil.	SL.
QUERCAMP	17/6/17		Church parade. 67 O.R.s arrived as reinforcements. Casualties Nil.	SL.
	18/6/17		Battalion inspected by Brigadier General Cunning 162nd Inf Bgde. 2nd Lt. C.S. MONRO awarded military Cross. 30.6.19 Col. BALFOUR AE.	

1577 Wt. W10791/1773 500,000 1/15 D. D. & L. A.D.S.S./Forms/C. 2118.

WAR DIARY
INTELLIGENCE SUMMARY
(Erase heading not required.)

Army Form C. 2118.

Place	Date	Hour	Summary of Events and Information	Remarks and references to Appendices
QUERCAMP	1917 15/6/17 contd		Battalion in training and 307586 Pte Murphy H. awarded Military Medal. Casualties Nil.	SL
	16/6/17		Lt Col Leah having returned from leave assumed Command (17/6/17). Training carried out. Organised games (5.30-7pm) 2nd Lt E F Leach & C.T. Howarth arrived as reinforcements. Casualties Nil.	SL
	20/6/17		Usual training carried out. Company Schemes. Rev. Capt. C.J. O'Higgins arrived for duty as R.C. Chaplain. 57 O.Rs arrived as reinforcements. Casualties Nil.	SL
	21/6/17		Range practice carried out by the Battalion. Casualties Nil.	SL
	22/6/17		Battalion route march. Casualties Nil.	SL
	23/6/17		Training carried out Company Schemes. Recreational training. 10 O.R arrived as reinforcement. Casualties Nil.	SL

WAR DIARY
INTELLIGENCE SUMMARY

(Erase heading not required.)

Army Form C. 2118

Instructions regarding War Diaries and Intelligence Summaries are contained in F.S. Regs, Part II. and the Staff Manual respectively. Title Pages will be prepared in manuscript.

Place	Date 1917	Hour	Summary of Events and Information	Remarks and references to Appendices
Our Camp	24/6/17		Battalion in training. Church Parade. Baths. Mk.	Sd.
"	25/6/17		Battalion scheme in the attack. Baths. Mk.	Sd.
"	26/6/17		Horse having in attack. Range practice carried out. 2nd Lt A.R. Alderton arrived for duty from 1st Bn. Kings Liv. Regt. 2nd Lt ? Hoson returned from Div. Sch. Casualties: Killed (2nd Lt Livesey) Baths. Mk.	Sd.
"	27/6/17		Brigade scheme of attack carried out. Casualties Mk.	Sd.
"	28/6/17		No training carried out. Boxing competitions. Casualties Mk.	Sd.
"	29/6/17		Brigade scheme again practised. Casualties Mk. Transport	Sd.
"	30/6/17		No training carried out. Moved to Mallen Copse. Casualties Mk.	Sd.

C. F. Booth
LIEUT.-COLONEL,
COMMANDING 1/8th (IRISH) BATTN. "THE KING'S" (LIVERPOOL REGT.)

SECRET.

Report on a Raid carried out on the night of the
5/6th June by the 1/8th(Irish)Battn.Kings Liverpool Regt.

The raid was preceded by a rapid bombardment of the part of the trench to be entered.

As soon as the barrage lifted the raiders rushed to the enemys parapet.

On arrival at the parapet the raiders divided into right and left party.

Two men of the left party under 2/Lieut. C.S.WHITEHEAD jumped into the trench but the remainder of the party were prevented by a strong hostile counter attack. The left party fought the Germans till every one of the party was wounded, when the party withdrew. Lieut. WHITEHEAD remained behind to see the whole of his party across, and although wounded assisted Cpl. BALFOUR to return to our trenches.

The right party also met with resistance but was more successful. One German was taken prisoner but he was too big and heavy to be dragged out of the trench and as he resisted stubbornly he was knocked on the head with a pistol butt to prevent him firing into the party as they returned.

No.307586, Pte. H.MURPHY accounted for at least five Germans himself and acted throughout with great dash and gallantry and at the end remained behind to carry back a wounded comrade.

Our casualties were :-

2/Lieut. C.S.WHITEHEAD and 7 other ranks wounded and
1 man missing.

The enemy was very alert and waiting for the raiding party. He is reported to be of fine physique, very tall and full of fight.

The enemys trench is reported to be from 6 to 7 ft.

deep, not revetted, and the bottom is covered with either planks or cement.

The entrances to the dug-outs are about 2ft. high only, very narrow, and it is only possible to get out of them by crawling.

1/8th (IRISH) BATTALION THE KING'S

(LIVERPOOL REGIMENT).

WAR DIARY

FOR THE MONTH OF

JULY 1917.

WAR DIARY

INTELLIGENCE SUMMARY

(Erase heading not required.)

Army Form C. 2118.

Place	Date	Hour	Summary of Events and Information	Remarks and references to Appendices
QUERCAMP	1/7/17		Battalion in training. Church Parade. Casualties Nil.	S.L.
"	2/7/17		Battalion moved to QUERY CAMP by train. At dusk the battalion again moved into billets as follows: HQrs GOLDFISH CHATEAU. A Coy. SCATTERED billets in YPRES. B Coy. L4 post. C Coy. RAMPARTS. D Coy. Dugouts in vicinity of Chateau. H.11.B.&3. Casualties Nil.	S.L.
GOLDFISH CHATEAU /YPRES.	3/7/17		Battalion in Brigade Reserve. Working parties. Consisted of Hdqrs. Casualties 1 wounded. GARDEN ST. taken in hand.	S.L.
"	4/7/17		" Working parties. NEW GARDEN ST continued. Major H LEECH returned from England & taken over duties of 2nd in Command. 2nd GASSLAW killed by shell. Casualties 1 Off. killed 1 O.R. wounded.	S.L.
"	5/7/17		" Training carried on under Coy arrangements. NEW GARDEN ST. & ARMYTAGE proceeded with. Casualties 1 O.R. wounded.	S.L.

Army Form C. 2118.

WAR DIARY

INTELLIGENCE SUMMARY

(Erase heading not required.)

Instructions regarding War Diaries and Intelligence Summaries are contained in F. S. Regs., Part II. and the Staff Manual respectively. Title pages will be prepared in manuscript.

Place	Date 1917.	Hour	Summary of Events and Information	Remarks and references to Appendices
GOLDFISH CHATEAU.	1/7/17.		Battalion in Brigade Reserve. Training carried out. NEW GARDEN ST & ARMITAGE continued. Working parties on Sumps. Cavalries No.	S.
"	2/7/17.		Training as before. Work continued on Dugouts & also NEW GARDEN ST & ARMITAGE. Cavalries(?)2 Horses, 1 Deep wounds.	S.
"	5/7/17.		Usual having proceeded with. NEW GARDEN ST. ARMITAGE. Cavalries. 3 Wounded.	S.
"	9/7/17.		Battalion relieves 1/5 Lancs Fusiliers in the Trenches. Disposition: Front line B & C Coy. Support A Coy. Reserve D Coy. Batt HQrs. POTIJZE. Cavalries. 2 Duty Horses sl.	
POTIJZE SECTOR	10/7/17.		Battalion in the Trenches. Usual maintenance work carried on. ARMITAGE to continue. 2 Rabals out on the Front. Cavalries. 1 Killed 3 Wounded.	S.

WAR DIARY
INTELLIGENCE SUMMARY
(Erase heading not required.)

Army Form C. 2118.

Instructions regarding War Diaries and Intelligence Summaries are contained in F.S. Regs., Part II. and the Staff Manual respectively. Title pages will be prepared in manuscript.

Place	Date	Hour	Summary of Events and Information	Remarks and references to Appendices
TOTITZE	1917		Battalion in the trenches.	
	11/7/17		Usual work on the trenches. Patrols out at night looking for areas to report. Casualties 4 wounded.	SL
	12/7/17		Maintenance work and DRAINAGE TRENCH work continues. Patrols have no special points to note. Casualties 1 wounded.	SL
	13/7/17		Work continued as much as possible. Enemy and back areas heavily shelled with gas shells which hindered the work on trenches. Our also paid work. Casualties 2 killed 10 wounded (Other rank)	SL
	14/7/17		Work continued. Heavy barrage on our line. Lieut. A.B. TOWLE killed. Casualties 6 O.R. wounded	SL
	15/7/17		Work continued. Patrols looking to report ? no enemy met with. Casualties nil.	SL
	16/7/17		Into Counsel refugee dug-outs front line. A & D Coys. Support B Coy. Reserve C Coy. Casualties (Other Ranks) 6 wounded	SL

WAR DIARY

INTELLIGENCE SUMMARY

(Erase heading not required.)

Army Form C. 2118.

Instructions regarding War Diaries and Intelligence Summaries are contained in F. S. Regs., Part II. and the Staff Manual respectively. Title pages will be prepared in manuscript.

Place	Date	Hour	Summary of Events and Information	Remarks and references to Appendices
POTIJZE	1917			
	17/7/17		Battalion in the trenches. Heavy barrage of enemy strong points and back area commenced.	
			Casualties Nil.	S4
	18/7/17		Heavy wire cutting barrage on enemy back area continues.	
			Casualties 1 killed 2 wounded.	S4
	19/7/17		Wire cutting takes. Heavy barrage on our lines. Capt R.P. KEATING & Capt P.G. FRANKLIN killed.	
			Casualties 2 Off killed 7 O.R. wounded	S4
	20/7/17		Battalion made a raid at 2.30 a.m. 2nd Lieut MICHAELIS in Charge. 2nd Lieut NAPP in charge of covering party. 2nd Lieut MONSON. Tanks met strong resistance & did not reach enemy trench. 2nd Lieut NAPP went forward & entered trench. The party did not meet any	

1577 Wt. W10791/1773 500,000 1/15 D. D. & L. A.D.S.S./Forms/C. 2118.

Army Form C. 2118.

WAR DIARY
INTELLIGENCE SUMMARY.
(Erase heading not required.)

Instructions regarding War Diaries and Intelligence Summaries are contained in F. S. Regs., Part II. and the Staff Manual respectively. Title pages will be prepared in manuscript.

Place	Date	Hour	Summary of Events and Information	Remarks and references to Appendices
POTIJZE	20/7/17		Battalion in the trenches. Battalion found their own stretchers. 2nd Lieut. MICHAELIS wounded. Battalion relieved by 1/5 Suffolk & Scottish & proceed to Boraillis.	Sd.
RED ROSE CAMP	21/7/17		RED ROSE CAMP. Battalion in Rest. Bathing parades after which Coy proceeded to WATOU No.3 area by march route taking one Hitch tent.	Casualties 2 O.R. killed, 13 wounded, 2 O.R. wounded Sch. 10 R. missing
WATOU No 3 AREA	22/7/17		Battalion in rest. Church Parades. Inspection & training parades under Coy arrangements. 2nd Lieut. McBell + H. CARBINES arrived as Reinforcement camp 19/7/17	Casualties Nil. Casualties Nil. Sch.
	23/7/17		29 O.R. arrived as reinforcements. Inspections & training parades under Coy arrangement.	Casualties Nil. Ch.

WAR DIARY

INTELLIGENCE SUMMARY.
(Erase heading not required.)

Place	Date	Hour	Summary of Events and Information	Remarks and references to Appendices
NATOU to SARPI	25/9/17		Battalion in Rest. Training carried on	Cavallie Hill Std.
CONCENTRATION AREA H.B.B	26/9/17		Battalion moved to Concentration area H.B.8. by MARCH ROUTE. Preparations made for forthcoming operations	Cavallie Hill Std.
	27/9/17		Preparations continued	Cavallie Hill Cd.
	28/9/17		Still preparing for advance	Cavallie Hill Cd.
	29/9/17		Preparations continued	Cavallie Hill Cd.
	30/9/17		Final preparations made for coming offensive. Letters from Byde and Divisional Bgde Commanders published and read to the troops together with message from the Commanding Officer. Copies attached. Brig. Gen. Stockwell D.S.O. Cdg. 164 Inf Bde visited the Battalion on his way up to the front line. Maj. Gen. Jeudwine C.B. Comdg. 55 th D. visited Battalion lines to wish success to Major Beech who was to command the Battalion in action. Order received for Lieut- Col E.C. Scott to remain behind and take command of all "B" Teams, Transport and other details of 164 Inf Bde concentrated at Transport lines. 2Lt Robinson, R.K. signalling officer was selected for command of the Bgde Forward Station in the coming operations	Cavallie Hill Std.

Army Form C. 2118.

WAR DIARY
INTELLIGENCE SUMMARY.
(Erase heading not required.)

Instructions regarding War Diaries and Intelligence Summaries are contained in F. S. Regs., Part II. and the Staff Manual respectively. Title pages will be prepared in manuscript.

Place	Date	Hour	Summary of Events and Information	Remarks and references to Appendices
Concentration area H & B	30/7/17	(cont'd)	— but was wounded on afternoon 30/7/17 while on route for front line. 2 Lt. Simpson was placed in charge of all Transport in the Brigade and became responsible for the bringing up of all supplies, ammunition during the operations. Battalion, as made up for battle (A Teams), left Concentration area, Burnt Farm, Veanertinghe at 9 p.m under command of Major H.L. LEECH 1/8 King's L'pool 2nd; the assembly trenches being reached without incident.	J.R.T.
	31/7/15		The operations of 31/7/17 & 1/8/17 will be given as a whole in the diary for August/17.	J.R.T.

D. C. J. Tooth
LIEUT.-COLONEL,
COMMANDING 1/8th (IRISH) BATTN. "THE KING'S" (LIVERPOOL) REGT.

A, B, C, D, & Details.

1/8 IRISH/OFFE/988.

In sending out to the Battalion the attached letters of the Divisional and Brigade Commanders, I desire once more to remind all ranks that they are fighting not only to break down the vaunted might of Germany and the militarism of Prussia, which have brought so much trouble on the world during the past three years, but that each one is also fighting for the freedom of mankind, for the security of his home, for the future safety of his mother, sister, sweetheart, wife, daughter and of all else that he holds dear and sacred.

That the fighting spirit of the Battalion is excellent I am fully convinced. Your good work in the trenches, your able construction of defences, your valuable patrolling, your steadiness under frequent heavy bombardments from front and flanks, in the most dangerous and difficult part of the whole Army front and your patience and cheerfulness through all the trials and hardships of the Winter, are proof that your Spirit is excellent and your heart in the right place.

Let each one go forward with the feeling and knowledge that he is winning, determined to play his part to the utmost of his ability, doing his level best to obey all orders implicitly, and, by his good work and splendid example of courage and devotion to duty, helping all to victory.

Let the name of the "Liverpool Irish" go down to posterity as a glorious and imperishable name, the name of a regiment in which each one nobly did his duty on this great occasion.

To every Officer, Warrant Officer, Non-Commissioned Officer and Private of the Battalion who is taking part in this, the first great engagement that you have been in since I have had the honour to Command you, I wish God Speed and Good Luck.

Lieut. Colonel.
Comndg. 1/8th(Irish)Batt. K.L.R.

In the Field.
29/7/17.

COPY.

TO ALL RANKS OF THE 55th (WEST LANCASHIRE) DIVISION.

        I believe everyone in the Division knows the importance of the operations we are about to undertake, and how immense their effect may be.

        I wish to impress on all ranks how greatly every man can help towards success by trying his utmost to stick to his job, and to go on, no matter at what cost, till the objective is gained and victory won. When two or three resolute men do this it is not only what they achieve individually that is of such value to their side, but it is the example they set to their comrades, and the influence they exert on those around them, that has such far-reaching effect.

        I am confident that every soldier, whether he is Officer, N.C.O., or private, in the West Lancashire Division is determined to uphold the great reputation of the Division and of his Regiment, and that each will do his duty.

        In any case where, during the attack, a soldier, although wounded, goes on to meet the enemy, or remains at his post, the case is to be brought to notice by the Commanding Officer in the form of a recommendation for immediate award. I shall be glad to recommend all such cases for favourable consideration for the award of the Military Medal to those concerned.

                        Sd/H.S.JEUDWINE.

                              Major General.

55th Division H.Q.,   Commdg. 55th (West Lancashire) Division.
  28th July, 1917.

-o-o-o-o-o-o-o-o-o-o-o-o-o-o-o-o-o-

COPY.   164th Inf. Bde. No. G.249.

I have little to add to the attached letter from the Divisional Commander.

I am confident that the fighting spirit of every unit in the Brigade and the single-minded determination to kill Germans and gain the objective, will end in the successful accomplishment of every task we are called upon to perform.

                        Sd/C.I.STOCKWELL.

                                Brigadier General.
28th July, 1917.   Commdg. 164th Infantry Brigade.

-o-o-o-o-o-o-o-o-

COPY.

The following telegram was received during the action:-

"Well done, One six four. I am very proud of what you did today. It was a fine performance and ~~was~~ no fault of yours ~~that~~ you could not stay.

                Genl. JEUDWINE".

I congratulate all units on having earned this praise which I know to be well deserved ".

                "Sd/C.I.STOCKWELL.
                        Brig.Genl.
8.40 a.m.   Commdg. I M B U E.
1/8/17.

C O P Y.

55th (WEST LANCASHIRE) DIVISION.

SPECIAL ORDER OF THE DAY.

3rd August 1917.

To all ranks of the 55th (West Lancashire) Division.

Before you went into action on the 31st July, I told you how confident I was that the Division would do its duty, and maintain its reputation and the reputation of the grand Regiments to which you belong.

You have done more than that.

The attack you made on the 31st is worthy to rank with the great deeds of the British Army in the past, and has added fresh glory to the record of that Army.

The courage, determination, and self-sacrifice shewn by Officers, Warrant Officers, Non-Commissioned Officers and men is beyond praise. It is a fine exhibition of true discipline, which comes from the mutual confidence of all ranks in themselves, their comrades, their leaders, and those under them. This in its turn is the product of hard training. Your doings on the 31st shew how well you have turned this training to account.

You captured every inch of the objectives allotted to you. It was not your fault that you could not hold all you took. You have broken and now hold in spite of weather ████████ and counter attacks a line that the enemy has strengthened and consolidated at his leisure for more than two years.

This will I believe be the beginning of the end. When your turn comes to go forward again you will know your own strength — and the enemy will know it too.

I am proud of what you have done, and am confident that with such troops ultimate victory is certain.

    Sd/H.S. JEUDWINE. Major General.
    Commdg. 55th (West Lancashire) Division.

XIX Corps No. G.820/9

The following telegrams of congratulations received by Fifth Army Commander yesterday, are circulated for information:-

"First Army send to Fifth Army heartiest congratulations on brilliant success.
    General HORNE".

"Hearty congratulations to you and Fifth Army on your great success from self and Second Army". "PLUMER".

"Very best congratulations on your success in the commencement of the Third Battle of YPRES AAA Bravo the Fifth Army.
    General RAWLINSON".

SECRET.   COPY NO........

1/8th (IRISH) BATT. "KING'S" (L'POOL REGT).

OPERATIONS — INSTRUCTIONS I.

Ref: Maps ST.JULIEN 28 N.W.2. Edit.5A. 1/10,000.
ZONNEBEKE, 28 N.W.1. Edit.5A. 1/10,000.

In the Field.
22/7/17.

1. Objectives and Distribution of Brigades.	1.	In the forthcoming operations in which the 55th Division will be employed, the allotment of Brigades and their objectives is as under:-
165 & 166 Inf. Bdes.		165 on Right and 166 on Left, will attack at ZERO and will occupy the BLACK/DOTTED GREEN LINE.
164th Inf. Bde.		At ZERO plus........ hours, 164th Inf. Bde. deployed on the Divisional front, will pass through the other two Brigades and will seize the GREEN LINE.
2. Concentration.	2.	On X/Y night, the Brigade will be concentrated about VLAMERTINGHE as laid down. 1/8th L'Pool R. about M.3.b.
		It is essential that throughout Y day there is no movement of any individual than is absolutely physically necessary.
		There will be no noise and no smoking during the hours of darkness on Y/Z night.
3. Jumping off Trenches.	3.	On Y/Z night the Brigade will move forward to the jumping off trenches, by routes to be detailed later.
		These are :- CONGREVE/LIVERPOOL line, with the newly dug trenches behind. Here the Brigade will be distributed as under:-
		Right Front Battn. 1/4th R.Lan.R. Left " " 2/5th Lan.Fus. CONGREVE/LIVERPOOL. Right Rear " 1/4th R.Lan.R. Left " " 1/8th L'Pool R. In rear of CONGREVE/LIVERPOOL - from LONE STREET incl. to THREADNEEDLE (excl).
4. Formation on leaving jumping off Trenches.	4.	At ZERO plus....... hours the Brigade will advance in artillery formation of Columns.
		1/8th L'Pool R. will advance in 4 lines of Columns of Platoons in file at 40 paces distance, (subject to modification with regard to mopping up parties).
5. Direction.	5.	The approximate direction of the advance is 55° GRID.

2.

6. Formation on reaching position of deployment.	6.	Deployment into line will take place as circumstances require before reaching the BLACK/dotted GREEN LINE.

When deployed into line, each Battalion will be in four waves at 30/50 yards distance; each Battalion on a two Company front; each Company on a front of two platoons.
In the case of the 1/8th L'Pool R. this formation will not be complete until such time as the Battalion has passed over the areas occupied by the Mopping-up Parties.
These Mopping-up Parties will follow immediately in rear of leading waves of Front Battalions. They will rejoin their own Battalions as the latter come up to them forming the rear waves. |
| 7. Dividing line between Battns. | 7. | The Battalion Right Boundary Line will be a line from the L of LONE FARM to D.13.Central; thence a line to junction of road and track at D.13.b.75.40; thence a line N.E. drawn through the E of HANEBEEK, passing S.E. of BOSTLER.
The Left Boundary Line is the line of Divisional Boundary. |
| 8. Objective. | 8. | The objective of 1/8th L'Pool R. as well as details of points to be mopped up, are laid down in Brigade Instructions issued, (164th Inf.Bde.No.B.F./4). |
| 9½ Dress, etc. | 9. | Instructions re Dress and Distinguishing Marks etc., as laid down in 164th Inf.Bde. No. G.S.I.460 dated 29th June, 1917,(circulated to all Officers on 7/7/17) are confirmed, excepting that the new Rifle Bomb Signal for S.O.S. will not be available. |
| 10. HEADQUARTERS. | 10. | (a) X/Y night and throughout Y day:-
  Batt.H.Qrs. N.8.b.70.10.
  Bde.H.Qrs.   RED ROSE CAMP.
(b) Y/Z night.
  Batt.H.Qrs. CONGREVE WALK - Concrete Elephant Dugouts.
  Brigade H.Qrs. |

Capt. & Adjt.
1/8th(Irish)Battalion K.L.R.

Issued at 2 p.m.
By Runner.
Copies to:-
 1. File.   8. Details and Signals Off.
 2. C.O.   9. Intell.Off.
 3. 2nd-in-Command 10.
 4. O.C. A Coy.
 5. " B "
 6. " C "
 7. " D "

1/8(IRISH)BATT. "KING'S"(L'POOL R).

Instructions II.

In the Field.
24/7/17.

1. **Distribution in "jumping off" trenches.**

    1. The 1/8th L'Pool R. will be formed up in the "jumping off" Trench in the following order from Right to Left:

    "A" Company: LONE STREET - to point 100 yards N. of ST.JEAN, WIELTJE ROAD (both incl).

    No. 1 Platoon.
    " 2 "
    Company H.Qrs.
    No. 3. Platoon.
    " 4 "

    "C" Company (Moppers Up) as detailed by O.C. 2/5th Lan. Fus.

    "B" Company & "D" from point 100 yards N. of ST.JEAN - WIELTJE ROAD to THREADNEEDLE STREET (both exclusive).

    No. 7 Platoon.
    No. 5 Platoon.
    Company H.Qrs.(B Coy).
    No. 6 Platoon.
    Company H.Qrs.(D Coy).
    No. 8. Platoon.
    No. 16 Platoon.

    Nos.14 & 15 (Moppers Up) as detailed by O.C. 2/5th Lan. Fus.

    -o-o-o-o-o-o-o-o-

    Battalion H.Qrs.   Concrete Elephant Dugouts, COSGRAVE WALK.

2. **Moppers Up.**

    2. The objectives of Mopping Up parties and the platoons allotted thereto are as under:-

    1. CAPRICORN KEEP and POND FARM (if not occupied by troops of 164th Brigade)

        No.12 Platoon.

    2. Dugout and trenches C.18.b.25,65.

        No.14 Platoon.

    3. Dugouts and emplacements in embankment, D.13.c70.85

        No.11 Platoon.

    4. Work about D.13.a.5.1. and Gun emplacements 100 yards N. of this point.

        No.9 Platoon.

2.

2. Moppers Up.
Contd.

    5. HINDU COT, D.13.a.27.20.
           No. 10 Platoon.

    6. Gun emplacements D.13.a.65.70. and SCHULER FARM.
           No. 15 Platoon.

Mopping up parties must clearly understand that they are responsible for putting down the fire of any hostile machine guns in their vicinity and for promptly dealing with any other situation or developement that may arise and which may be unprovided for.

    It is their duty constantly to keep their Company Commander informed of their whereabouts and the progress of their work; as well as to give full information as to the tactical and other possibilities of the area being mopped up.

3. Objective
of Battn.

    3. The objectives of the 1/8th L'Pool R. is the line of Supporting Points Nos. 4, 5, 6, & 7. This line is to be made into a strong support line to the whole Brigade front by the construction of lines of trenches in the intervals between the points,- the Supporting Points themselves being constructed by R.Es.

    These lines of trenches are to be dug by 1/8th L'Pool R; who will also find Garrison for the Supporting Points as soon as completed by R.Es.

Garrison of
Supporting
Points.

Garrison of Supporting Points.

    No.7.   No. 1 Platoon (less 2 Secs) and 1 Lewis Gun.
    No.6.   No. 4. Platoon (less 2 Secs) and 1 Lewis Gun.
    No.5.   No. 6. Platoon (less 2 Secs) and 1 Lewis Gun.
    No.4.   No. 8. Platoon (less 2 Secs) and 1 Lewis Gun.

    1 Machine Gun is also allotted to each of the above.

4. Front Line
Consolidation.

    4. Two Companies, A & B, will be held in readiness to assist the Front Line Battalions to consolidate their positions and will also find garrisons for the Line of Supporting Points.

    "A" Company to assist 1/4th R.Lan.R. on Right.
    "B"   "   "   "   2/5th Lan.Fus. on Left.

These Companies will only be used to assist the Front Line Battalions if and as required by Os.C., Battalions concerned. If not required they will continue to fulfil the role of the 1/8th L'Pool R., viz:- the consolidation of the line of Supporting Points.

    If required to assist the two front line Battalions they will rejoin their own unit immediately their work if front is completed.

    As soon as objectives have been gained, the 1/8th L'Pool R. becomes the immediate support to the whole Brigade Front.

2.

5. Capture of enemy guns.	5. It is possible that Troops going to the Brigade's furthest Objective will have the opportunity of capturing enemy guns, or of rendering them useless by rifle, Lewis Gun, and Machine Gun fire. These opportunities must be boldly seized by patrols within the limits of our artillery barrage.
A complement of Gunners has been attached to the Brigade for the purpose of serving any captured guns.
Early information of any such capture is urgently required.
6. Liaison.	6. "A" Company is responsible for constant and close liaison with 1/6th M.Lan.R., "B" Coy. with 2/5th Lan. Fus., "D" Coy. with 4/5th Black Watch (118th Bde).
"D" Coy. will also be responsible for establishing our left flank on the line of Divisional Boundary, should the necessity arise.
7. Communications.	7. The following trenches will be used for IN and OUT traffic.

IN : STRAND & LONE.
OUT : PAGODA & GARDEN.

Communication from Companies to Batt.H.Qrs. by Visual and runner, supplemented by a Lucas Daylight Lamp at Left Front Company H.Qrs.
Battalion Runner Relay Posts will be established as follows:-

For Left Companies in the vicinity of D.13.a.70.60.
For Right Companies about D.13.Central.

Communication from Battalion H.Qrs. to Brigade Forward Station will be by Visual, Telephone, and Runner.
Brigade Forward Station will be at SOMME.
All important messages will be sent in duplicate by two different routes or means of transmission; those of _special_ importance will be sent in triplicate by three different routes or means of transmission. Messages will be carried in right hand breast pocket, in which nothing else will be carried.
All runners must realise the vital importance of getting their messages through quickly and at all costs. |
| 8. Dumps. | 8. Main Brigade Dump - junction of BRIGHT TRENCH & CORDUROY WALK, C.66.c.70.65.
Advanced Brigade Dump: About D.13.c.1.5.
Forward Brigade Dump : Left - CORDUROY WALK.
Right- BALLIOL.
When these latter have been established they will be handed over to charge of Battalions. |

4.

9. Medical Arrangements.	9.	Regt. Aid Post will be established at POTIJZE on Y/Z night and will move forward with Batt. H.Qrs. to CAPRICORN TRENCH and POND FARM. Later it is intended to occupy position in or about D.13.Central.
10. Tanks.	10.	For action of Tanks see 164th Inf.Bde. B.P./6 It is essential that all ranks should realise that the TANK acts independently, that its movement must not be allowed to affect or modify the action, direction etc. of assaulting troops. If there should be any exception to this general rule it will be the subject of a specific and detailed order. Otherwise the only modification of action by the Infantry in relation to TANKS will be made under the direction of the responsible officer on the ground as a result of communication with the TANKS in the field. The card giving "Tank Coloured Discs and Light Code" must be studied by all Officers and N.C.Os. The three general signals given on the front page must be known to all ranks.
11. Artillery.	11.	Details of Artillery Barrage not yet known. The Shrapnel barrage under which the Brigade will advance will creep forward at the rate of 100 yards every 4 minutes.
12. M.Gs.	12.	Details will be issued later.
13. Trench Mortars.	13.	Details will be issued later.
14. Prisoners.	14.	See Administrative notes etc. Strength of fighting troops will not be depleted for the purpose of bringing back prisoners. Prisoners will be sent back in small parties under escort of one slightly wounded man.
15. Bde.H.Qrs.	15.	Brigade H.Qrs. will be in POTIJZE Dugout until objectives have been gained, when it will move forward to Advanced Brigade H.Qrs. in the neighbourhood of RAT FARM.
16. Reports.	16.	Battalion H.Qrs. will move in rear of Batts. by line parallel to and 100 yards to left of ST. JEAN – GRAVENSTAFEL ROAD. On arrival at the crossing of the FREZENBERG line, H.Qrs. will be established in CAPRICORN TRENCH. On objectives being gained, H.Qrs. will move forward to vicinity of POND FARM.

ACKNOWLEDGE.

Issued at 9.20 a.m.
By Runner.
Copies to:-
1. File.
2. C.O.
3. 2nd-in-Command.
4. Capt. V.S. WARD.
5. O.C. A Coy.
6. " B "
7. " C "
8. O.C. D Coy.
9. " Signals.
10.

Capt. & Adjt.
1/8th (Irish) Batt. K.L.R.

SECRET.   COPY NO....

1/8th(IRISH)BATT."KING'S"(LIVERPOOL REGT).

OPERATION ORDER NO.108.

Ref.Maps: ST.JULIEN 28 N.W.2.   Ed.5A. 1/10,000.
          ZONNEBEKE, 28 N.W.2. Ed.5A. 1/10,000.
          OPERATIONS MAP, FREZENBURG, 1/10,000.

                                                In the Field.
                                                27/7/17.

(1) Information.   (1) On Z day the 55th Division will take part in
                        a general attack.
                        The 15th Division will attack on the right,
                        the 39th Division on the Left. Divisional
                        boundaries and dividing lines between Brigades and
                        Battalions are shewn on maps already issued.

(2) Disposition   (2) The 164 Brigade will take up a position in
    of Brigade   CONGREVE/LIVERPOOL TRENCH by 2 a.m. on Z day.
    for Attack   At ZERO plus 4 hours 40 minutes, the 164 Brigade,
    and times.   deployed on the Divisional Front, will advance
                        and at ZERO plus 6 hours 20 minutes will pass
                        through the 165 and 166 Brigades, who will have
                        taken the enemy first and second line systems,
                        (165 on right, and 166 on left) and will
                        capture and consolidate the enemy third line system
                        (GHELUVELT - LANGEMARCK LINE) up to and including
                        the GREEN line, and will push forward posts to
                        about the line TORONTO - AVIATIK FARM.

                        The attack will be made behind creeping
                        barrage moving at the rate of 100 yards every 4
                        minutes. The barrage will finally halt, covering
                        the final consolidation, 200 yards beyond the line
                        of outposts (BLACK DOTTED LINE) and will cease at
                        ZERO plus 8 hours 20 minutes.

                        In the event of the enemy having evacuated
                        the GRAVENSTAFEL SWITCH and the ZONNEBEKE - STADEN
                        Line, the 164 Brigade, after the protective
                        barrage in front of the GREEN line ceases, will
                        establish a line of resistance along the
                        GRAVENSTAFEL SPUR, in touch with the 15th Division
                        on the right about GRAVENSTAFEL, and on the left
                        with 39th Division on GREEN line.

                        The dispositions of Battalions will be as
                        under:-

                            Right Front Battn.   1/4th K.Lan.R.
                            Left   "   "   2/5th Lan.Fus.
                            Right Rear   "   1/4th R.Lan.R.
                            Left   "   "   1/8th L'Pool R.

                        When objectives have been gained the 1/8th L'Pool
                        R. will become Brigade Support. The 1/4th
                        K.Lan.R. will become Brigade Reserve.

(3) Formation and   (3) The Battalion will be disposed on a two
    Distribution   Company frontage, each Company on a frontage of
    of Battalion.   2 platoons. The dividing line between Companies
                        during the advance will be a general line
                        starting from a point in LIVERPOOL TRENCH,
                                                          (100 yards

2.

(3) Formation and Distribution of Battalion.

(3) 100 yards N. of ST.JEAN - WIELTJE ROAD, passing through LYTHAM COT, BOSSAERT FARM, (to Left Coys) E. of POND FARM (POND FARM to right Coys) E. of SCHULER FARM, (SCHULER FARM to right Coys). E. of KEIR FARM.
Right Front Company (A Coy) LONE STREET incl. to Dividing Line.
Left Front Company (B Coy) from Dividing Line to Divisional Left Boundary.
These two Companies form the first two waves. The Right Rear Company (C Coy) and the Left Rear Company (D Coy) will form the last two waves as the battalion reaches the ground held by them after mopping up.
The Battalion will advance in artillery formation of platoon columns in file up to the BLACK LINE, whence it will advance in successive waves at 40 yards distance.
The leading wave will follow the rear wave of the 2/5th Lan. Fus. at a distance of 50 yards.

(4) Moppers Up.

(4). The 1/8th L'Pool R. will mop up all defences on the left Battalion front as far forward as SCHULER FARM inclusive, as per Instructions No.2. issued 24/7/17.
Mopping Up parties (C Coy. and 2 platoons D Coy) will take up their position in the assembly trenches with the Left Front Battalion (2/5th Lan. Fus) and will advance in rear of the first wave of that battalion. Mopping up parties will ensure reaching their allotted objectives at the moment the first wave reaches them, and will vigorously deal with any of the enemy remaining in them. They will also reconnoitre and clear up any other point in the vicinity which may be occupied by the enemy. They will further be prepared to go to the assistance of any other mopping up party on conclusion of their own task.

(5) Objectives.

(5) The objectives of the 1/8th L'Pool R. are:-

(a) To act in immediate support to the Left Front Battalion and to ensure the capture of the GREEN Line.
(b) After the ~~objective~~ Green Line has been gained:-
 (1) To assist in the consolidation of the GREEN Line.
 (2) To form a support to the whole Brigade Front and to dig in a support line on a general line passing through E of KEIR Fm. - SCHULER Fm.
 (3) To provide garrisons for the supporting points numbered 4,5,6, & 7, when these are constructed and completed by the Divisional R.Es.

Immediately the GREEN Line has been gained, O.C. Coys. will ensure the re-organisation of their commands and will proceed to the following tasks:-

A Coy. Assist in the consolidation of that portion of the GREEN Line held by the 1/4th E.Lan.R.

B Coy. Assist in the consolidation of that portion of the GREEN Line held by the 2/5th Lan. Fus.

3.

(5) Objectives. (contd)	(5) **C Coy.** Will construct a series of small tactical posts on the general line D.20.a.10.72. to D.13.b.27.20.(incl) to form in conjunction with the supporting points 6 & 5, a strong support line in rear of the Right Front Battalion.
These tactical posts will themselves be protected by a system of trenches in their rear to be dug immediately after, or simultaneously with the tacticalposts.
This Company will establish touch with the 6th Camerons in the vicinity of supporting points No.7.

D Coy. Will construct a similar series of small tactical posts and support trenches on the general line D.13.b.27.20.(excl) to D.7.c.central, forming a strong support line in rear of Left Front Battn.
This Company will establish touch with the 4/5th Black Watch in vicinity of Cross Road junction S.E. of WINNIPEG.

The Officers Commanding A & B Coys. will, on completion of the consolidation of the GREEN line immediately place themselves at the disposal of the Officers Commanding C & D Coys, and will assist in the construction of the support line, A to report to C, B to report to D. |
| (6) Garrisons of Supporting Points. | (6) As soon as the supporting points 4,5,6 & 7 are constructed by the Divisional R.Es. A & B Coys. will receive orders to garrison these posts on the basis of 1 Platoon (less 2 sections) including 1 Lewis Gun to each Post.
 A Coy. being responsible for 6 & 7.
 B "   "   "   "   4 & 5.
Should the Officers Commanding A & B Coys. find before receipt of order as above, that the supporting points have been constructed, it will be their duty to occupy them without waiting for orders.
One machine gun will be added to the garrison of each post on the order of O.C. 1/8th L'Pool R. |
| (7) Responsibility of Company, Platoon, and Section Commanders. | (7) In the course of these operations, many situations may arise which cannot be foreseen or provided against. In these circumstances Commanders of Companies, Platoons, or Sections on the spot must be prepared to act with promptitude resource, and resolution.
In every case where mopping up or consolidation has to be done, it is imperative that patrols and scouts be sent out to front and flanks to search for enemy, protect the working party from surprise, and keep touch with neighbouring units, platoons sections etc.
All Officers are reminded views of the paramount importance of and necessity for personal reconnaissance on reaching their objectives and before digging in.
Early information on every situation that arises during the operations is urgently required and must be forwarded to Batt.H.Qrs. with the least possible delay. |

4.

(8) **Communications.** (8) During the advance communication will be maintained by runner and visual.

When the GREEN Line has been taken the following posts will be established :-

(1) Batt. Command Post at or about POND FARM in telephonic communication with Brigade Forward Station at SOMME FM.
(2) Runner relay posts in the vicinity of D.13.a.75.60. for Left Companies, and about D.13. Central for Right Companies. Company Commanders will report location of Company H.Qrs. as speedily as possible.
(3) Visual will be established wherever possible but will only be used for important messages which must be kept short.

All important messages will be sent in duplicate by two different routes or means of transmission; those of special importance will be sent in triplicate by three different routes or means of transmission. Runners will carry all messages in the right hand breast pocket in which nothing else will be carried.

All Signals Stations will be marked with a triangular blue and white board, size 18". Troops will be careful not to bomb any dugouts marked in this way.

Aeroplanes on contact work can be recognised by the following markings:-
(1) Rectangular attachment on right lower plane.
(2) A white dumb-bell on either side of body of plane.

Only infantry who have reached most advanced portions of the Brigade objective will indicate their position to contact aeroplanes. This will be done by
(a) White Flares.
(b) Watson Fans.

Flares will be lit in the bottom of a trench or behind a parapet. Watson Fans will be used open and turned over at intervals of about 30 seconds so as to shew alternately the white and coloured sides. Contact aeroplanes will call for these signals by means of the KLAXON Horn and by firing a WHITE VERY LIGHT. The KLAXON Horn may not always be audible but as this will be the only occasion upon which very lights will be fired from the air flares must be lit and fans shewn by the most advanced infantry on seeing the signal. Times at which contact planes will be in the air will be notified later. The 118th Infantry Brigade on the Left will signal the gaining of the LANGEMARCK TRENCH system from D.7.b.1.1. to C.6.b.80.05. by Golden Rain Rocket. All Messages will be timed. All ranks must be warned that times will be written in clock times and not with reference to ZERO hour.

5.

(9) Liaison. (9) The following points of liaison have been arranged with the Brigade on our Left:-

BORDER HOUSE, ROAD JUNCTION, S. E. of WINNIPEG, D.7.c.34.55.

O. C. D Coy. will be responsible for establishing liaison at these points. O. C. A Coy. will maintain close liaison with 1/4th E. Lan. R. and O. C. B Coy. with 2/5th Lan. Fus. During the advance O. C. C Coy. will be responsible for establishing immediate touch with the 6th Camerons when the task of consolidating support line has been commenced.

(10) Tanks. (10) As per instructions issued. All ranks must be warned that on no account must they divert from their objective or line of advance by bunching round Tanks or conforming to their movements.

(11) Dumps. (11) Brigade Dumps will be established as follows:-

Main Dump - Junction of MILNER TRENCH & CONGREVE WALK. C.28.c. 20.05.

Adv. Dump. - About D.13.c.1.8.

Forward Dump - Left - SCHULER FARM.

(12) Prisoners) (12) Will be sent to the rear without loss of time, under the escort of slightly wounded men if available. Escorts must be kept as small as possible.

(13) Enemy Documents. (13) Two men per Company will be detailed to search systematically for and collect, enemy documents, maps, correspondence etc. These will be collected and put into sandbags which will be labelled ENEMY DOCUMENTS - URGENT. The label on sandbags will be marked with the location of the place where the documents were found. If taken from enemy dead, the word "DEAD" will be added to the label. These bundles will be passed to Battalion H. Qrs. as quickly as possible and from these to Advanced Brigade Dump.

(14) Medical. (14) The Regimental Aid Post at ZERO hour will be at I.4.a.6.4. POTIJZE WOOD. During the advance the Medical Officer will move forward in rear of the centre of the Battalion and will establish an Aid Post adjacent to Battalion H. Qrs. CAPRICORN TRENCH and later in vicinity of POND FARM. The O. C. Advanced Dressing Station will immediately be notified of the establishment of these posts by R. A. M. C. Runner.

6.

(15) Synchronisation of watches.	(15)	Watches will be synchronised between 5 p.m. and 7 p.m. daily. On Y/Z night 2/Lt. S.ROTHWELL will synchronise H.Q. and Company watches at Brigade H.Qrs in WYELTJE DUGOUT at 2 p.m.
(16) Zero Hour.	(16)	Will be notified later.
(17) Batt.H.Qrs.	(17)	Batt.H.Qrs. will move in rear of Battn. by line parallel to and 100 yards to left of ST.JEAN/ GRAVENSTAFEL ROAD. On arrival at the crossing of the FREZENBERG Line H.Qrs. will be established in CAPRICORN TRENCH. On objectives being gained Batt.H.Qrs. will move forward to vicinity of POND FARM and later to D.15.Central.
(18) Reports.	(18)	To Batt.H.Qrs.

Attention is directed to the following instructions which have already been issued.

    164th Inf.Bde.No.B.P./4. Amplification of Scheme.
    1/8 IRISH OPERATION INSTRUCTIONS NO.1.
      "   "   "   "   "   " 2.
      "   "   ADMINISTRATIVE   "   " 1.
      "   "   "   "   " 2.
    164th Inf.Bde.No.B.P.13. Memorandum on forthcoming operations

ACKNOWLEDGE.

Issued at 4 p.m.
By Runner.
Copies to:-

1. 164th Inf.Bde.
2. 1/4th K.Lan.R.
3. 2/5th Lan.Fus.
4. 1/4th N.Lan.R.
5. 164 M.G.Coy.
6. 164 T.M.Bty.
7. 6th Camerons.
8. 4/5th Black Watch.
9. O.C. A Coy.
10. " B "
11. " C "
12. " D "
13. C.O.
14. 2nd-in-Command.
15. Adjutant.
16. Capt.F.S.WARD.
17. Signalling Officer.
18. Intell.Off.
19. M.O.
20. T.O.
21. Q.M.
22. Sgt. AITCHISON.
23. War Diary.
24. File.

Capt. & Adjt.
1/8th(Irish)Batt.K.L.R.

1/8th (Irish) Batt. K.L.R.

From No. 308250 Pte. A. SMITH,
No. 5. Platoon.

To O.C. "B" Company.

Narrative of Action, 31/7/17 - 1/8/17.

I, as a Platoon Runner was with No.5.Platoon on the morning of July 31st and advanced quarter right, leaving the ESTAMINET on our right, towards the FREZENBURG LINE. We advanced in Artillery formation and I was sent by 2/Lt.J.E.FENN, my platoon Commander to get in touch with No.7.Platoon. This I did and reported to 2/Lt.FENN. I was then sent to the Left to try and get in touch with the BLACK WATCH. This I was unable to do - meeting only one wounded man of that Regt. who told me that nearly all the BLACK WATCH were wiped out. I assisted him and returned to my Platoon. We carried on until we reached the FREZENBURG LINE; there we deployed from artillery formation into line and advanced a few hundred yards and then halted to wait for our barrage. I went forward to gain touch with the 2/5th Lan.Fus. and found them to be about 50 yards in front. I returned to the platoon and reported; shortly afterwards the barrage commenced and we again advanced. We assaulted and took HINDU COTT. and from thence we advanced and took SCHULER FARM. From thence, Capt.WARD took a party, of which I was one, to form a line of resistance on the left of SCHULER FARM. The remainder of our platoon went to the right to WURST FARM to assist party of the 2/5th Lan.Fus.

The Bosche counter attacked from left and right and we were compelled to retire. During the retirement, Cpl.JONES, one of our wirers was wounded and I bandaged him up and placed him in a shell hole. I was by myself and encountered another of our men wounded and I also saw to him. I continued to retire until I met an M.G. team looking for "B" Coy. of the "Irish". I directed them to the nearest strongpoint and accompanied them. Here I found Major LEECH, Capt.WARD, 2/Lt.HODSON, and the party in the Strong Point held the position until nearly surrounded by the enemy, when we evacuated the position.

We withdrew to the BLACK LINE, and whilst withdrawing the enemy directed M.G. and L.G. fire on us and we suffered heavily. L/Cpl.COOPER and myself, not being able to find any more of the Irish remained with the Liverpool Rifles in the front line until they were relieved at about 3 p.m. on 2/8/17. After relief we rejoined our unit at the Transport Lines.

(Signed). A. SMITH

No. 308250.
No. 5. Platoon.   B Company.

1/8th(Irish)Batt.K.L.R.

From Sgt. BIRTWISTLE, No.6. Platoon.

To   O.C.   B Coy.

Narrative of Action, July 31st/Aug1lst/1917.

Left LIVERPOOL TRENCH and advanced in artillery formation passing BOSSAERT FARM on our left; soon after passing the latter spot we came under M.G. fire from all directions. We took cover in different shell holes under orders from our Company Commander, who soon after leaving this spot decided to find out exactly where we were and proceeded to a building which afterwards we found out to be VANHEULE FARM. It thus appears that we had lost direction a little. From here we moved away from the road in a direction right, for about 200 yards to a gap in the wire, and went through the gap. Here Capt. BUDER was killed. As we did not know where we were, we moved the platoon back to VANHEULE FARM and myself and Cpl. HETHERINGTON went out to reconnoitre. I proceeded up the road until I reached a trench crossing same. Here I found a Cheshire Regt. who could give me no information of my own regt. I came back to the platoons.

Cpl. HETHERINGTON then went out and crossed the STEENBEEK for about 150 yards. He could find no trace of any one and I met him about 200 yards in front of the farm where I had gone to observe and found out positions. It was then about 7 p.m. We were ordered to stand to somewhere about this time by an Officer of the Cheshire Regt. who said the enemy were expected to counter attack against ST.JULIEN, VANHEULE Fm. being the H.Wrs. for the 116 & 118 Bdes. No attack was made and we were ordered to move forward by the Adjts. to try and find our unit. It was about midnight and we had only 14 men left, of which 4 were taken by the Chess. for stretcher bearing. The remaining 10 went on but before reaching the stream we met a corporal of our own unit who told us that the Batt. had been relieved. We thus came back to our own lines.

(Signed).   BIRTWISTLE Sgt.

No.6 Platoon.   B Coy.

1/8th(Irish)Batt. K.L.R.

From Pte. T. GREGSON, No.7. Platoon.

To O.C. "B" Company.

Narrative of Action 31st July/1st Aug 1917.

We commenced about 8.20 a.m. from LIVERPOOL TRENCH on July 31st, in charge of Lieut. C.W. TOMS. We worked our way to the right in Artillery Formation and continued until we came under Machine Gun and Rifle Fire, which was particularly severe on the ST. JEAN ROAD about 500 yards in advance of the BLUE LINE. We were held up for at least half an hour, then we went forward to our objective; we were then informed by Lieuts. TOMS & ORCHARD that we were 12 minutes in front of our own barrage. We then fell back about 100 yards, at the same time working slightly to the right for safety until the barrage had lifted. There we found about 5 of the enemy concealed in a large concrete dugout, apparently used as Headquarters containing maps etc. These were handed by me to Cpl. ABBOTT to be forwarded to the Officer. We then proceeded to our objective and found that the enemy was massing his troops for a Counter Attack, as he could be seen chiefly on the Right and Left, advancing towards us in massed formation. We were "digging in" under heavy gun fire, but as we were very weak and in danger of being surrounded, we were ordered by Lieut. TOMS to fall back. This movement gave us a better position and slight reinforcements, enabling us to hold the enemy in check for about an hour.

Major LEECH then came up and viewed the position and placed a few men on the Left and Right. The centre was being held by Machine and Lewis Gun fire from a concrete dugout. This position was held until all the ammunition was exhausted and Major LEECH gave the order to "fall back". The time would be about 4.30 p.m. and it would be about 5 p.m. when we reached the BLACK LINE that had in the meantime been dug behind. Here we remained until relieved in the early hours of 1st Aug. 1917.

Signed,

(Signed).

T. Gregson.

7 Platoon.
1/8th(Irish)Batt. K.L.R.

1/8th(Irish)Batt. K.L.R.

From Pte. J. SHANE, No. 8. Platoon,

To O.C. B Coy.

Narrative of Action 31st July/1st Aug. 1917.

At 8.20 a.m. on Tuesday July 31st, 8 Platoon, B Coy. commanded by 2/Lt. DAVIES, left the assembly trench and commenced to advance. We advanced to the ridge behind the FREZENBURG LINE when we were held up by M.G. fire sustaining many casualties. We lay down and waited for the barrage to lift and then advanced to the next ridge, where 2/Lt. DAVIES was wounded and I lost sight of him. The remainder of the Company advanced to SCHULER FARM which we captured and sent several Germans down the line with our wounded. Lieut. ORCHARD and most of our N.C.Os. were hit whilst holding this position. Capt. WARD came along and took a party away to the left; I dont know what became of them. We held on for some hours when the Germans commenced to counter attack, which lasted about 1½ hours. We then found there was nobody on our left, so we withdrew to the BLACK LINE where we stood to all night and part of the next day. The BLACK LINE was also defended by the 165 Brigade. About midday Wednesday, we learned that our Brigade had been relieved and had taken up position in the old front line so we went and rejoined our Battalion.

(Signed) J. SHANE

8 Platoon.
B Company.

"A" COMPANY.

Company H.Qrs.
No. 1. Platoon.
" 2   "
" 3   "
" 4   "

=0=0=0=0=0=0=0=0=

1/8th(Irish)Batt.K.L.R.

From Pte.J.EVANS, No.14 Platoon.

To O.C.   D   Coy.

Narrative of Action 31st July/1st Aug.1917.

On the morning of July 31st we left LIVERPOOL TRENCH and advanced to our objective in the rear of No.13 platoon of the 2/5th Lan.Fus.   All went well until we were about 300 yards passed BOSSAERT FARM when a large shell burst just in front of our platoon, killing one man and seriously wounding 3 others.   I myself was knocked down with the concussion and partly buried with earth. As soon as I recovered from the shock I managed to see if I could find my platoon but not being able to see if I could find them I went forward in the direction of BORDER HOUSE. On the way I met Pte.WILSON of 14 Plat. and he told me the platoon had gone on and that he was wounded so I went on again and came across Pte.A.R.TAYLOR a Lewis Gunner of 14 platoon who was wounded in the leg and hand.   I dressed his wounds and left him to make his way back.   I then went on and got in touch with D Company, who were taking cover behind a ridge and reported to the Company S.M. what had happened.   Learning that, Cpl. ANKERS, has been detailed to go and see if BORDER HOUSE had been cleared,   I followed him but when we got there we lost touch with one another and I then tried to find my way back again to D Coy. and made enquiries off an Officer of the Royal Sussex Regt. and he told me that I had better stay with his men for a while as the enemy was preparing for a counter attack, and he was getting his men into position to beat it off.   I stayed with them a couple of hours and then thought I had better try and make my way back to my own Battalion so I wended my way over to the right and came across Captain JONES and about 20 men on the left of the road near SPREE FARM. During the time that I was with them Capt.JONES left us with Cpl.ELLIOTT to go and see the Colonel of the Lan.Fus. and when they came back we were told that Capt.JONES had been wounded.   He stayed with us until about midnight and then left us to go and have his wounds dressed, leaving Mr.FENN in charge.   We stayed where he left us until reinforced relieved the next day about 1.30 p.m. proceeding to the WIELTJE, where we joined up with the rest of our Battalion under Capt.MONKS.

We were relieved next morning.

(Signed)   J. EVANS
307997
No. 14 Platoon.

1/8th(Irish)Batt.K.L.R.

From O.C. A Coy.

To Adjutant.

Narrative of Action, 31/7/17 - 1/8/17.

On the morning of July 31st at 8.30 a.m. we left COLGREVE WALK to attack the German line. We advanced in artillery formation under shell fire until we got beyond WIELTJE and we went further along when the enemy opened out with a machine gun barrage so we took what cover was available, but lost a few men, including 2 or 3 N.C.Os. When the enemy ceased firing for a short time we advanced through the 165 and 166 Brigades in extended order and then the enemy opened fire again and we suffered more casualties. We took cover again behind a mound of ground and a few yards ahead discovered a sniper in a shell hole and threw a bomb at him and 2 men rushed the shell hole and took him prisoner. After that we advanced under Capt. BODEL further along and we captured more prisoners. Later we got in touch with some of the 1/4th R.Lan.R. near SOMME FARM where we discovered a battery of Field Guns and we rounded up more of the enemy who were hiding in shell holes. They surrendered without shewing fight. The german dugouts were strongly made, but our artillery had played havoc with them and smashed them. We advanced further along under our own artillery barrage and we got as far as SCHULER FARM which was strongly fortified with barbed wire, cut in several places by our shell fire. At this point I lost touch with Capt. BODEL because we had to take cover from snipers and German aeroplanes, which were very active at the time (12 noon). I was under cover when I met Pte. COSGROVE who was going down for reinforcements so I went with him in order to ensure getting the news to H.Qrs. and informed the C.O. He ordered 3 or 4 machine guns into action but in the meantime our men had retired to the BLACK LINE and dug in. We then held this ground with the aid of other troops in the Division. Later on our artillery opened out but they dropped short on our trenches and Capt. JONES was wounded but stayed with us for a few hours in command. In the morning we were relieved and went to our original front line which was shelled at intervals without any damage as far as I know. We were relieved about 3 p.m. by the 2nd Royal Irish Rifles.

Cy.Sgt.Maj. Cook

for O.C. "A" Coy.

1/8th(Irish)Batt. K.L.R.

From Pte. DAVIES. No. 1. Platoon.

To O.C. A Company.

Narrative of Action 31st July/1st August. 1917.

    On July 31st we left CONGREVE WALK about 3.30 a.m. under the Command of 2 Lt. E.F. LYNCH and Sergt. HARDY. Forming up in artillery formation with the 1/4th R. Lan. R. on our right we advanced across the open. After reaching the German front line 2/Lt. LYNCH was wounded and he passed orders to Sergt. HARDY to carry on. Proceeding half right No. 1. Platoon were badly hit by a shell and all the Bombers with the exception of one were badly wounded. The Lewis Gun and ammunition were blown away, No. 2. of the gun being wounded. On recovering the gun we moved on till we got to the FREZENBURG LINE, held by the 9th King's. We continued our advance under the barrage, losing Cpl. POWERS who was in charge of the Lewis Gun. Ptes. DAVIES & BONNER were the only ones left with the gun and proceeded on to our objective. After holding out here some hours against enemy attacks, we received orders to fall back. We then lost touch with the Company and came back to the 5th S. Lancs. in FREZENBURG LINE and reported to the Officer i/c who told us to stand by till further orders and to have our gun ready for action. Here we stopped the night when we received orders the following morning to go back to our old front line and report to 164 H. Qrs. bringing back the Lewis Gun and Spare parts.

(Signed)   DAVIES

307800. No. 1. Platoon.

1/8th(Irish)Batt.K.L.R.

From 303478 Pte.H.COSGROVE. No.2.Platoon.

To O.C. A Coy.

Narrative of Action 31st July/1st Aug:1917.

On the morning of the 31st July No.2.Platoon went over to attack and advanced 200 or 300 yards beyond the BLACK LINE where we came under machine gun fire which wounded 3 or 4 men in the Platoon, these being the first casualties. At that time we were still in artillery formation but immediately swung out to skirmishing order and shortly afterwards we captured a battery of 4 field guns which I think were subsequently recovered by the enemy. From that point we lost all semblance of a platoon but carried on under the command of Capt. BODEL and 2/Lt. WRAY, being held up in shell-holes at intervals by the fire of distant machine guns and snipers. One sniper we found held us up from a distance of 15 yards but he was wounded by a bomb thrown by L/Cpl. COPLIN and we captured him. From this point we advanced to a large mound of earth about 100 yards long, by 10 feet high. Here Capt. BODEL sent a message down for reinforcements. It was about 11 a.m. and we were about 150 strong, the majority 1/8th(Irish)K.L.R., but a good number of the 2/5th Lan. Fus. and 1/7th R.Lan.R. were with us. Capt. BODEL, after discussing the situation with the other officers present decided to carry on with the attack, although we were out of touch with the left and right flanks and couldn't see any signs of troops in our rear.

We pushed forward again, getting well peppered from the left until we reached WURST FARM where we were again held up. We occupied shell holes on the East side of this place and 5 enemy planes came over flying very low directing the fire of their 5.9 guns. This battery was probably within 1000 yards of the position we were holding. Intense M.G. fire, artillery, and the aeroplane machine gun fire withered us so we went forward again to the cover of some trees and bushes. I found a sniper sitting in a tree at a distance of 80 yards and brought him down ; a falling twig gave his position away. At this time I found Lieut. ORCHARD lying out in the open with severe wounds, unable to move so with the help of 4 German prisoners of the 456 Regt. I removed him to the building in our rear. This place was reinforced with concrete and contained 2 rooms, one equipped as an Aid Post and the other being Officer's sleeping quarters in this room. I placed Lieut. ORCHARD and my prisoners and found 7 more wounded men whom I brought in. I went to bring 2 more wounded but they were killed by explosive bullets before I could reach them. I found a wounded German who told me we had broken the line; shortly afterwards I discovered the enemy advancing in skirmishing order on our left flank, 200 yards away, and about 80 strong. Acting upon the orders of Lieut. ORCHARD I dumped all my equipment and made a bolt of it back to H.Qrs. with the information. On the way down I met Pte. HOLDSWORTH and took him down with me in case I didn't succeed in getting through. Arriving at the 2/5th Lan. Fys.H.Qrs. I found the

C.O. of that Battalion, also Major LEECH, Capt. JONES, Capt. WARD, and other Officers, to whom I reported. I was posted to watch the enemy and report movement whilst a defensive line was formed behind me. The M.G. Corps went out 100 yards in front with their guns and opened out on the enemy. Stragglers began to come in from the GREEN LINE and we turned them into the ridge we were holding. Our 18 pdrs. then opened out with shrapnel, but they fell short of the M.G.C. and I had to retire from my position to the firing line. Major LEECH and Capt. WARD went forward to the Machine Guns and I never saw them again. I was detailed to work with the stretcher bearers and worked with these men until 6 a.m. the following morning.

(Signed) H. COSGROVE

203475.
No. 2 Platoon.

1/8th (Irish) Batt. K.L.R.

From   Pte. R. LEESE, No. 3. Platoon.

To O.C.   "A" Company.

Narrative of Action 31st July/1st Aug. 1917.
_____

Having reached LIVERPOOL TRENCH early in the morning of the 31st July we advanced further right to CONGREVE WALK TRENCH, and there assembled. At 8.30 a.m. we commenced to go forward till we reached our objective, but before we reached this we had great difficulty in keeping the artillery formation owing to rough "going". After we had passed the enemy's first line of trenches our platoon Commander (a Sergt) was wounded. After this we came under very heavy shell fire and from this point we had many casualties, and the platoon was somewhat broken up. However, the few who were left, including myself, reached our objective and commenced to consolidate when we had to retire owing to heavy M.G. fire and shell fire. I then came across one of our machine gunners, Pte. CHURCH, who had his leg broken, and owing to there being no stretcher bearers in that vicinity for a time, I got two bayonets which I used as splints. He lay there some considerable time until we got him to one of the Tanks. From there the Stretcher bearers took him to the Aid Post. After this the platoon was nowhere to be seen and I got attached to the North Lancs for about 2 hours, before I came across some of our Company who were getting relieved. I joined in with them and we made our way to the WIELTJE Dugout, being relieved next morning.

(Signed)   R LEESE

No. 3. Platoon.

1/8th (Irish) Batt. K.L.R.

From Pte. H. JACKSON, No. 4. Platoon.

To O.C.   A   Coy.

Narrative of Action 31st July/1st Aug. 1917.

We proceeded to take up position behind LIVERPOOL TRENCH on the night of 31st July, 1917, and at 8.30 a.m. next morning we started to advance in artillery formation until we reached WIELTJE. There we had 2 casualties, one killed and one wounded. We went a bit further and another man was wounded and we then passed the enemy first, second and third lines. There we had another one wounded. We went on a bit further on and were shelled very badly, altho' there was a machine gun in action against us on our left. We were told to take cover and got our Lewis Gun into action and opened rifle fire on "Fritz". Going on a bit further we got another one wounded and the enemy shelling increased and was very heavy. We all got broken up and I got into the trenches a bit further on but where the others went to I do not know. About 3 hours after I went to look for my platoon but could not find it and was looking for them for about 2 hours. I then assisted wounded to safety. By this time it was about 1 a.m. and the Brigade Bombing Officer whom I met told me to stay there and act as a stretcher bearer and runner, which I did, until he told me to go and join the platoon at NEW JOHN ST. That would be about 9.15 a.m. and I spent the remainder of the time in our front line until we got relieved.

(Signed)   H. JACKSON

No. 4. Platoon.

O/988.

HEADQUARTERS,
    164th INFANTRY BRIGADE.

Reference your G.270 of the 3rd inst.

Herewith copy of further narrative,
just received from 2/Lieut S. Rothwell.

25/8/17.

Lieut. Colonel.
Commdg. 1/8th(Irish)Batt. K.L.R.

COPY.

Ward B.6.
High St Military Hosp.
C-on-M.
Manchester.
15/8/17.

Dear Colonel Heath,

Many thanks for your letter just received. The whole war as far as I know it is as follows :-

We arrived in the Assembly trenches without any casualties and everything went well until about 2-30 a.m. when Andrews of the L.Fs came to our dugout and told us that they had lost five Lewis Guns and one team. We lent them four guns. Up to this time we had only had one casualty.

At the appointed hour we got ready to go over the top. Everybody was in the best of spirits and the men went over singing.

The ground was very hard to recognize but we managed to find the way. Before we got to the Black Line a machine gun opened out on to us from the right, but we got through. By this time we, with Headquarters, had lost sight of the rest of the Battalion, so we made straight for Pond Farm. This we eventually reached.

As soon as we got there Ward and myself went forward to try and find out where the rest of the Battalion was.

We got to Schuler Farm and found Fenn and Orchard with about 30 men of D Coy including Sgt Major Greenwood. Orchard was badly wounded and was unable to carry on. Fenn and Sgt Major Greenwood were getting their men together. From what they told us they had had a hard fight for Schuler Farm but eventually had gained it. Ward and I then got the men together and took them across the road to where the Green Line was. Fenn stayed at Schuler with about ten men. Just as we had got the men out and they were commencing to dig in a machine gun opened on our left flank - evidently Gravenstaeel Switch - and laid a lot of men out. We got down into shell holes and tried to locate the gun. We could'nt do it however. The gun kept firing from our flank and we suffered heavily through it. Then there was some rifle fire from the same direction. By this time we had only about six men left, so we decided to give information to the tanks whom we saw about 200 yards in our rear. We left Sgt Major Greenwood in charge and made a dash for the tanks. In passing, I ought to tell you that the wire in front of Gravenstafel Switch was very strong and hardly damaged. We got back to the tanks and found one out of action and the other making his way back towards Wieltje. We managed to stop him and told him as much of the situation as possible and he promised to help. We then decided to get back to Pond Farm and make a report. On the way there we met the Tanks Observation Officer and told him the whole situation. He seemed rather lost and did'nt know quite where he was.

When we got back to Pond Farm we made the report and then Major Leech decided to go across to the L.Fs who were at Spree Farm. We got there and were just getting the report through to Brigade when a runner came through to the Fusiliers with a message that the Boche was counter attacking.

We got together all the men that we could see and I was going to take them forward when a message came through that we had four machine guns at Somme. Major Leech then told me to go there and get the M.Gs into action whilst he and Ward would go forward. I went to Somme and found the M.G Officer and helped him to get his guns into action. By this time the enemy was attacking in force and our men were retiring.

When I had got the guns into action I went back to Somme to try and get the Artillery on. I found that the Artillery could not get a message through so I sent a runner back to their Battery. Then an aeroplane came over and we also gave him the message.

I stayed at Somme until everyone else had left and then I went back to Spree Farm. Whilst I was at Somme I saw Major Leech and Ward going forward. This was the last I saw of them.

When I got back to Spree Farm I found Col Best Dunkerly, Andrews and Jones. I told them what was going on and we prepared to make a stand at Spree Farm. Some R.Es had come up by this time and so we collected them and got behind the parados of the trench at Spree Farm. We managed to get two M.Gs and a L.G. and about 30 men. Very soon the enemy started to come near and started to bring rifle fire to bear upon us. We had to be very careful as we were running short of ammunition, but we managed to hold him. He shelled us with havies but did not do much harm as he was not on the right range.

In this part there were two old Boche lines so we split the force up into two. Col Best Dunkerly and myself held the front trench whilst Jones and Andrews held the rear. Andrews came forward to speak to the Colonel and was killed. We still held on and then our Artillery found the range and opened fire. This kept the Boche rifle fire down a bit, but his Machine Guns and Snipers were still very active.

Later on in the afternoon Colonel Best Dunkerly was hit very badly and I was left in the front trench with about 25 men. I did'nt know what had happened to the people in the rear trench. I still held the trench all thrugh the night and by morning things were more or less quiet, except for Snipers and shells. We were up to our waists in water however, and it was not very comfortable. Still we held on. At about 9 a.m. on the 1st a rumour came round that the 164 Brigade was relieved. This rumour kept coming along and I thought that we had been forgotten in this isolated trench.

I then decided at 10 oclock to make a dash to the trench in rear - about 100 yards, to see if they had any news and also to see how they were getting along. It was whilst going there that I got hit. I asked the people there if they knew anything of the relief, but they did'nt.

They told me that Jones had been killed, but I am glad to hear that it is not true.

I was feeling very bad from the wound, and my arm was useless, so I made my way to the Dressing Station.

On my way down I saw Fenn holding a trench on the North side of the road just at Spree Farm. He seemed all right so I came along down.

That is absolutely all that I know of the battle. There were two or three things went wrong as far as I can see. First, I was astonished when Ward and myself were at Schuler Farm to see four enemy aeroplanes come over and have a look at our position. There was not one of ours in sight. Secondly, the tanks were nearly all out of action, and what were in action were trying to get back as quickly as possible. Thirdly, the wire in front of the Gravenstafel Switch had not been cut and was a large obstacle.

I am, Sir, I have the honour to be, Sir
Your obedient servant.
(sd) S. ROTHWELL.

OFFICERS.

2/Lt.B.E.ROBINSON.	wounded m30/7/17.	
k Major H.LEECH.	wounded and missing, believed killed 31/8/17
Capt.H.S.DUDER.	killed 31/7/17
" F.E.BODEL.	" "
k Lieut.E.F.G.ORCHARD,	Wounded and Missing, believed died of wounds. 31/7/17.
2/Lt.A.S.HARRIS,	Missing, believed killed 31/7/17.
k " F.A.WRAY.	" " " "
k Capt.F.S.WARD,	Wounded and Missing, believed prisoner 31/7/17
Lieut.C.W.TOMS.	" 31/7/17.
k 2/Lt.D.J.B.McCABE,	" and missing, 31/7/17.
" C.BFIELD.	" 31/7/17.
" H.MARSDEN	" "
" R.L.DAVIES.	" "
" F.J.WRIGHT.	" "
" E.F.LYNCH.	" "
" C.J.HOWARTH.	" "
Capt.J.F.JONES.	" 1/8/17.
2/Lt.S.ROTHWELL.	" "

Other Ranks.

Killed .... 27.
Wounded........190.
Missing........ 87.
            ———
              304

In addition to these, the following detached other ranks casualties are reported:-

422 Field Coy.

2 killed.   6 wounded.   2 acc.injured.   2 missing.

164 M.G.Coy.

3 wounded.

164 T.M.Bty.

2 wounded.

55th Div.Signals.

1 wounded.

-0-0-0-0-0-

CONFIDENTIAL.

164/J.5

WAR DIARY

OF

1/8TH (IRISH) BATTALION THE KING'S
(L'POOL REGT.)

from August 1st 1917

to August 31st 1917.

WAR DIARY

INTELLIGENCE SUMMARY.

(Erase heading not required.)

Army Form C. 2118.

Place	Date	Hour	Summary of Events and Information	Remarks and references to Appendices

I. of YPRES	31/7/17		Narrative of operations attached.
			The following are also attached:
			1. Copy of letter from Capt & Adjt J.F. Toms to Lt. Col. Heath.
			2. Copies of " 2 " 's " 9/Lt S. Rothwell (Intelligence Officer) to Lt. Col. Heath & fighting around
			3. Special report on "Capture of SCHULER FARM"
			    " " " " " WURST FARM.
			4. Narrative of events from
			    a. Senior Surviving Officer, N.C.O. & man from each Company.
			    b. Senior Surviving Officer, N.C.O. & men from each platoon.
			5. Consolidated list of casualties for whole operations.
				Instructions I + II for operations
				2. Battalion operation order No 108.
				3) Message from L. Col. Heath to Baton.
				C.S.
				
				C.S.

AUGUST YPRES Original front line	1/8/17		Survivors of Battalion — 9/Lts R.B. Hodson & J.E. Fenn & some 160 O.R. — re-established in original front line STRAND C.T. to WIELTJE. Capt A.J. Morks took over command of battalion & commenced to reorganise it for further action. Hot meals sent up to men. Weather very unfavourable. Almost perpetual rain — whole area a "sea of mud". Battalion ordered to return to former transport lines in vicinity	
	2/8/17			

WAR DIARY
INTELLIGENCE SUMMARY.
(Erase heading not required.)

Army Form C. 2118.

Place	Date	Hour	Summary of Events and Information	Remarks and references to Appendices
Original Front Line Trench	2/8/17		of VLAMERTINGHE on relief by 8th Royal Dublin Fusiliers. Relief completed about 2.0 p.m. In the evening while battalion then moved to billets & camp in the WATOU AREA. 'A' Coy (i.e. All Ranks who had been in action) were conveyed in Motor-Lorries, 'B' team (i.e. remainder) proceeded by march route.	C.L.
WATOU AREA (billets & camps)	3/8/17		Battalion resting. Capt. A.T. Monks takes over duties of 2nd in Command. 2/Lt Allison " " " " Adjt. 2/Lt Hodson " " " Command "A" Coy. 2/Lt Fenn " " " " "B" Re-organisation & re-equipment of battalion commenced. Correct details of casualties compiled. Narratives of events during the operation 31/7/17 - 1/8/17 obtained from surviving Officers & N.C.O.s.	C.L.
	4/8/17		Work of cleaning, re-organising & re-equipping progresses. Weather very rainy. Copy of "SPECIAL ORDER OF THE DAY" of 55th Division attached. Reinforcement: 17 O.R.	C.L.

WAR DIARY
INTELLIGENCE SUMMARY.
(Erase heading not required.)

Army Form C. 2118.

Place	Date	Hour	Summary of Events and Information	Remarks and references to Appendices
BONNINGUES	5/8/17		Batt. moved to billets at BONNINGUES (Ref. Map HAZEBROUCK 5A. 1/100,000) Proceeded to ARCLES by march route, thence by train to AUDRUICQ & thence by motor-lorries).	C.L.
	6/8/17		Work of re-organisation & re-equipment known favorably progressed. Attention now to be concentrated on the training of specialists. No training area at present available. — Companys training in vicinity of billets	C.L.
	7/8/17		Divisional Commander addressed all ranks who had taken part in action of 31/7/17 – 1/8/17. Copy of address attached. 2/Lt. A.A. Carbery returned from Brigade H.Q. & takes over command of "B" Coy. 2/Lt. G. Suridis " " " " " " " " duties of Y/sgt. 2/Lt. A.R. Allerton takes over command of "D" Coy vice 2/Lt. A.R. Allerton Battalion in training in vicinity billets.	C.L.
	8/8/17		Battalion in training 2/Lts. BALL & CARBINES + 148 O.R. arrived as reinforcement.	C.L.

WAR DIARY
INTELLIGENCE SUMMARY

Army Form C. 2118.

Place	Date	Hour	Summary of Events and Information	Remarks and references to Appendices
BONNINGUES	9/8/17		Battalion allotted training area some 2000ᵗ N. of BONNINGUES. Area very suitable for attack schemes, firing of Lewis Guns + rifle Grenades. Platoon attack schemes + firing of Lewis Guns on QUÉRY field firing range.	CL
	10/8/17		S.O.R arrived as reinforcements. Battalion in training in area.	CL
	11/8/17		2/Lt. Carbines to 4th Army Infantry School. Training.	CL
	12/8/17		2/Lt. Henn takes over command of "C" Coy. Church parade + inspection.	CL
	13/8/17		Training.	CL
	14/8/17		2/Lt Carbines returned from 4th Army Infantry School - course cancelled. Training. Successful Battalion attack practise. Capt. Whitaker R.A.M.C. proceeded to England on leave.	CL
	15/8/17		Usual training. Lt. Col. Nboth assumes command of Brigade. Capt. A.T. Marks 200 mins command of Batt. Reinforcements 2/Lts W. Hornby; A.G. Rao. M.B. Jones.	CL
	16/8/17		Training. Capt. Brand R.A.M.C. arrived for duty as M.O. vice Capt. Whitaker R.A.M.C.	CL

WAR DIARY
or
INTELLIGENCE SUMMARY.

Army Form C. 2118.

Place	Date	Hour	Summary of Events and Information	Remarks and references to Appendices
BONNINGUES	16/9/17 (ctd)		Result of inter Brigade Football Competition. 1/4 K.O.Y.L.R. 2. 1/8 K.O.Y.L.R. 1.	Cd
	7/8/17		Brig. Gen. C.L. Stockwell having resumed command of 164 Inf. Bde. Lt. Col. E.C. Heath resumed command of the Battalion & Capt A.J. Monks resumed duties of 2 i/c Command.	Cd
			Training as usual.	
	17/8/17		Training	
			Following Officers arrived as reinforcements	Cd
			2/Lt. O.T. Heathcote 2/Lt. F.A. Stone 2/Lt. H.J. Raynard
			2/Lt. F.A. Childs " A.K. Hewitt " M. Curtis
			" C.A. Baker " F.H. Kelt " K. Kendrick
			2/Lt. O.T. Heathcote takes over command of "C" Coy vice
			2/Lt. Fenn transferred to "B" Coy.	
	19/8/17		Church parade	
			Divisional inter-battalion Cross Country Run. Team of 30 entered from battalion. 1/5 S.Lanc R seemed 1st place with 8679 points. Battn secured 4th place with 6350 points. Other units of the Brigade placed

WAR DIARY
INTELLIGENCE SUMMARY
(Erase heading not required.)

Army Form C. 2118.

Place	Date	Hour	Summary of Events and Information	Remarks and references to Appendices
BONNINGUES	19/8/17	(am)	11th, 12th & 18th respectively. Capt. Brand R.A.M.C. returned to 1/3rd W.Lancs. F.D. Reinforcements: 2/Lt W.K. Cotton, 2/Lt F.E. Abloh, 2/Lt F.I. Hawey.	Cd.
	20/8/17 21/8/17		Training as usual in area. Battalion Sports Meeting held under ideal weather conditions. In the athletic event some very keen contests were seen. Prizes distributed by Brig. Gen. C. Stockwell D.S.O. to 2/Lt A.R. Geage, 2/Lt T.S. Gogsby, " W.J.C. Grayson, " F.J. Chadwick, " H.G. Speary, " A.W. Tickling, " W. Lake. Reinforcements:	Cd. Cd.
	22/8/17		Brigade Athletic Sports & Horse Show. Weather ideal. In the mounted events the battalion compared more than favourably with other units of Brigade. 1st Prize was gained for "best Limber" & 1st Prize for "Best Cooker". On the total points gained battalion was placed 2nd among the 5 units of the Brigade competing.	Cd.

1577 Wt.W10791/1773 500,000 1/15 D.D.&L. A.D.S.S./Forms/C. 2118.

WAR DIARY
INTELLIGENCE SUMMARY
(Erase heading not required.)

Army Form C. 2118

Place	Date	Hour	Summary of Events and Information	Remarks and references to Appendices
BONNINGUES	23/9/17		Training continues. Field firing in Quarry Range.	CLS
	24/9/17		Training somewhat hindered by unfavourable weather conditions. Capt & Adjt. J.F. Jones returned from hospital. 2/Lt G Stevens returned to 164th Infantry Brigade H.Q. to take up duties of Intelligence Officer.	CLS
	25/9/17		Training. 2/Lt C.A. Barker becomes attached (temporarily) to 164th T.M. Battery. Concert arranged for Batt. Divisional Pierrot Troupe & Orchestra performed.	CLS
	26/9/17		Church parades & inspections	CLS
	27/9/17		Training. The following NCOs were awarded the Military Medal (Authority DRO. No.766 dd 23/8/17) 305757 Sgt. W. Howarth 305155 Sgt. D. Foster 305314 L/Sgt J. Rimmer 305296 Cpl. S. Cooper 306237 Pte. R. Marsh 308541 Pte. E.P. Hughes.	JJJ

Army Form C. 2118

WAR DIARY
or
INTELLIGENCE SUMMARY
(Erase heading not required.)

Place	Date	Hour	Summary of Events and Information	Remarks and references to Appendices
BONNINGUES	2/8/17		Capt (Major) L. DUCKWORTH, 1/4 Loyal North Lancs Regt. Assumes main command, joins for duty. Capt A.T. MONKS assumes command of D Company. Capt H.D.F. BRAND, R.A.M.C. reports for duty as M.O. vice Capt H. WHITTAKER to 1/3rd W. LANCS F.A. 2/Lieut G. SURTEES returns to Bde Headquarters as Brigade Intelligence Officer. The following awards were notified under authority D.R.O. No 770 dtd 26-8-17. 2/Lieut J.E. FENN Military Cross 305891 C.S.M. GREENWOOD. T. D.C.M. 305179 Sgt. E.W. ELLIOTT M.M.	

WAR DIARY
or
INTELLIGENCE SUMMARY

Army Form C. 2118

Place	Date	Hour	Summary of Events and Information	Remarks and references to Appendices
BONNINGUES	28/8/14		Training as usual.	
	29/8/14		Firing on "B" Range. 3 Practices. 1. Application. 2. Application. 1. Rapid.	
	30/8/14		Training.	
	31/8/14		Training continues. 2/Lieut. F. BURNIE. 3rd. King's reported for duty 30/8/14. and posted to "B" Company.	W.S.

E.B. 100b

LIEUT.-COLONEL,
COMMANDING 1/8th (IRISH) BATTN. "THE KING'S" (LIVERPOOL) REGT.

1/8th (IRISH) BATT. "KING'S" (LIVERPOOL REGT).
------------------- o -------------------

Narratives of Action 31/7/17 - 1/8/17.

        Battalion H.Q.
        Adjutant.
        Intelligence Officer. *2 Letters.*
        Special report re Capture of SCHULER
        FARM and fighting round WURST FARM.

-o-o-o-o-o-o-o-o-o-o-o-o-o-o-o-

1/8th (IRISH) BATT. "KING'S" (LIVERPOOL REGT).

Narrative of Operations 31/7/17 - 2/8/17.

Ref. Map: FREZENBURG SHEET 1/10,000 (attached).

---

1. **Concentration.** The time spent in the concentration area passed without incident.

2. **Assembly.** The march to the Assembly positions in LIVERPOOL TRENCH and CONGREVE WALK and the Assembly Trenches on the night 30-31/7/17 were carried out without a hitch. There was no confusion during the assembly and the enemy artillery was exceptionally quiet.

3. **The Attack.** At 8.30 a.m. on the 31/7/17, the Battalion, (less C Coy. and 2 plats. "B" Coy. which were attached to 2/5th Lan. Fus. as "Moppers Up") commenced its advance in small columns (artillery formation) from the CONGREVE WALK - LIVERPOOL TRENCH LINE, in rear of the 2/5th Lan. Fus.
   The "going" was very bad, numerous trenches and other obstacles being encountered, especially in the vicinity of our own and the enemy original front lines. This caused difficulty in maintaining the formation which however was very good on the whole, as far as the BLUE LINE. Here, particularly in the neighbourhood of BOSCAERT FARM (C.23.b.12.30.) the enemy artillery fire was very heavy, causing many casualties and a little disorganisation. Two platoons of "B" Company lost direction here and moved to VANHEULE FARM and there remained for some hours under orders of the 118th Brigade. At this time there was an irregular hostile artillery fire over the whole of the area between the BLUE and BLACK LINES.
   In spite of this the advance as far as the BLACK LINE was well carried out according to Programme and touch was maintained on right and left.
   Immediately on passing the BLACK LINE however, the whole Battalion came under very heavy artillery, M.G. and rifle fire and heavy casualties were sustained. The hostile M.G. fire was particularly deadly and appeared to come from the high ground in the neighbourhood of SOMME, from HINDU COTT and from the direction of SCHULER FARM, and from our Left front.
   Nevertheless the leading columns were well up to the allotted time, the majority having to wait some minutes as the 2/5th Lan. Fus. were ahead of the time allotted for the first lift of the barrage. During this pause several Officers were hit by snipers concealed in a row of trees about C.13.d.6.6. in spite of the fact that they wore khaki uniform.
   At 10.10 a.m. opening into extended order, the Battalion commenced its advance behind the 2/5th Lan. Fus. being very well organised in spite of numerous casualties. At this juncture heavy artillery and M.G. fire was experienced from all directions.
   Casualties were very heavy and platoons became very seriously depleted in numbers. No check, howvere, was

(made

made in the advance. The enemy dugouts were everywhere found to be made with fero-concrete, exceptionally strong and with few exceptions, undamaged by our fire preparatory artillery fire. Most of them contained numbers of the enemy who speedily surrendered on being approached with the bayonet.

POND FARM and trenches in vicinity, HINDU COTT. BORDER HOUSE and dugouts at C.12.d.7.3. were all duly "mopped up" and prisoners and documents sent to the rear according to Programme. The "Moppers-Up" of "D" Coy. attacked the line of dugouts at C.13.b.7.9. capturing some 150 prisoners.

The 2/5th Lan.Fus. has also suffered very heavy casualties and by this time the larger portion of the 1/8th (Irish)K.L.R. had become absorbed into the leading waves of the 2/5th Lan.Fus. This was done in order to ensure the taking of the GREEN LINE.

The barrage was very ragged and not dense enough to prevent hostile M.G. firing.

By this time H.Qrs. had reached and been established at POND FARM.

Meanwhile the leading wave had been held up by M.G. fire from the emplacements D.13.a.80.30. to D.13.a.60.80. and SCHULER FARM, where the enemy was offering a determined resistance. These emplacements consisted of a concrete gallery with concrete M.G. emplacements branching off into the W. side. They were undamaged by our fire and the wire W. of them was uncut. They were eventually taken by a determined attack, a number of the enemy being killed and a large number captured. (see O.C. "C" Coy's narrative).

By this time WINNIPEG had been taken but SCHULER FARM was still holding out, and heavy casualties were sustained from M.G. fire from here and from the high ground around WURST FARM and from the direction of GRAVENSTAFEL.

SCHULER FARM was next attacked and taken (see narratives of Os.C. "B" & "C" Coys. and "Special Report on Capture of SCHULER FARM etc". 2/Lt. FENN).

But the M.G. fire and artillery had been so heavy that it had reduced our numbers to a low figure and caused much disorganisation. However the remnants of platoons having reached their objectives commenced to dig in in the neighbourhood of SCHULER FARM and KANSAS CROSS - WINNIPEG ROAD.

Owing to the heavy fire communications were very bad and the majority of runners sent with messages never reached their destinations.

Owing to this the position was not clear at H.Qrs. and Capt. WARD went forward to ascertain the situation. On learning that only very small parties of the 2/5th Lan.Fus. had reached the GREEN LINE he ordered "B" Company to push forward to WURST FARM and D Coy. to occupy the GREEN LINE in vicinity of FOKKER FARM.

Both these places were reached and consolidation commenced (see "Special Report on Capture of SCHULER FARM & Fighting around WURST FARM").

Thus at 12.30 p.m. the situation was as follows:-

Small force of "B" Company with 2/5th Lan.Fus. consolidating on GREEN LINE in neighbourhood of WURST FARM and "D" Company 1/8th(Irish)Batt.K.L.R. consolidating GREEN LINE in vicinity FOKKER FARM with a few small parties of 2/5th Lan.Fus. in GREEN LINE between these 2 main parties. All attempts to get into touch with Battalion on left failed. Remainder of the Battalion digging in near SCHULER FARM. Battalion H.Qrs. had meanwhile moved to SPREE FARM on account of heavy enfilade fire of M.Gs. on POND FARM.

3.

Hostile fire on our positions now became very heavy being apparently directed by low flying aeroplanes which appeared over our positions from 12.30 p.m. till 2 p.m.

About 2 p.m. under cover of artillery and M.G. barrage the enemy counter attacked in force, using several battalions in 3 - 6 lines extended to approximately 3 yards interval. The main thrust appears to have been directed as shown on attached map.

The party at WURST FARM, now reduced to 3, therefore withdrew to the KANSAS CROSS - WINNIPEG ROAD and after firing on the advancing enemy from here fell back to our position W. of SCHULER FARM.

The remainder of our force opened Lewis Gun and rifle fire inflicting heavy losses on the enemy until all ammunition was expended and then withdrew to our position by the emplacements W. of SCHULER FARM. The force here had by this time learnt that the right flank of the Battalion on our left rested at BORDER HOUSE, and therefore our left flank was "in the air".

Major LEECH, the Commanding Officer, having arrived at this critical period thereupon further organised the position for defence and endeavoured to form a defensive flank on the left bending back to BORDER HOUSE.

Sufficient men were not available for this and before reinforcements could be brought up from the BLACK LINE the enemy counter attack swept on this, our last position.

2 M.Gs. had been brought up and these supplemented by Lewis Guns and Rifle fire inflicted heavy casualties on the advancing enemy. When all ammunition had been expended and not until then, the survivors of the mixed force from SCHULER FARM, now almost surrounded by the enemy, made their way back to the BLACK LINE, fighting all the way whenever a little ammunition could be procured. Heavy casualties were sustained from enemy artillery fire during the withdrawal.

In CAPRICORN TRENCH the remnants of the Battalion were reorganised by Capt. JONES and 2/Lt. FENN (the only remaining Officers in addition to 2/Lt. R.M. HODSON who however had reached the BLACK LINE father South).

On the night 31/7/17 orders were received for the Battalion to return and hold our original front line.

Copy of letter from Capt. J.F. JONES, Adjutant.

To

Lieut. Colonel E.C. HEATH, Commdg. 1/8th L'Pool R.

My Dear Colonel,

Thanks for your letter. I intended to write you as full an account as possible before, but I have been knocked about so much since leaving the line that I have not been able to make time.

Yesterday's performance was a magnificent one, and I am glad to hear that it is appreciated by "Army" and so on. The General must feel very proud of the Brigade for they took their objectives in fine style and heldon to them for many hours under adverse circumstances. The withdrawal to the BLACK LINE was of an orderly character so far as the remarkably few who withdrew are concerned, and a stout resistance was put up there and an attempt made to advance our line again slightly in front of this position.

Perhaps I had better tell you what I know of the show from the beginning - which is not too much for communications, as was nearly certain in a show of this kind, were not of the best. The advance to the BLACK LINE so far as effected the Lan. Fus. and ourselves was almost without incident. Very few of the enemy and our own casualties were seen. As soon as we passed the BLACK LINE a perfect hell of M.G. fire was turned upon us from high ground in vicinity of our objectives, but no check in the advance was caused, altho' casualties were very severe. At this portion of the engagement we had bad luck with our H.Qrs., particularly Signallers who were widely extended, and, with about two exceptions did not get up to our Headquarters at POND FARM. I fear that most of them became casualties, together with a number of runners and pioneers. Leech decided to liase on our way with Right Batt. of the Division on our left at BORDER HOUSE - we did so, finding CAMBRIDGESHIRES occupying CAPITAL TRENCH up to a point about C.18.b.05.65. which was the most advanced point at which we ever gained touch with the left.

We moved on to POND FARM and established our Battn. H.Qrs. there - 2/5th Lan. Fus. opening at SPREE FARM.

At about 11.15 we passed about 50 prisoners down to Brigade, together with documents which were taken from them. The situation at that time (about 11.15 a.m.) was not clear, so WARD and ROTHWELL went up to reconnoitre. They found the Right fairly well established, but on the left our advance had been held up by the enemy wire roughly at D.7.d.55.65. to Divisional Boundary on Left. The trench behind was held and heavy machine gun fire was being turned upon us from it.

There was no touch with troops on left, and small bodies of enemy troops could be seen working to a position opposite to our exposed flank.

Isolated stragglers from the HERTS came in about this time (12 noon) with very serious reports as to the losses they had suffered and suggestions which seemed to indicate that they had entirely failed to attain their objective.

2.

A youth named STOCKWELL, 164 M.G.Coy. who had reported at our H.Q. about an hour earlier with a tripod only, now received four machine guns, and two of these were immediately diverted to form protection on left.

AT 1 p.m. the enemy had worked round sufficiently to be able to enfilade us at POND FARM with M.G. and considerable sniping was being done. We transferred our H.Q. to SPREE FARM.

A verbal report was received that WURST FARM had been occupied but this was not confirmed.

WARD had found ORCHARD severely wounded, holding SCHULER FARM with 3 men. They had to eject the enemy.

Frequent attempts were made to get reports as to situation from leading Companies, both our own and L.Fs. being forward and no attempt to make Support Line being possible.

Early in the afternoon the Brigade Major came up, and it was decided to try to form a general line, HILL 35 - BORDER HOUSE. LEECH and WARD went forward to attempt this - COLONEL DUNKLEY and myself remained in charge of H.Q. I did not see either LEECH or WARD again, I heard that they had been wounded and probably taken prisoner.

At about 5 p.m. men began to fall back from Front Line on our right and our men conformed. Working parties of R.Es. for supporting points, who did not report until after 5 p.m. also began to make their way to the rear.

The conduct of Col. DUNKLEY at this junction was magnificent. He rallied the few men of the L.Fs. who came back, added his H.Q. personnel and at once formed a firing line in the vicinity of SPREE FARM.

I found that CAPRICORN TRENCH North of the road, was not occupied by any troops for a distance of about 250 yards. I immediately assumed Command of the R.Es. and threw them into the gap. I maintained touch with the L.Fs. and had just arranged with Colonel DUNKLEY to advance our line behind CAPRICORN - in accordance with orders from Brigade - when I heard that he was wounded and wanted me. I ran across and had almost arrived at his position when I was blown head over heels up into a little trench and wounded in several places in the thigh (7 p.m.)

Unfortunately both Col. DUNKLEY and myself were hit by our own gunners.

I had already lent ROTHWELL to Lan. Fus. as they had no officers, so he remained.

I looked after the remnants of our Battalion which I tried to pull together and the R.Es. The 5th M.Lan.R. ultimately came up and took over the line, so I handed over Command of the men of our Battalion to NH. (about 30 all told) and arranged with 5th M.Lan.R. that they should remain in the line to assist them until orders were received from Brigade. I then "walked" down to WILTJE to get my hurts dressed - I had not had a real opportunity until that time - (about 10.30 p.m.). I intended to go back but was evacuated.

I have the honour to be,

Sir,

Your obedient Servant,

(Signed) J. F. JONES
Captain.

1/8th(Irish)Batt.K.L.R.

Special Report on Capture of SCHULER FARM,

and fighting around WURST FARM.

No.5 & 7 platoons marched a point on the WINNIPEG - KANSAS CROSS road as indicated on attached map, Lt. TOMS being in Command.

The force numbered two Officers and about 30 O.Rs.

Lieut.ORCHARD joined us with C.S.M.GREENWOOD, of "D" Coy. and about 10 men, and the whole party lined the road. We studied the barrage map and found we were ten minutes in front of our own barrage. We found our position to be 100 yards to the left of SCHULER FARM.

Lieut.ORCHARD took Command of the operations, and suggested surrounding the farm, as enemy movement was noticed.

The force was divided into three parties, the first taking the road under Lieut.ORCHARD, the second under myself, attacking the front, the third under Lt.TOMS, outflanking from the right.

My party having the shortest distance to go, reached the wire surrounding the farm, and we took up a position this side of the wire, and all shell holes, in order to allow all my party to get up. There were two entrances. All this time the right and left flank parties were doing their outflanking movements. No opposition being given I passed the word down, "When I blow the whistle I want every man to charge".

We reached the farm without difficulty and searched it, finding 5 unarmed prisoners. While engaged in searching the prisoners about 10 other ranks of IMPUTE joined us, who appeared to be part of Company H.Qrs. because one of the men was carrying a pigeon.

Lieuts. ORCHARD & TOMS arrived at this moment and then heavy machine gun and rifle fire was opened on us. We immediately took cover behind the little hill to the left of the farm, and began digging in, this being the support line IMPOSE was to hold and consolidate.

Lieut.ORCHARD was wounded here, and Lt.TOMS went back to explain the situation, and delivered his message after being wounded. At this point an Officer of IMPUTE came up with a few men, and asked for Lt.ORCHARD. He bandaged him and here we suffered further casualties.

The german prisoners assisted our wounded men back. An Officer of IMPUTE said he would push forward to WURST FARM, taking with him about 10 men.

At this point Capt.WARD, accompanied by 2/Lt.ROTHWELL arrived and advised me to go forward and assist IMPUTE to consolidate.

A party of IMPUTE about 20 strong, under a C.S.M. came forward on the right and took up a position behind two small mounds on the right, and in rear of WURST FARM.

On crossing the road, Capt.BODEL joined my party, and took command, and the party reached the officer of IMPUTE sitting in a large shell hole, to the right of the trench,

2.

which surrounds WURST FARM. Here they discussed the situation. It was decided to send two messages back, one by pigeon to Division, the message being written by the Officer of IMPUTE, who stated he would sign himself and for Capt. BODEL. Capt. BODEL wrote a message and sent it back by runner at 12.35 p.m. We arrived at WURST FARM about 12.10 p.m.

The runner was unable to deliver the message owing to HEADQUARTERS of IMPOSE having moved, and being unable to find them he handed me the message back, on the 2/8/17, when he rejoined his unit, having lost his way and joining the 166 Brigade. Attached is the message for your information.

Capt. BODEL, taking a runner, went out personally to try and get in touch with the left, runners being previously unable to do so. I did not see Capt. BODEL again until we returned to the road where he rejoined us. Taking the party the route as indicated on map, we searched the trench in front of WURST FARM. It was brushwood and floored with planks, and badly damaged. The dugouts were untouched and contained boxes of bombs.

My party consisted of:-

    Cpl. Foster.   B Coy.
    " Rooney.   " "
    " Abbott.   " "
    L/Cpl. Cooper.   " "
    Pte. Hurst   " "
    " Evans   and one man of "A" Coy.

Enemy aeroplanes flying low were locating our positions by means of very lights, the result being that we were heavily shelled, from ridge on left. This was the last I saw of the officer of IMPUTE until 2/Lt. DICKINSON joined us. He had been wounded in the arm and appeared very weak.

I gave orders to my men to open fire on all visible targets and not to waste their ammunition, being very short of it. All this time machine guns were active and we suffered heavily. I lost all my party as a result, except Cpl. FOSTER.

The few remaining men of IMPUTE retired running back towards the road altogether. The result was that they attracted heavy machine gun fire. 2/Lt. DICKINSON, seeing this, stood up in the shell hole and shouted, "Come along lads, don't go back, but put up a fight for it", and it was just as he said this that he was shot along with his runner, the two remaining being myself and Cpl. FOSTER.

I told the Corporal to go back, shell hole at a time, doing the same myself. We succeeded in reaching the road and here found Capt. BODEL and an officer of IMPEL with a Lewis Gun team.

The party was now 3 Officers and about 6 other ranks.

Capt. BODEL was killed on the road and four men wounded badly.

These were bandaged and tried to get back.

The Officer of IMPEL took his gun and fired to the left, the enemy attacking there.

This party retired and then Cpl. FOSTER and myself did the same. I reached our lines and reported the situation to Capt. JONES, it being now 5.30 p.m.

(Signed) J.E. FENN

2/Lt.

1/8th(Irish)Batt.K.L.R.

From Intelligence Officer.

To Adjutant.

Narrative of action 31st July/1st Augl 1917.

I beg to report that I was wounded this morning by a Sniper in the left shoulder. The attack went very well until we crossed the BLACK LINE, when we lost direction slightly. H.Qrs. reached POND FARM alright, and Capt. WARD and myself got in touch with all that was left of D Coy. We found them at SCHULER FARM. ORCHARD was wounded. Whilst we were there the enemy started a flank attack and we were obliged to take up a position on the GRAVENSTAFEL ROAD. Meanwhile WARD and myself went back to report to Major LYNCH.

We sent the report on to Brigade H.Qrs. and then conferred with the Lan.Fus. Whilst this was going on a report came through that the enemy was attacking in force on our flank. I went up to the Brigade Forward Station and got the machineguns into position. We were driven back to the BLACK LINE, where Col.DUNKLEY, ANDREWS, JONES, and myself got together with all the men we could and held the enemy back. ANDREWS was killed, and I believe JONES was also killed. Col.DUNKLEY was badly wounded.

I have not seen Major LYNCH or WARD since I went to the Forward Station. We held the position till this morning, when I heard we had been relieved.

I was going to get confirmation of this when I was wounded. As I was coming down I saw 2/Lt.FINN with about 40 of our men holding a position North of WIELTJE - KANSAS CROSS Roads, on the BLACK LINE.

I have nothing further to report,

I beg to remain, Sir,

Your obedient Servant.

(Signed. S. ROTHWELL
2/Lt.

Pigeon Message ~~OC "B"~~ Cay.
~~Special~~ report

~~Copy~~

Message Form.

...............Division.

Map reference or mark own position on Map at back.

I am at...... WURST F.M.

I am at............................and am consolidating.

I am at............................and have consolidated.

I need :—Ammunition.
  Bombs.
  Rifle Grenades.
  Water.
  Very lights.
  Stokes shells.

Enemy forming up for counter-attack at..............................

~~I am in touch with..................on Right/Left at..............................~~

I am not in touch on ~~Right~~/Left. Have sent out scouts

Am being shelled from... front heavily

I estimate my present strength at............rifles.

Hostile { Battery ✓ / Machine Gun ✓ / ~~Trench Mortar~~ } active at... from Ridge on Left

Send reinforcements

(Signed)

Time 12.35 P.M. Name... F.E. Bodel Capt
Date 3/11/17 Platoon... OC 'A' Company
Place.............. Battalion... IMPOSE

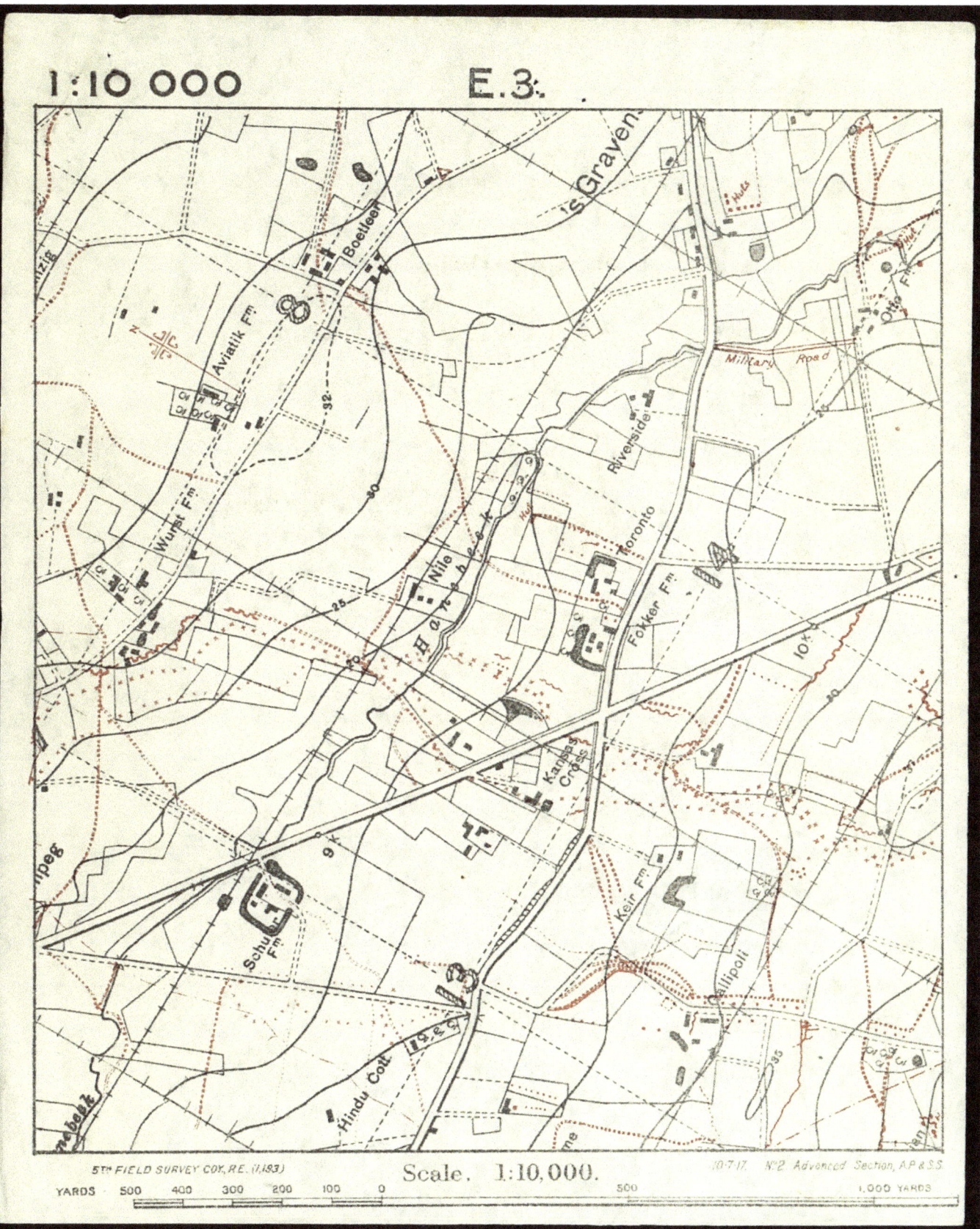

1/8th (IRISH) BATTALION "KING'S" (L'POOL REGT.)

SPECIAL ORDER

TO ALL RANKS OF THE LIVERPOOL IRISH (1/8th K.L.R.)

By your glorious work on the 31st July/1st August, you have earned the congratulations of all your commanders, and have gained the praise of the whole world. The English press is full of the gallant deeds of the lads of Lancashire.

You knew that you were going to win, you know now that you have won. You have once again beaten the Germans, you have yourselves snatched from them the central portion of a long strip of strongly defended territory, through which you have advanced our line by many hundred yards.

Never again will you have to do "Sentry-go", in DURHAM TRENCH, EDGE TRENCH, or the "DEAD END".

Never again need you look for Germans in WHITE COTTAGE, ARGYLE FARM, L.P.E. or WELL COTTAGE !

Never again can they snipe at you from CAMBRAI TRENCH, from KAISER HILL, or from the WHITE SAP !

You, by your own work, have changed all that. You have forced the enemy out of his strong positions, and by your own deeds have changed the whole aspect of the war on the YPRES front.

You conducted yourselves right gallantly on that great day, and have made your name for ever glorious in the history of war, and in the annals of the British Army.

That the price of victory is at times severe is unfortunately unavoidable, and I deplore with you, the loss of so many gallant friends and brave comrades.

To the relatives and friends of those who have fallen, I offer, on your behalf as well as on my own, our heartfelt and deepest sympathy. May it be some comfort to them all to know that those they loved fell in the supreme and proudest hour of their lives - winning - in the noblest cause for which man ever fought.

Signed. E. C. HEATH.
Lieut. Colonel,
Com dg. 1/8th (Irish) Batt. K.L.R.

In the Field.
6/8/17.

COPY.

Index to Map

A. Schuler Fm.
B. Shell holes to left of A.
C. Hill behind which party took cover
D. Point where Capt Boder was killed.
E. Shell hole where Lieut Dickinson was killed.
F. A large shell hole where Capt Boder & Lieut Impute drowned plans. Runner was sent back messages were sent back by pigeon & runner.
G. Trench Surrounding Wurst Fm.
H. Wurst Fm.
I & J. Mounds behind which Impute took cover

COPY.

Ward B.6.
High St Military Hosp.
C-on-M.
Manchester.
15/8/17.

Dear Colonel Heath,

Many thanks for your letter just received. The whole war as far as I know it is as follows :-

We arrived in the Assembly trenches without any casualties and everything went well until about 2-30 a.m. when Andrews of the L.Fs came to our dugout and told us that they had lost five Lewis Guns and one team. We lent them four guns. Up to this time we had only had one casualty.

At the appointed hour we got ready to go over the top. Everybody was in the best of spirits and the men went over singing.

The ground was very hard to recognize but we managed to find the way. Before we got to the Black Line a machine gun opened out on to us from the right, but we got through. By this time we, with Headquarters, had lost sight of the rest of the Battalion, so we made straight for Pond Farm. This we eventually reached.

As soon as we got there Ward and myself went forward to try and find out where the rest of the battalion was.

We got to Schuler Farm and found Fenn and Orchard with about 30 men of D Coy including Sgt Major Greenwood. Orchard was badly wounded and was unable to carry on. Fenn and Sgt Major Greenwood were getting their men together. From what they told us they had had a hard fight for Schuler Farm but eventually had gained it. Ward and I then got the men together and took them across the road to where the Green Line was. Fenn stayed at Schuler with about ten men. Just as we had got the men out and they were commencing to dig in, a machine gun opened on our left flank - evidently Gravenstafel Switch - and laid a lot of men out. We got down into shell holes and tried to locate the gun. We could'nt do it however. The gun kept firing from our flank and we suffered heavily through it. Then there was some rifle fire from the same direction. By this time we had only about six men left, so we decided to give information to the tanks whom we saw about 200 yards in our rear. We left Sgt Major Greenwood in charge and made a dash for the tanks. In passing, I ought to tell you that the wire in front of Gravenstafel Switch was very strong and hardly damaged. We got back to the tanks and found one out of action and the other making his way back towards Wieltje. We managed to stop him and told him as much of the situation as possible and he promised to help. We then decided to get back to Pond Farm and make a report. On the way there we met the Tanks Observation Officer and told him the whole situation. He seemed rather lost and did'nt know quite where he was.

When we got back to Pond Farm we made the report and then Major Leech decided to go across to the L.Fs who were at Spree Farm. We got there and were just getting the report through to Brigade when a runner came through to the Fusiliers with a message that the Boche was counter attacking.

We got together all the men that we could see and I was going to take them forward when a message came through that we had four machine guns at Somme. Major Leech then told me to go there and get the M.Gs into action whilst he and Ward would go forward. I went to Somme and found the M.G Officer and helped him to get his guns into action. By this time the

-2-

enemy was attacking in force and our men were retiring.

When I had got the guns into action I went back to Somme to try and get the Artillery on. I found that the Artillery could not get a message through so I sent a runner back to their Battery. Then an aeroplane came over and we also gave him the message.

I stayed at Somme until everyone else had left and then I went back to Spree Farm. Whilst I was at Somme I saw Major Leech and Ward going forward. This was the last I saw of them.

When I got back to Spree Farm I found Col Best Dunkerly, Andrews and Jones. I told them what was going on and we prepared to make a stand at Spree Farm. Some R.Es had come up by this time and so we collected them and got behind the parados of the trench at Spree Farm. We managed to get two M.Gs and a L.G. and about 30 men. Very soon the enemy started to come near and started to bring rifle fire to bear upon us. We had to be very careful as we were running short of ammunition, but we managed to hold him. He shelled us with Havies but did not do much harm as he was not on the right range.

In this part there were two old Boche lines so we split the force up into two. Col. Best Dunkerly and myself held the front trench whilst Jones and Andrews held the rear. Andrews came forward to speak to the Colonel and was killed. We still held on and then our Artillery found the range and opened fire. This kept the Boche rifle fire down a bit, but his Machine Guns and Snipers were still very active.

Later on in the afternoon Colonel Best Dunkerly was hit very badly and I was left in the front trench with about 25 men. I did'nt know what had happened to the people in the rear trench. I still held the trench all through the night and by morning things were more or less quiet, except for Snipers and shells. We were up to our waists in water however, and it was not very comfortable. Still we held on. At about 9 a.m. on the 1st a rumour came round that the 164 Brigade was relieved. This rumour kept coming along and I thought that we had been forgotten in this isolated trench.

I then decided at 10 oclock to make a dash to the trench in rear - about 100 yards, to see if they had any news and also to see how they were getting along. It was whilst going there that I got hit. I asked the people there if they knew anything of the relief, but they did'nt.

They told me that Jones had been killed, but I am glad to hear that it is not true.

I was feeling very bad from the wound, and my arm was useless, so I made my way to the Dressing Station.

On my way down I saw Fenn holding a trench on the North side of the road just at Spree Farm. He seemed all right so I came along down.

That is absolutely all that I know of the battle. There were two or three things went wrong as far as I can see. First, I was astonished when Ward and myself were at Schuler Farm to see four enemy aeroplanes come over and have a look at our position. There was not one of ours in sight. Secondly, the tanks were nearly all out of action, and what were in action were trying to get back as quickly as possible. Thirdly, the wire in front of the Gravenstafel Switch had not been cut and was a large obstacle.

I am, Sir, I have the honor to be, Sir
Your obedient servant.

(sd)S ROTHWELL.

55th (WEST LANCASHIRE) DIVISION,

SPECIAL ORDER OF THE DAY,

3rd August, 1917.

To All Ranks of the 55th (West Lancashire) Division.

      Before you went into action on the 31st July, I told you how confident I was that the Division would do its duty, and maintain its reputation and the reputation of the grand Regiments to which you belong.

      You have done more than that.

      The attack you made on the 31st is worthy to rank with the great deeds of the British Army in the past, and has added fresh glory to the record of that Army.

      The courage, determination, and self sacrifice shewn by Officers, Warrant Officers, Non-Commissioned Officers and men is beyond praise. It is a fine exhibition of true discipline, which comes from the mutual confidence of all ranks in themselves, their comrades, their leaders, and those under them. This in its turn is the product of hard training. Your doings on the 31st show how well you have turned this training to account.

      You captured every inch of the objectives allotted to you. It was not your fault that you could not hold all you took. You have broken and now hold in spite of weather and counter attacks a line that the enemy has strengthened and consolidated at his leisure for more than two years.

      This will I believe be the beginning of the end When your turn comes to go forward again you will know your own strength, - and the enemy will know it too.

      I am proud of what you have done, and am confident that with such troops ultimate victory is certain.

H. S. Jeudwine
Major General,
Commanding 55th (West Lancashire) Division.

ADDRESS OF THE DIVISIONAL COMMANDER TO
1/4th R. LAN., 1/8th L'POOL R, &
164th T.M. BATTERY.
3/8/17.

General Stockwell, 164th Infantry Brigade,
8th Irish, 4th King's Own, and Trench Mortar
Battery.

The other day before you went into action I sent round to tell you that I was quite sure that you would uphold the reputation of your new regiments, and of your Brigade, and of your Division.

Now I have to tell you that you did a great deal more than that. What you did on the 31st July was a magnificent piece of work, grand and striking, worthy to be remembered hereafter with the old fights of your Regiments have gone through, and that the British Army has on its colours already.

It was a great example of determination and discipline, and by discipline you know what I mean - it isn't bright buttons and clean boots - that is a sign of it, but what means a great deal more than that. Discipline means confidence in oneself and in each other. It means confidence which a man has in himself and in his weapons. It means the confidence that a man has in his leaders and it means the confidence that these officers have in you.

That is what makes the Army, or a Division, or a Brigade, of a section, or 6 or a dozen men - I don't care what it is, that, coupled with the determination to get through, shews you what it means. It is done with hard work, and I know what you and your Officers have had under General STOCKWELL. Many a time you have come out of the trenches on Rest, and I suppose some of you have thought that there was not much rest about it. Well now, you fellows, you know now that the training you had was for your benefit and has borne good fruit. It has borne fruit for the nation, for the country, for the Army, for the Division, and for the Brigade. You got right up to your objectives, every one of them !! That is the fruits if discipline, given the material, given you fellows who mean to get through. That of course is the bottom of everything. I am proud of your determination, I am proud of the spirit you shew. I am proud of the way you did things - you did everything the Brigade was asked to do.

It wasn't your fault, or of anyone in the Brigade that you couldn't stay there. It was a magnificent fight and I am very proud to be able to hand down to General STOCKWELL the very high praise of General HUBERT GOUGH, Comdg. the 5th Army. It is a thing to be proud of and I believe it to be the highest praise I have yet seen.

I believe this advance we have started is beginning again. What you tackled the other day was three lines of trenches that the enemy has strengthened and consolidated for, to my knowledge, 2 years, for I have known that front for 2 years, and I know the industry he has put in it. You have got through that and the rest after that ought not to be so hard.

I believe the battle we begun to be the beginning of the end, but it is no use prophesying. We have only to work and hammer away at his lines and bring the war to an end as soon as we can, but there is no doubt that it will have a great effect on the war.

I cannot tell you how much I regret the loss of the fine young fellows who have fallen. A more honourable ending they could not have had. And you fellows will remember that I know, when you go into action again.

When you do, if you only act as you have begun, there will be no doubt but that you will win, and I am sure that you will.

Once more I congratulate you heartily, on the example you have set and the fighting spirit you have shewn, and I thank you, I tell you I thank you from the bottom of my heart, I am proud to have fellows like you under my Command.

-o-o-o-o-o-o-o-o-o-o-o-o-o-o-o-o-

"D" COMPANY.

Company H.Qrs.
No.14 Platoon.
" 15 "
" 16 "

1/8th (Irish) Batt. K.L.R.

From O.C. D Coy.

To Adjutant.

Narrative of Action 31st July, /1st Aug. 1917.

---

which consisted of 1 platoon & Coy. H.Qrs. D Company/advanced from the junction of THREADNEEDLE STREET and LIVERPOOL TRENCH at 8.30 a.m. on the 31st July, 1917. The remaining platoons were attached to the 2/5th Lan. Fus. as "mopping up" parties. We took up a position at C.18.c.7.6. just to the rear of CAPRICORN TRENCH. At this juncture the enemy artillery fire was very heavy. As we crossed CAPRICORN TRENCH we found the 2/5th Lan. Fus. still occupying the trench. We crossed the trench, passing through the Lan. Fus. and on to BORDER HOUSE, and FORTUIN which we proceeded to mop up in conjunction with the Battalion on the left - the Cheshire regt. A number of prisoners were taken here. The next position to be attacked was a line of dugouts at C.18.b.7.9. and more prisoners were taken here, about 200, several of whom were wounded. We then proceeded to dugouts at C.12.d.7.3. and on to WINNIPEG which we mopped up with the CHESHIRE and CAMBRIDGE REGIMENTS, which Regts. then took the crest in front of VAN TIRPITZ FARM. D Coy. proceeded along the main ZONNEBEKE ROAD (leaving a Lewis Gun and team, at D.7.d.0.4.) to the attack on SCHULER FARM from which strongpoint we had been fired upon. Also heavy machine gun fire was brought to bear on us from the direction of WURST FARM. Lieut. ORCHARD (O.C. D Coy) divided us into two parties and he led one to a frontal attack and I led the other to attack from the rear along the ZONNEBEKE ROAD. Lieut. ORCHARD was severely wounded as we took the position together, getting several prisoners and wounding several by our fire. We proceeded to dig in along the GREEN LINE. This would be about 11.40 a.m. About 11 a.m., I noticed the Germans retiring very fast from FOKKER FARM, TORONTO, and dugouts at D.14.a.9.8. in the direction of POETLEER FARM. There would probably be about 200 of the enemy. They were not wearing equipment. Two Coys. of the Lan. Fus. arrived about 12.10 p.m. and I sent them forward to take the GREEN LINE; also a few of B Coy. At 12.30 p.m. I noticed the Left Battalion retiring from the crest towards WINNIPEG. Shortly afterwards the enemy made his counter attack, preceded by a heavy barrage directed by flare lights.(white). from the Infantry. I took up a position at A.B. (see accompanying map). By this time the enemy had occupied WINNIPEG. One of our Tanks now engaged the enemy but after about 10 minutes retired in the direction of HINDU COT (one of our aeroplanes had been over at 12 noon and fired the single flare but as I had no ground flares I could do nothing). Four enemy aircraft now appeared flying low, using his machine gun and directing the fire. Small parties of our troops had now occupied the GREEN LINE and WURST FARM. We held the attacking force of the enemy off until every round was expended (I had 2 Lewis Guns, 8 men, 4 pans of S.A.A. for gund). We then fell back to SCHULER FARM. I here rallied a party of the L.Fs. and we again engaged the enemy.   We lost men fast. The enemy snipers did heavy damage.   In the retirement we lost Sgt. NAYLOR who had been doing fine work.   We then fell back on C Coy. who were holding a position slightly to the rear and we took up a position about D.13.Central. line C.D.E.F. (see map).   This was about 2.30 p.m.   Our advanved posts were now beginning to be driven in and the enemy was breaking through on the right.   We rallied our men who were falling back and got two M.Gs. into position (Sgt. KIRKHAM incharge).   These guns did fine execution amongst theenemy but we lost heavily,   No. 1 of the gun being shot down 4 times.   Capt. BODDINGTON hadtaken charge of the Strong Point and 2/Lt. HODSON was 2nd i/c, both doing fine work.   Major LEECH and Capt. WARD came to the position but both were wounded about 6 p.m. - Major LEECH sniped through the head, and Capt. WARD through the arm. We held on to the position until S.A.A. was all expended, having used the men's bandoliers for the machine guns. Shortly afterwards we fell back, to SOMME, where the same thing occurred, and then back to the BLACK LINE.   The men fought finely but we met the enemy as he was preparing a strong counter attack. At D.13.c.8.9. there is a large crater across the road and for about 100 yards on either side the road is in bad condition.   The enemy was armed with light machine guns, the heavy guns co-operating from the CRAVENSTAFEL SWITCH.   The men wore steel helmets,,great coat rolled, bandolier style, and a light pack on the back. A great number of snipers were used.

(Signed) T. GREENWOOD.

C.S.M. D Coy.

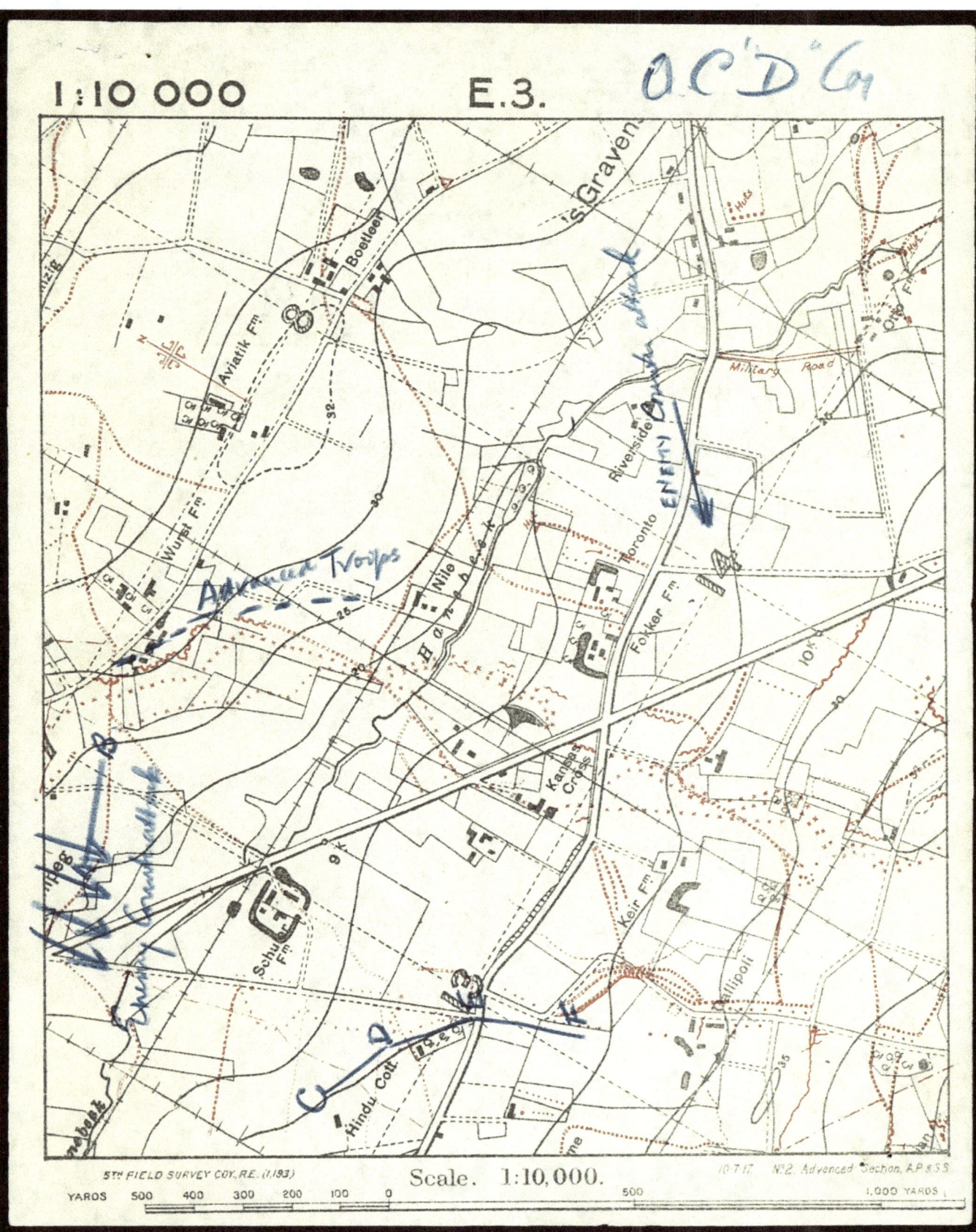

Message Form.

...............Division.

Map reference or mark own position on Map at back.

I am at..

I am at..and am consolidating.

I am at..and have consolidated.

I need :—Ammunition.
        Bombs.
        Rifle Grenades.
        Water.
        Very lights.
        Stokes shells.

Enemy forming up for counter-attack at..

I am in touch with............................on Right/Left at............................

I am not in touch on Right./Left.

Am being shelled from..

I estimate my present strength at.................rifles.

Hostile { Battery / Machine Gun / Trench Mortar } active at..............................

Time   a.m. (p.m.)   Name..

Date..   Platoon................. Company....................

Place..   Battalion..

1/8th(Irish)Batt.K.L.R.

From   L/Cpl.MORRIS, 15 Platoon.

To O.C.   D Coy.

Narrative of Action 31st July/1st Aug. 1917.

No.15 Plat.

At ZERO hour of the 164 Brigade, which was in CONGREVE WALK commenced its advance under 2/Lt.HARRIS in a column 2 deep.   All went well up to our own front line where we found ourselves in front of the Lan.Fus. A platoon Sergt. of 11th Plat. Lan.Fus. called to us to stop.   The word was passed up to Mr.HARRIS and he stopped us for about 3 minutes.   All the platoon was in close touch and we had only one casualty up to the BLUE LINE.

We then made forward as far as BRIDGE HOUSE, when a shell dropped at the rear of our platoon, wounding or killing all the rifle grenadiers and Lewis Gunners. Here the platoon lost a little formation but we made towards the BLACK LINE, the enemy shelling being at its height.   Here L/Cpl.UPSON and 2 men were wounded, also platoon Sergt. (Sgt.MONKS).   I bandaged them up and carried all into a dugout about 30 yards behind BRIDGE HOUSE.   There I noticed a battery emplacement but no guns; plenty shelling around them and a few direct hits on the emplacements.   Just by were three concrete dugouts, which were in the best of condition.   When I entered one of them I became very bad, which I suppose would probably be from the effect of one of our gas shells which the artillery had sent over before the attack.   I then made up the GRAVSTENAFEL ROAD, where I noticed the enemy machine guns very active and a great many of our lads in shell holes suffering from machine gun wounds.   I then made my way to the left, coming into contact with Cpl.ROBINSON, Mr.HARRIS and only 9 other ranks.   We were then about 20 yards in front of the LIVERPOOL SCOTTISH.   We formed up in the best formation possible, owing to suffering so many casualties we only had one line, we then made forward under our barrage. We went a short way before we were held up from a Strong Point about 300 yards in front of the BLACK LINE.   We again made forward, Mr.HARRIS still leading and made a dash for this Strong Point, capturing a great many prisoners and 3 officers. We continued to SCHULER FARM, our objective.   An enemy's machine gun was still in action, firing on the entrance which stopped us from entering at the front.   We then consolidated just behind SCHULER FARM and while we were digging in I noticed three German aeroplanes firing rockets towards us.   2/Lt.HIDSON and men were on our left, also digging in. After being there about an hour the Germans made a counter attack, and flanks fell back.   Mr.HARRIS then told us to fall back, which was to concrete emplacements behind SCHULER FARM, where we formed a strong point.   Here we met C.S.M. GREENWOOD, Lieut.HODSON, Capt.BODDINGTON (L.F.) and formed a defensive flank with Lewis Guns and Machine Guns.   The Bosche was still attacking in waves and every so often they stopped and sent up rockets, for artillery, which kept up a heavy fire.

Later Major LEECH and Capt. WARD came up; every man was kept busy firing. We had to empty pouches for the machine gun belts. The Bosche was now very near to us; Major LEECH made towards a flank where he received a wound in the head. Four machine gunners were sniped through the head while firing the gun. The Bosche was only about 15 yards away from us, and Capt. EODDINGTON shouted to us "Get back to the BLACK LINE". Capt. WARD was left lying on the ground badly wounded. We had a lot of casualties whilst withdrawing and we got caught in the barbed wire. We stopped in the BLACK LINE all night until we were told that the 164 Brigade had been relieved and we then made our way back to our old front line, reported to Capt MONKS and stayed there until relieved.

(Signed). MORRIS

307957 L/Cpl.
15 Platoon.

1/8th (Irish) Batt. K.L.R.

From Cpl. ROTHWELL, No. 16 Platoon.

To O.C. D Coy.

Narrative of Action, 31st July/1st Aug. 1917.

On the morning of the 31st July, our platoon, No. 16. were assembled in LIVERPOOL TRENCH, near its junction with THREADNEEDLE STREET, the Cambridgeshires being in touch on our left. At ZERO hour plus 4 hours 40 minutes, we got an order from our Coy. Officer Lieut. ORCHARD, to go over the top. Everything went alright. When passing our old front line we had three casualties, but we still carried on, No. 16 Platoon keeping in touch with the people on our left, until we reached BORDER HOUSE. We then extended out into battle formation and pushed on, my platoon Commander Sgt. NAYLOR leaving L/Cpl. ANKERS and 3 men behind to get in touch with the Cambridgeshires. It was then that we noticed that Mr. McCABE was wounded, but still carrying on. L/Cpl. ANKERS then returned to his platoon and reported that all was well on the left of our platoon. We kept pushing on till we reached SCHULER FARM, were the fighting was very severe, many of the Irish being wounded and killed. It was here that L/Cpl. ANKERS was told by the C.S.M. to take a number of prisoners. Whilst taking these prisoners he noticed 2/Lt. DAVIES lying in a shell hole, badly wounded. He stopped and dressed him and then proceeded. He met a great number of the wounded Irish and North Lancs. and stopping his prisoners, he told them in the best way he could to carry all the wounded down. Cpl. ROTHWELL of the Lewis Gun Section was going on alright till we passed the Scottish who were lying in shell holes and had not dug in; the enemy's machine gun and sniping fire being very severe. When we got to our objective Sgt. NAYLOR was wounded, a shell bursting near him, and I found that the Cambridgeshires had not got up, leaving us exposed with nobody on our left. The enemy was preparing for a counter attack and we took up our position in a shell hole and waited for the enemy to come, which they did in waves. By this time our platoon had suffered badly in casualties; my section held on firing on the enemy, inflicting heavy casualties on him, till the Irish were outnumbered and somebody shouted to withdraw. In doing so two of my men got lost, leaving me with three men, including myself. We then went off to Capt. JONES and reported to him and he told us to get just behind a ridge where we dug in. Here I met L/Cpl. ANKERS returning from taking the prisoners. Capt. JONES was wounded whilst proceeding to the Lan. Fus. with L/Cpl. ELLIOTT, our heavy shells dropping short killing two of our men. Capt. JONES handed over orders to 2/Lt. FENN and told him he was going to try and get on to our artillery about dropping shells short. He told Mr. FENN to look after the Irish - what was left of us. We stayed here until we got relieved, when we got orders to go to our old front line, NEW JOHN ST. where we reported to Capt. MONKS.

(Signed) Rothwell Cpl.
No. 16 Platoon.

"C" COMPANY.
------------0------------

Company H.Qrs.
No.9 Platoon.
" 10   "
" 11   "
" 12   "

-0-0-0-0-0-

1/8th(Irish)Batt.K.L.R.

From O.C. "C" Company.

To Adjutant.

Narrative on Action 31st July/1st August. 1917.

I have the honour to place before you my report of the fighting on the 31st July, 1917.

As "Moppers-up" to the 2/5th Lan.Fus. my Company (C Coy). left the jumping off trench at 8.30 a.m.

Our advance was good until we approached a point about C.23.b.80.40. (map attached). Here we came under a very heavy barrage of the enemy's artillery. Moving quickly, we reached the BLACK LINE at 9.35 a.m.

In the CAPRICORN SUPPORT we found the 1/10th King's (Scottish) Liverpool Regt. At this point a number of our wounded were seen. A heavy fire from snipers and enemy machine guns was playing round us all this time, while waiting for our barrage to left (at 10.10 a.m. by the clock). We suffered heavy casualties. I found this was due to the snipers whom I located in the row of trees (8 in number) which are to the right of CAPRICORN KEEP. I directed Lewis Gun and rifle fire onto these trees. Our fire was of good effect. These snipers had caused the loss of 2 Officers of my Company, my Company Sergeant Major, besides a number of other ranks of my Company. Many of the casualties of the BLACK LINE were caused by this fire of the enemy from this particular point. I personally reported this matter to the Officer Commanding 2/5th Lan.Fus.

Following our barrage, we moved to our objectives under a very heavy barrage of the enemy - his snipers and machine guns were active also. Moving to our objectives, POND FARM had been cleared of the enemy. Then HINDU COT - Here a "Tank" was doing very good work - and enabled us to move forward to the MACHINE GUN EMPLACEMENTS at D.13.a.80.30. to D.13.a.60.80.

These Emplacements were giving a fight. A Tank came up and helped to clear this place of the enemy. The Dugouts were bombed and a number of the enemy killed. A large number of prisoners were taken. When searching these dugouts a bundle of papers was found burning on the stove. At this place, the enemy appeared to have his Battalion H.Qrs. These emplacements were found to be well preserved, very little damage had been done to the concrete work and the wire in front was in very good condition - very little damage being done to it by our artillery. From here we moved to SCHULER FARM. The hedges around the FARM were very little damaged, for it was behind this cover that O.C. A Coy.(Capt. BODEL) and myself organised our Companies. SCHULER FARM was surrounded searched and found to be unoccupied. At this point we found three dead horses (on the left of SCHULER FARM). From this we concluded that the enemy had been moving his guns, for they were heavy horses.

Eventually we succeeded in reaching a line on the KANSAS CROSS - WINNIPEG road - in front of SCHULER FARM. I decided to take up a line at this point. During this time the enemy were busy sniping and firing at us with machine guns. The machine gun fire appeared to come from our flanks and our front. The snipers' fire was coming from the trees on the KANSAS CROSS - WINNIPEG ROAD. A message was sent to Headquarters at 12.30 p.m. giving our position. While we were making good our line four of the enemy aeroplanes were flying low immediately over our line. From this I concluded they were seeking information prior to a counter attack on our particular sector. Both our flanks were falling back, and at 2.40 p.m. took up a position in the MACHINE GUN EMPLACEMENTS in rear of SCHULER FARM. At 2.45 p.m. the Brigade Major of the 164th Inf. Bde. visited my position. I informed him of my plans and acting on his orders my men were placed behind the wire in rear of my position. I was reinforced by 3 guns of No.2.Section of the 164 M.G.Coy. At 3.30 p.m. the enemy approached in force immediately on my front. We held to our position until our ammunition was finished, then were forced to fall back to the BLACK LINE. I reported to the Officer Commanding the 1/4th N.Lan.R.

While falling back the enemy put up a severe fire from his machine guns and a heavy barrage of artillery. This barrage of the artillery seemed to be directly on our position. While the enemy approached our position in the counter attack it was very noticeable that he lifted his barrage by signal from the Infantry. The signal was a small white light. In my opinion the light if fired from the rifle and from the rifle of the front line of the advancing troops. The line of his barrage was on the line of lights. While we were holding the MACHINE GUN EMPLACEMENTS, 3 lights were fired directly at our position. Very soon after these lights were fired, the enemy's artillery dropped shells within a few yards of where I was. I remained in my position in the BLACK LINE until I was informed that the 164 Brigade had moved to CONGREVE WALK. I reported at that point but was ordered to report to Brigade H.Qrs. WIELTJE at about 4 p.m. on Aug. 1st 1917. I reported to Capt. MONKS of my Regiment at 4.15 p.m. 1/8/17 The Battalion were holding the line NEW JOHN ST. to LONE TRENCH and were relieved at 2 p.m. on Aug.2nd. I moved out of the position with my Company.

Before closing my report I beg to draw your attention to the fact that when we were attacking I do not remember seeing any of the enemy armed with a rifle and bayonet.

It was not until the enemy counter-attacked that his troops carried the rifle and bayonet. It is my opinion that he left his troops to defend themselves with the bomb as these were very plentiful. A number of revolvers were found in the dugouts.

At a point D.13.c.20.70. there was a strong brickwork, the top of which is made like a bee hive. This may be either a machine gun emplacement or an observation post. It was in very good condition.

I have the honour to be, Sir,

Your obedient Servant,

(Signed) R. B. HODSON

O.C. "C" Company.

1/8th(Irish)Batt.K.L.R.

From Sergt. FRASER, No.9.Platoon.

To, O.C. C Coy.

Narrative of Action, 31st July/1st Augt 1917.

On the morning of Tuesday, July 31st, we advanced from CONGREVE WALK at about 8.15 a.m. in artillery formation so as to take up our position at an unnamed strongpoint about a mile and half past the BLACK LINE.

Prior to our reaching our position we were very heavily shelled with 5.9s and machine gun fire was directed at us from the enemy on the Right of RAT FARM. The severe fire of the enemy caused our platoons to intermingle one with the other, although I do not consider that we had many casualties, up to the time of reaching RAT FARM.

After leaving this point we advanced in open formation (to prevent casualties) on a right incline so as to take up our position in the BLACK LINE.

I noticed that after advancing about 500 yards past RAT FARM we encountered heavy shelling, and Machine Gun fire which caused us very heavy casualties, with the result that by the time we reached the BLACK LINE, I do not think we were of more than half strength.

After a stay of ten minutes in the BLACK LINE, (during which time we collected our men together) we advanced together with the 2/5th Lan.Fus. towards our objective.

It was between the BLACK LINE and our objective that I noticed the enormous amount of sniping which was going on by the enemy, and which was causing fairly heavy casualties, and as a result when we reached our objective, we had to take cover whenever we could as it was quite impossible to dig in owing to the machine gun fire and sniping. Directly we reached our objective we at once opened out with Rifle Fire. I heard orders from someone for the Lewis Guns to fire, but so far as I know, I neither saw or heard any. Still I do not consider that had Lewis Guns been there they could possibly have been used, owing to his sniping being so severe.

We held our objective for about an hour, after which I noticed the only officers left were Capt. JONES, 1/8th K.L.R. C.O. and Adjutant of the 2/5th Lan.Fus.

At this time I noticed that the enemy were advancing in mass formation with the intention of making a flank movement on our left. It was quite noticeable that had we held on we should have been surrounded.

An order was here given by an Officer to retire to the BLACK LINE and to there make a stand; this we did until relieved.

After holding the line for 2 hours, the C.O. of the 2/5th Lan.Fus. and the Adjt. of the "Irish" were wounded, but the Adjt. of the Irish did not leave his post until about 4 hours afterwards, during which time he gave every encouragement to the men who were now left.

2/Lt. J.E. FENN, then took Command of our part of the line until we were relieved, when we retired to our original fire trench at the top of NEW JOHN ST.

(Signed) FRASER-Sgt.
No.9.Platoon.

1/8th(Irish)Batt. K.L.R.

From Pte. RAINFORD, No. 10 Platoon.

To, O.C. C Coy.

Narrative of Action, 31st July/1st Aug. 1917.

On the morning of the 31st July, we advanced in artillery formation from CONGREVE WALK, No. 10 platoon being on the right of number 9 platoon. Everything went alright until we got about 100 yards off RAT FARM, and then we got heavily shelled, causing many casualties and at the same time we lost touch with the 2/5th Lan. Fus. and went on to the FREZENBURG LINE, where we again established touch with the 2/5th Lan. Fus. We stayed there a few minutes and were fired on by machine guns and snipers and had many casualties. We then carried on to SPREE FARM where we took many prisoners and stopped a number of them from firing. We once again carried on until we got to our objective where we dug in but had only got two or three feet deep when we received the order to retire to a strong point, from whence we opened fire with our rifles and machine guns. We had been defending this strong point for about one hour when we received another order to retire to the BLACK LINE, owing to the insufficiency of men to hold out, and to a flank movement by the enemy on the right, which placed us in danger of being surrounded.

We stayed in the BLACK LINE until relieved on the following day at about 3 p.m.

(Signed). RAINFORD
306055.
No. 10 Platoon.

1/8th (Irish) Batt. K.L.R.

From Cpl. JONES, No. 11. Platoon.

To, O.C. "C" Coy.

Narrative of Action 31st July/1st Aug. 1917.

On the morning of Tuesday July 31st. 1917. we advanced from CONGREVE WALK at 8.10 a.m. in artillery formation. We were led over by 2/Lt. C.J. HOWARTH, following No. 10 Platoon of the 2/5th Lan. Fus. During this time we were being very heavily shelled, which caused the Lan. Fus to open out and owing to this we lost touch with them. The Officer in charge of this platoon then made for RAT FARM, which continued to the WIELTJE ROAD. During these operations we were shelled continually by 5.9s. and the platoon extended. Afterwards, we advanced along the WIELTJE ROAD until we were stopped by M.G. fire. We then made a left incline and advanced about 100 yards towards the BLACK LINE. By this time we had had a number of casualties including the platoon Officer and Sergeant, and most of the men. I was instructed by the Officer to carry on, which I proceeded to do, and met the Battalion at the BLACK LINE. After waiting about ten minutes at this line for the barrage to open, we advanced towards our strong point, situated about POND FARM, to the right of it. This point was taken by this Battalion and afterwards we advanced to our objective which we reached with about one third of the Battalion and what was left of the Lan. Fus. Owing to heavy machine gun fire on our left (which was exposed) we were unable to dig in and had to take what cover we could in shell holes. We held this line for practically an hour until ordered to cease fire by an officer on account of the enemy coming over dressed in khaki and with sandbag hats. On this ruse being discovered the Officer immediately ordered rapid fire, which was continued for about 7 minutes and caused heavy casualties to the enemy. Afterwards we were ordered by an Officer to withdraw, which we did, as far back as the BLACK LINE where we dug ourselves in and soon afterwards machine guns arrived with plenty of ammunition. At this point the enemy was very strong on our right, with rifle fire which caused a few casualties, including the C.O. and Adjutant of the Lan. Fus. and our own Adjutant, which left us with only one of our officers. We were continually shelled by the enemy, but held on to the BLACK LINE by the Liverpool, Scottish. We were relieved early next morning.

(Signed). JONES Cpl.
No. 11 Platoon.

1/8th(Irish)Batt.K.L.R.

From Pte. GOODWIN,
     No.12 Platoon.

To, O.C. "C" Company.

Narrative of Action, 31st July/1st Aug: 1917.

On the morning of the 31st July, 1917, we advanced in artillery formation from CONGREVE WALK. We had very little shell fire to contend with until RAT FARM was reached, when the shelling became very strong but our casualties were slight. We moved to the left of the ST.JEAN road and carried on, passing more lines of trench work, then came to an embankment which ran on both sides of the road. We noticed a farm or strong point burning. On coming back I was told that it was an AID POST. We carried on, making for POND FARM. On arrival, there was nothing to be found except a few dead Bosche. We went forward, still on the left of HINDU COT and commenced digging in, four or five hundred yards West of KANSAS CROSS - WINNIPEG ROAD. After digging in for some time we had to move back a little and fix up a strong point, owing to the enemy making a counter attack on us. We put up a good fight with them until it was found necessary to fall back to the BLACK LINE, where we held back the enemy. We had several casualties in the fight, and also caused the enemy many.

(Signed).   Goodwin

                                      308454.
                                      No.12 Platoon.

"B" COMPANY.

```
Company H.Qrs.
No.5 Platoon.
 "  6    "
 "  7    "
 "  8    "
```

1/8th Liverpool Regt.
Sep 1917

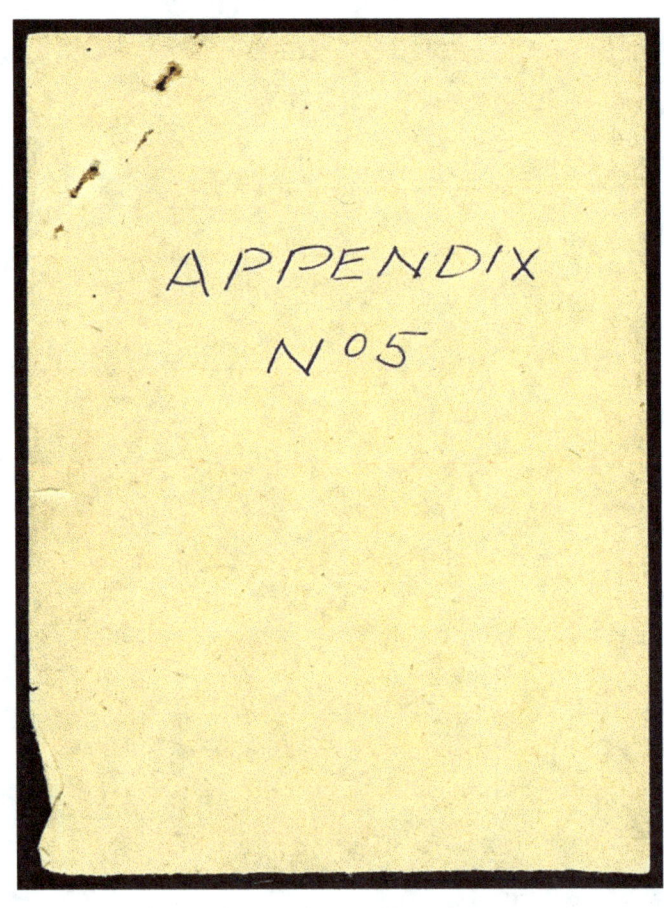

Vol 29

Confidential.

WAR DIARY

OF

1/8TH (IRISH) BATTALION THE KING'S
(L'POOL REGT.)

from 1st Sept, 1917
to 30th " "

WAR DIARY or INTELLIGENCE SUMMARY

Army Form C. 2118

(Erase heading not required.)

Instructions regarding War Diaries and Intelligence Summaries are contained in F.S. Regs., Part II. and the Staff Manual respectively. Title Pages will be prepared in manuscript.

Place	Date	Hour	Summary of Events and Information	Remarks and references to Appendices
BONNINGUES	1.9.17		Training. Battalion Attack formations and movements on Training area about 2000' N of BONNINGUES. Casualties Nil.	W.H.
	2.9.17		Church Parades and Inspections under company arrangements. 2/Lt. (Temp/Lieut.) J.O. COOK 4th NORFOLKS arrived for duty 1-9-17 and posted to "B" Company. Casualties Nil.	W.H.
	3.9.17.		Training. Battalion practice attack against new system of hostile defence. Casualties Nil	W.H.
	4.9.17.		Training. Brigade Attack Scheme in which this Battalion acted as enemy. Casualties Nil Lieut. J.O.S.I. Northcote proceeded on course of instruction to G.H.Q. Lewis Gun School, Le Touquet 3-9-17.	W.H.
	5.9.17.		Training. Brigade in the attack. Casualties Nil	W.H.
	6.9.17		Training. Platoon and Company attack schemes. Casualties Nil	W.H.
	7.9.17		Training. Platoon and Company attack schemes. Casualties Nil	W.H.
	8.9.17		Training. Platoon and Company attack schemes. Casualties Nil	W.H.
	9.9.17		Distribution of Medal Ribbons by G.O.C. 164th Brigade. (Trial attack of 164th Y.M.B. 8-9-17.) Casualties Nil.	W.H.
	10.9.17		Church Parades and Inspections under Company arrangements. Divisional Training. 2nd Lieut. L.E. Fenn to 164th Y.M.B. 8-9-17. C.A. Baker from. Casualties Nil.	W.H.

1875 Wt. W593/826 1,000,000 4/15 J.B.C. & A. A.D.S.S./Forms/C. 2118.

WAR DIARY or INTELLIGENCE SUMMARY

Army Form C. 2118

Place	Date	Hour	Summary of Events and Information	Remarks and references to Appendices
BONNINGUES	11-9-17		Training. Platoon Attack Schemes. M.G. demonstration for all Officers on GUEMY RANGE at 5.30 p.m. Lieut. J.F. Jones.) Entitled to wear the badges of the rank of O.S.I. Northcote) Captain pending notification in the London Gazette. 2nd Lt. M. Curtis. Returned from XIX Corps Bombing School 9-9-17. Lieut. T.G.A. Cook. to 5th Army Musketry School 9-9-17. Lieut-Col: E.C. Heath having proceeded on short-leave. Command to assumed by Major L. Duckworth from 11-9-17. Casualties Nil.	
	12-9-17		Training. Platoon and Company Schemes. Lt.Col. Heath returns & resumes command of Bn. W.H. Platoon Schemes, Field Firing Practice on GUEMY RANGE.	
	13-9-17		Training. Company Inspections prior to moving to forward area. Capt. O.S.I. Northcote from G.H.Q. Lewis Gun School 11-9-14. 2.Lt. P.R.P. George & 2.Lt. T.S. Godby. to XIX Corps Infy. Schl. 12-9-14. 2.Lt. A.W. Hickling to XIX Corps Lewis Gun School. 12-9-17. Lieut. T.G.A. Cook from 5th Army Musketry School 13-9-17. Casualties Nil.	W.H.
GOLDFISH CHATEAU YPRES	14-9-17		Battalion moved to YPRES, NORTH AREA.	O.O. No. 115. Attached.
	15-9-17		Training under Company arrangements. Captain & Revd. W.J. ALCOCK. attached as R.C. Chaplain 15-9-17. Casualties Nil.	W.H.
	16-9-17		Church Parades. Camp shelled by A.V. Shells. and bombed by fleet of eleven hostile aeroplanes. Casualties 10.O.R. Wounded. (one of which Since D.G.W.)	W.H.
	17-9-17		Company Parades and Platoon Retires. Casualties Nil. "B" Coy. under Captain R.B. Hodson. move to forward area.	O.O. No. 116 attached. W.H.

WAR DIARY
or
INTELLIGENCE SUMMARY
(Erase heading not required.)

Army Form C. 2118

Place	Date	Hour	Summary of Events and Information	Remarks and references to Appendices
GOLDFISH CHATEAU YPRES.	18-9-17		Final preparations before moving to Battle Front. Casualties Nil.	
	18/19.9.17	Night	Battalion relieve 1/10th Liverpool Scottish in CONGREVE/LIVERPOOL TRENCH. O.O.'s Nos. 117, 118, & 119. Also extracts from 164 Inf. Bde Order No 135. Attached.	W.D. O.O.149.
TRENCHES.	19.9.17		Batt. move from CONGREVE/LIVERPOOL TRENCH to assembly position at 8.30 p.m. Batt. Hdqrs. taken over at FORT HILL at that time.	J.G.
TRENCHES.	20.9.17		Narrative of operations attached. The following are also attached. & Narrative of events from (a) O.C. "A" Coy. (b) 2nd in Command "D" Coy. (c) Narrative from 1, 2, 3, 6, 6, 7, 9 and 10 Platoons.	J.G.
TRENCHES	21.9.17		SCHULER FARM captured at 4.30 p.m.	J.G.
TRENCHES	22.9.17		Whole front line now extended and consolidated, and strong points strengthened. All counter attacks were broken up.	
TRENCHES	23.9.17		Batt. relieved by Relieving between 11.30 p.m. and 1.30 a.m. 24/9/17 by the 2/6 North Staffs	

WAR DIARY
~~INTELLIGENCE SUMMARY~~

Army Form C. 2118

(Erase heading not required.)

1917.

Place	Date	Hour	Summary of Events and Information	Remarks and references to Appendices
Vlamertinghe No 2 Area	24/9		Batt. left St. Jans by light railway entrained at Vlamertinghe. 2 Copies of Orders of the Day. attached.	J.C.
			1) Letter 21st Sept. congratulating division on its work, from Fifth Army, Corps Commander and Major General Commanding.	
			2) Letter 23rd Sept. congratulations from V Corps.	
Vlamertinghe	25/9		Entrained at Vlamertinghe at 8 pm. detrained at Poperinghe then marched 2 miles and motor lorries to WATOU AREA. O.O. 120	J.C.
WATOU 3 AREA	25/9		Battalion resting. Reorganising and re-equipment of battalion commenced. 2nd Lieut R.E. Robinson and 2nd Lt James joined us with 196 men as reinforcements. Also 2 Lt. B. Daniels, 2 Lt L. McPoland and 2 Lt A. Wilson arrived for duty. Batt. moves to BAYPAUME WEST by rail from HOUPOUTRE Station. Copy of "Special Order of The Day" attached.	J.C. O.O.121 J.C.
	26/9		Batt. arrives here in camp at 10 am.	
LECHELLE AREA	27/9		Consolidated list of Casualties for whole operation attached.	J.B.
	28/9		Major L. Duckworth assumes command of Batt, vice Lieut Col. E.C. Heath on leave. Work of cleaning, re-organising and re-equipping progresses.	
"	29/9		Weather fine. Copy of "Special Order of the day" of 55th Division attached.	J.C.

WAR DIARY
or
INTELLIGENCE SUMMARY

Army Form C. 2118

Place	Date	Hour	Summary of Events and Information	Remarks and references to Appendices
LECHELLE AREA	29/9		Work of reorganisation still continues & attention devoted to training of specialists and general training of the Battalion. An excellent area around "F" Camp facilitating training. Special attention being given to training of Junior Officers & N.C.Os.	F.C.
	30/9		Church Parades and Inspection C.R.E. at Camp R.C. at YPRES Church	F.C.

R. Buckworth
Major
Comm⁹ 1/8th (Irish) Bn. "The King's" (L'pool Regt.)

SECRET.   COPY NO. 15

1/8th (IRISH) BATTALION "KING'S" (L'POOL REGT).

OPERATION ORDER NO. 115.

Ref: BELGIUM, Sheet 28 N.W. 1/20,000.
HAZEBROUCK 5A, 1/100,000.

In the Field.
13/9/17.

(1) The 164th Inf. Bde. will move to the YPRES, NORTH AREA, on the 14th September.

(2) This Battalion will move in the order:-

        H.Qrs.
        A Coy.
        B "
        C "
        D "

to the entraining station - AUDRUICQ, via:-
TOURNEHEM - ROAD JUNCTION immediately S.E. of JOUARQUES CHURCH - E of RECQUES - BLANC PIGNON.

The Starting Point at ROAD JUNCTION immediately S.E. of JOUARQUES CHURCH will be passed at 6.56 a.m.

Entrainment at AUDRUICQ will be commenced at 9 a.m. for departure at 9.45 a.m.

The following distances will be maintained:-

    During march to Entraining station.   100 yards between Coys.
    EAST OF POPERINGHE..................   200 " " "
    WEST OF POPERINGHE..................   500 " " Battns.

(3) Transport will move to entraining station in accordance with attached table.
The 4 vehicles entraining at 10.45 a.m. will not leave BONHUM USS until personnel of 2/5th Lan. Fus. are clear. Transport detraining at PESELHOEK will move from there by the SWITCH ROAD - NORTH OF POPERINGHE and the main POPERINGHE - YPRES ROAD.

(4) Supply, Ordnance, Lorry and postal arrangements have been issued.

A C K N O W L E D G E.

Capt. & Adjt.
1/8th(Irish)Batt.K.L.R.

Issued at 6 p.m.
By Runner.
Copies to:-
1. File.
2. 164th Inf Bde.
3. C.O.
4. 2nd-in-Command.
5. O.C.   A Coy.
6. "   B "
7. "   C "
8. "   D "
9. "   Details and Signals.
10. Intell.Off.   13. Q.M.
11. M.O.   14. R.S.M.
12. T.O.   15. War Diary.

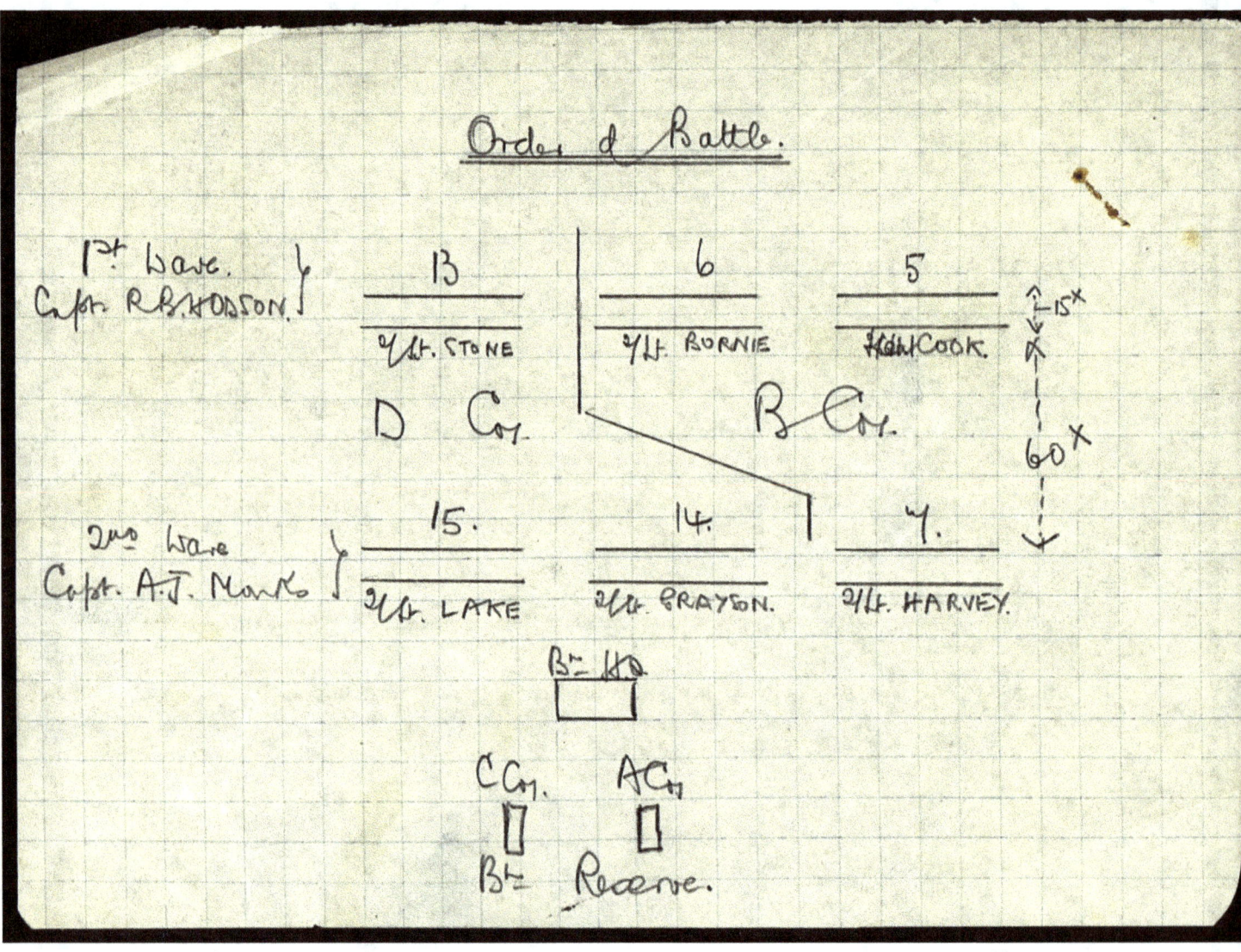

SECRET.   COPY No. 8

1/4th (HANTS) BATT. K.R.R.
OPERATION ORDER NO.119.

Ref: French Map ZANDVOORDE 1/10,000.
        GHELUVELT 1/10,000.

                                        In the Field,
                                        18/9/17.

(1) This Unit will move to its assembly position
    on the night of the 19/20th Sept. Coys. will
    be in position in accordance with attached
    diagram by 5 a.m.   Movement along the line
    of assembly after that hour must be restricted
    to a minimum.

(2) Leading waves will be in a position about 150
    yards short of the line marked "+5" on the
    barrage map.

(3) Movement from INVERNESS COPSE will be in the
    order:-
        D Coy. (less one platoon).
        1 Platoon D Coy.
        Batt. H.Qrs.
        B Coy.
        A Coy.
                        via No.6 Track, and will
    commence at 8.30 p.m. Platoons will move at
    100 yards distance.

(4) Assembly positions for Coys. will be reconnd.
    on the night 18/19th Sept. and dividing point
    of Sectors mutually agreed upon with O/6th L
    Fus.

2.

(5) O.C. Coys. will report arrival at
Assembly positions to Batt. H.Qrs.
by runner as early as possible.

(6) Batt. H.Qrs. will close at LIVERPOOL TR.
at 8.30 p.m. and will open at PORTHILL
(approx. C.19.b.20.50) at that time.

A C K N O W L E D G E.

J.F. Jones
Capt. & Adjt.
1/5th (Irish) Batt. K.L.R.

Issued at 11.5 p.m.
Copies to:-
1. C.O.
2. A Coy.
3. B "
4. C "
5. D "
6. Details and Signals.
7. 164th S.A.Bde.
8. 2/5th Lon. Fus.
9. 2/4th Lond. R.
10. War Diary.
11. File.

SECRET. COPY NO. 11

1/8th (IRISH) BATTALION "KING'S" (L'POOL REGT).

OPERATION ORDER NO. 116.

Ref: 1/10,000. Trench Map.
1/20,000. Sheet 28 N.W.

In the Field.
17/9/17.

(1) "B" Coy. less one platoon and one platoon "D" Coy. under Capt. R.E. HODSON, will move with 2/5th Lan. Fus. from this Camp to positions in old German front line system and old British Front line system on the night 17th/18th inst.

(2) 2/Lieut. F. BURNIE with guide will report to O.C. 166 Inf. Bde. at WIELTJE Du out at 5 p.m. 17th inst. together with guides and will ascertain area available. He will detail guides to meet platoons on ST. JEAN - WIELTJE Road where it crosses COW REVE/LIVERPOOL TRENCH.

(3) Movement will be by platoons at 100 yards distance - commencing at 7.30 p.m.

(4) Route will be as indicated by O.C. 2/5th Lan. Fus. under whose command the Company will pass on leaving this Camp.

(5) Capt. R.E. HODSON will report the location of the Company to these H.Qrs. immediately it is known.

(6)- DRESS - Fighting Order (as amended).

(7) Administrative arrangements as already issued.

A C K N O W L E D G E.

Capt. & Adjt.
1/8th (Irish) Batt. K.L.R.

Issued at 3.30 p.m.
By Runner.
Copies to:-

1. 164th Inf. Bde.
2. 166th " "
3. C.O.
4. 2nd-in-Command.
5. O.C. 2/5th Lan. Fus.
6. B Coy.
7. D "
8. T.O.
9. G.K.
10. Files.
11. War Diary.

SECRET.   COPY NO. 16.

1/8th (IRISH) BATT. "KING'S" (L'POOL REGIMENT.)
OPERATION ORDER NO. 117.

Reference:-   1/10,000.   Trench Map.
               1/20,000.   Sheet 28 N.W.

                                          In the Field,
                                          17/9/17.

(1) This Battalion will take over its Battle Front on the night 18/19th Sept. relieving the 1/10th Liverpool Scottish.
One Officer and one N.C.O. per Coy. and the Intelligence Officer for Headquarters will make the necessary reconnaissance on the night 17/18th inst.

(2)(a) "B" Coy. less one platoon and one platoon "D" Coy. under Capt. F.B. HOBSON will take over the Battle Front. Capt. HOBSON will arrange details of relief with 1/10th Liverpool Scottish. There will be no movement until after dark.
The Battalion less "B" Coy. less one platoon and one platoon "D" Coy. will move to CONGREVE/LIVERPOOL TRENCH. Diagram showing dispositions will be issued later.

(3) The Battalion will move from its present Camp by platoons at 100 yards distance in the order:-

         Headquarters.
         A Company.
         C "
         One Platoon B Coy.
         D Coy. less one platoon.

   by No.6. Track.
Headquarters Company will move at 7.45 p.m.

(4) Battalion H.Qrs. will close at this Camp at 7.45 p.m. on the 18th Sept. and will open at CONGREVE/LIVERPOOL TRENCH at that time and date.

   A C K N O W L E D G E.

                                          J.F. Jones
                                          Capt. & Adjt.
                                          1/8th(Irish)Batt.K.L.R.

Issued at 11.30 p.m.
By Runner.
Copies to:-
1. 164th Inf. Bde.
2. 1/10th Scottish.
3. C.O.
4. 2nd-in-Command.
5. O.C. "A" Coy.
6.   "   B "
7.   "   C "
8.   "   D "
9.   "   Details and Signals.   14. R.S.M.
10. Intelligence Officer.   15. File.
11. M.O.   16. War Diary.
12. T.O.   17.
13. Q.M.

SECRET.   COPY NO. 3.

1/8th (IRISH) BATTALION "KING'" (L'POOL REGT).

OPERATION ORDER NO. 118.

Ref: Maps FREZENBURG 1/10,000.
        GRAVENSTAFEL 1/10,000.   In the Field.
                                                                              18/9/17.

(1) **INFORMATION.** (1). On Z day the 55th Division will take part in a general attack on the enemy's positions. The objective will be the GREEN Line. The 9th Division will attack on the Right, the 58th Div. on the left. Divisional boundaries and dividing lines between Bdes. and Battns. are as shewn on maps issued.
It is probable that the opposing Division (2nd Guards Res. Div) has it's three Regts. in the line; that each Regt. has one Battalion in front line, one in support, and one in immediate reserve, and that those Battns. in immediate reserve are located West of the PASSCHENDALE RIDGE.

(2) **DISPOSITION** (2) The attack on the GREEN Line by the 55th Division
    OF 55th   will be made on a front of two Bdes; 165th on right,
    DIVISION.   and 164th on left. The 166 Bde. will furnish a Battalion to each of the above as Bde. Res. – that for 164th Bde. being the 1/5th R. Lan. R.
                      The remainder of 166 Bde. forms the Divisional Reserve.

(3) **DISPOSITION** (3) The 164 Bde. will attack on the frontage shewn on the
    OF BDE. FOR   map distributed to the sectors as under:-
    ATTACK.

                     1/4th R. Lan. R. & 1/4th N. Lan. R.   KEIR.
                     2/5th. Lan. Fus.   COTTS.
                     1/8th L'Pool R.   SCHULER.
the 2/4th London Regt. (of 173 Bde) will operate on our immediate left, and will assist in the taking of SCHULER FARM. The 174 Bde. are responsible for the capture of the high ground on the left of 173 Bde. including CLUSTER HOUSES.

(4) **FORMATION &** (4) 2/5th Lan. Fus. in four waves.
    OBJECTIVES.   Objective: 1st Wave.   Dotted RED Line.
                              2nd   "   YELLOW Line.
                              3rd & 4th   "   GREEN Line, seizing GREEN House as an advanced Strong Point.

                 1/8th L'Pool R. Two Coys. – formed in two waves.
                 Objective : 1st Wave – Area up to Dotted RED Line.
                                      including N. end of SCHULER GALLERIES.
                                2nd Wave – Area up to YELLOW Line –
                                      two platoons detailed for capture of SCHULER FARM in co-operation with 2/4th London R.
Two Coys. will be in the hands of O.C. 1/8th L'Pool R for the purpose of :-
(a) ensuring gaining of his objective.
(b) supporting 2/5th Lan. Fus. to the extent of 1 Coy. in gaining their objective.
(c) carrying forward ammunition.
(d) establishment of defences in depth along S. bank of HANEBEEK to protect left flank of the Bde.

(5) **JUMPING OFF** (5) The Jumping Off Line for the 1st Wave will be marked
    LINE.   out by a line of posts with circular heads, painted white and shewing the number of platoon and frontage. These will be placed in position on Y/Z night.
The posts shewing boundary of each platoon will be joined with tape.

2.

(6) PLAN OF ATTACK. (6)	**1st Wave (objective - Dotted RED Line)**, will cover the whole Battalion front - the Right moving by the boundary line shewn on map, in close touch with 2/5th Lan. Fus., the left moving via the HANEBEEK and keeping touch with 2/4th Lond.R.

Capt. HODSON. B Coy. less 1 plat.(on Right) & 1 plat. D Coy (on left).

This wave, moving 50 yards behind the barrage will advance to the Dotted RED Line - will mop up and garrison all positions or Strong Points in its area.

The special duty of the Right Platoon is to seize SCHULER & ALLERIES (n. end) in conjunction with 2/5th Lan. Fus.

The special duty of the Left Platoon is to seize and garrison the works and trenches about D.7.c.20.10. and D.13.a.30.95.

The centre platoon must assist by every means in its power the other two platoons in gaining their objectives.

Capt. MONKS. D Coy. less 1 plat.(on left. one plat. B Coy. (on right).

2nd Wave (objective YELLOW Line). On the barrage lifting from the Dotted RED Line, this wave will follow it at a distance of 50 yards and will advance to the attack of SCHULER FARM.

The platoon on right will turn the position via the Southern entrance.

The platoon on left will turn it by the Northern entrance, with in conjunction with a platoon of the 2/4th Lond.R. who will advance against it, accompanied by 2 Tanks, along the WINNIPEG - KANSAS CROSS ROAD.

The centre platoon will operate by fire against the front of the position, and on the flanks being turned it will be used in such a way as O.C. 2nd Wave may direct, either as a close support to either of the other platoons, or to rush the position from the front. The approximate frontage of platoons when extended is 50 yards.

Each wave will be in two lines at 15 yards distance. The second will, follow the first at a distance of 50 yards. Should the 1st wave encounter unexpected difficulties, it will be the duty of the 2nd wave to ensure that the 1st Wave attains its objective.

"A" & "C" Coys. 4 additional Lewis Guns.

Battalion Reserve etc. These two Coys. forming the Battalion Reserve will remain in close proximity to Battn. H.Q. The Os.C. will reconnoitre suitable positions and after placing their Coys. will personally, report to Battn. H.Q.

(7) ACTION ON REACHING DOTTED RED LINE. (7)

On reaching the RED Dotted Line, and as soon as the 2nd Wave has closed up to the barrage, the 1st Wave will be reorganised and distributed in depth in such a way as to ensure the safety of the Left flank of the Battalion. Adequate garrisons will be allotted to the strong points and a thorough reconnaissance will be made of all dugouts and concrete emplacements.

Men are on no account permitted to go into any of these, except when ordered for a period of rest when off duty. All such posts will be defended at all costs by occupying shell hole and other positions outside and on the flanks.

(8) ACTION ON REACHING YELLOW LINE. (8)

On reaching the YELLOW Line, the 2nd Wave will be reorganised. A garrison, probable strength one plat. will be allotted to SCHULER FARM, the remainder of the wave being distributed in depth, with special reference to the safety of the Left flank of the Battalion. The defence of SCHULER FARM will be so arranged as to sweep with fire the front of units on Right and Left, and to command fully the Valley of the HANEBEEK over an arc which included R of RIVERSIDES on Right, and O of OLIVE HO on Left. If such command cannot be obtained it will be necessary, on the barrage lifting from the GREEN Line, to create a Strong Post about 0.13.b.35.20.

3.

As soon as the barrage permits, patrols will be pushed out to furthest limit possible to clear any remaining enemy from the front of our position.

(9) PATROLS RECONNOITRING & STRONG.
(9) On the barrage ceasing, reconnoitring patrols will be sent out to get in touch and maintain touch with the enemy. Immediate report as to enemy's presence will be rendered to Batt.H.Q. by whom the necessary Strong Patrols will be ordered.

(10) MACHINE GUNS.
(10) One sub-section 164 M.G.Coy. is allotted to the Battn. and will remain close to Battn.H.Qrs. until ordered forward.

(11) CONSOLID-ATION.
(11) Consolidation of captured ground will be energetically taken in hand and will mainly consist of:-
(i) linking up shell holes in the positions selected for defence.
(ii) erecting blocks to cover entrances on enemy sides of concrete shelters, and providing a covered way round to the entrance.
(iii) wiring.
Parties of R.E. will be detailed to assist in the consolidation (including wiring) of:-
wiring from N. of SCHULER FARM to the HANEBEEK.

(12) BRIGADE RESERVE.
(12) RESERVE BATTALION (1/5th R.Lan.R.) will be timed to move from its assembly position so as to arrive in the area AISNE - HINDU COT - POND FARM about the time assaulting troops are due on the final objective (GREEN Line).
The role of this Battalion will be to deliver an immediate counter stroke against any hostile counter attack which may penetrate the front or flanks of the Bde. To ensure rapidity of action close liaison must be maintained with front line troops by means of patrols, and the front must be kept under continuous observation. If the final objective should not have been gained, the reserve Battalion will, without halting, move on in support of the assaulting troops and ensure the attack being driven home to the GREEN Line.

(13) CAPTURED MACHINE GUNS.
(13) All Machine guns captured, if they cannot be usefully employed are to be got back as soon as possible. If impossible, must be broken up. To remove the lock only is insufficient.

(14) LIAISON
(14) Commanders of Flank Platoons of each wave will be responsible for close touch being maintained throughout with units of flanks. Liaison will specially be made with 2/5th Lan.Fus. prior to ZERO and again at SCHULER GALLERIES, and on the YELLOW Line. On the Left, liaison will be made with 2/4th Lon.R. on the SCHULER GALLERIES - WINNIPEG ROAD, and at SCHULER FARM.

(15) COMMUNIC-ATIONS.
(15) (a) Bde.H.Qrs. will be at WIELTJE.
Battalion H.Qrs. at about C.18.b.20.65.
Cable Head at BRIDGE HOUSE.
(b) A Bde.Forward Station will be established on the night of 18/19th Sept. at POND FARM.
On the night 19/20th Sept. a line will be laid from Battle H.Qrs. to Bde.Forward Station for use after ZERO.
(c) During the advance communication will be maintained by runner and visual.
(d) The Batt.Forward Party under the Signalling Officer, will follow in rear of 1st Wave and will establish a Forward Command Post at a point in SCHULER GALLERIES approximately C.13.a.55.80. A line will be established from Battle H.Qrs. to Forward Command Post.
(e) (over)

4.

- (e) **Runner Relay Posts.** A Relay Post between Battle H.Q. and Forward Command Post will be established at C.13.a.00.80.
- (f) **Bde. Visual Receiving Station** at C.23.c.6.8. (Call Reserve). This Station may send after ZERO. Other Bde. Stations will be in CAPRICORN KEEP and at BRIDGE HOUSE.
- ( ) **Power Buzzer.** will be established at Forward Command Post.
- (h) **Four Pigeons** will be drawn from Bde. Forward Station after 10 p.m. on night 19/20th Sept.
- (i) All important messages will be sent in duplicate by two different routes or means of transmission; those of special importance will be sent in triplicate by three different routes or means of transmission. Runners will carry all messages in the right hand breast pocket in which nothing else will be carried.
- (j) **Contact aeroplanes.** The contact aeroplane of the 55th Division can be recognised by a white rectangular attachment on both lower planes and a white dumb-bell on either side of body of plane. Whenever the aeroplane calls for Signals by sounding KLAXON HORN or firing a White Very Light, the most advanced lines of Infantry will:-
    - (a) light flares in the bottom of a shell hole.
    - (b) shew Watson fans - white and coloured sides alternately 30 seconds.

    The contact aeroplane will call for Signals at:-
    ZERO plus 1 hour.
    "   "   2 "
    "   "   2½ "
    but flare and fan signals will be made by front line Infantry whenever the Divisional aeroplane calls for them.
- (k) All messages will be timed. All ranks must be warned that times will be written in clock time and not with reference to ZERO hour.
- (l) Station Calls - as issued to all concerned.

(17) **DUMPS** (17) As per Administrative Instructions Nos. 1 and 2.

(18) **PRISONERS** (18) Will be sent down to the rear without loss of time under the escort of slightly wounded men if available. The escort will not exceed 10% of the number of prisoners, excepting in the case of small numbers, when there will never be less than 2 men escorting.
All prisoners will be searched immediately they are captured to ensure that they have no weapons concealed. No personal effects such as decorations, watches, trinkets etc. identity discs, pay books, mess tins, water bottles, haversack etc. will be taken from the prisoners, nor will they be searched for papers of tactical importance by the fighting troops, whose only duty in this connection will be to see that papers are not done away with by prisoners before they reach the Divisional Cage.
Wounded Prisoners will be evacuated to the Cage in the ordinary way and will not be retained for examination at the Dressing Station.
A Divisional Cage has been established immediately W. of ST. JEAN on south side of YPRES/ST. JEAN Road at I.3.a.6.6.

5.

(19) MEDICAL (19).   Location of Regtl Aid Post. will be issued later.

(20) SYNCHRONISATION (20). To be issued later.
    OF WATCHES.
    ----

(21) ZERO HOUR (21).   To be issued later.

(22) BATT.H.Qrs.(22)   Will be established at C.18.b.20.65.

(23) REPORTS. (23)   To Battalion H.Qrs.

                -o-o-o-o-o-o-o-o-o-o-o-o-

            Attention is drawn to the following which have
            been issued:-

                164th Inf.Bde. Notes on Conference .505.
                   "   "   Q.P.1. Scheme and Instructions.
                   "   "   Q.P.3. Prisoners of War.
                   "   "   Q.P.5. Communications.
                   "   "   Q.P.7. Medical arrangements.
                   "   "   Appendix "A".
                1/8th(Irish)Batt. Order No.116.
                   "   "   "   117.
                   "   "   Administrative Instructions Nos.1 &
                                                                  2.

        A C K N O W L E D G E.

                                        Capt. & Adjt.
Issued at 5 p.m.   1/8th(Irish)Batt.K.L.R.
By Runner.
Copies to:-

    1. 164th Inf.Bde.
    2. File.
    3. War Diary.
    4. C.O.
    5. 2nd-in-Command.
    6. O.C. A Coy.
    7. "   B "
    8. "   C "
    9. "   D "
    10. "   Details and Signals.
    11. Intell.Off.
    12. 1/5th Lan.Fus.
    13. 2/4th Lond.Regt.
    14. 1/5th W.Lan.R.
    15. Q.M.
    16. T.O.
    17. M.O.
    18. R.S.M.
    19. 164 M.G.Coy.
    20.

            -o-o-o-o-o-o-o-o-o-o-o-

SECRET   COPY NO ----

OPERATION ORDER NO 119.

The Battalion will be relived tonight 23/24th inst as hereunder :-

      Schuler Farm))
      Schuler Galleries)   by   LANK

      Fort Hill   by   LARK.

On relief the Battalion will move via No 6 Track to Wieltje for Vlamertinghe No 2 Area. If possible trains will be arranged from St Jean Station, details of which will be notified later.

Two guides (Battalion Runners) will be at Battalion Headquarters of LANK at CALL FARM, CALL RESERVE, at 6.30 p.m. 23rd Sept and will guide incoming platoons to Front Line Company Headquarters. O.C. Front Line will arrange to have guides from each post waiting for arrival of reliefs.

The Battalion Runners who guide the reliefs will act as guides ~~for outgoing platoons for outgoing platoons~~ for outgoing Platoons to Wieltje.

All Trench Stores, S.A.A. Wire cutters in the line will be handed over and receipts taken.

Completion of relief will be reported to Battalion Headquarters by runner as quickly as possible after relief.

                                        s d. J.F. Jones
                                                Capt & Adjt.
Issued at :- 5. p.m.   for O.C. IMOSE.

Copies to:-

1 C.O.
2 164 Inf. Brigade.
3 O.C. Front Line.
4 File.
5 War Diary.

SECRET.   COPY NO .....

1/8th (IRISH) BATTALION "KING'S" (L'POOL REGT).

OPERATION ORDER NO 113.

Ref: BARRAGE MAP.   In the Field.
                                                        9/9/17.

1. **Information.** (1) On Z day the 55th Division will take part in a general attack. The 9th Division will attack on the Right and the 58th Division on the Left.
   The 55th Division will attack with the 165th Infantry Brigade on the right, and the 164th Infantry Brigade on the left.
   The 174th Infantry Brigade will be on the left of 164th Infantry Brigade.
   The Brigade frontage and dividing line between Battalions are as shown on Barrage Map.

2. **Disposition of Brigade for attack and times.** (2) The 164th Inf Bde will take up positions in the British Front Line and positions 100 yards in rear of it by 3.55 a.m. on Z day. Dispositions of Battalions will be as follows

   Right Batt. for 1st Objective. 1/4th K.Lan.R
   "   "   " 2nd   "   1/4th R.Lanc.R
                British Front Line.
   Left Batt for 1st Objective   2/5th Lan.Fus
   "   "   " 2nd   "   1/8th L'poolR
        100 yards in rear British Front Line.

   At ZERO, 1/4th K.Lan.R on the right, and 2/5th Lan.Fus. on the left will advance from our front line and gain the BLUE Area.
   At ZERO plus 25 minutes 1/4th R.Lanc.R on the right, and 1/8th L'pool R on the left will move from Assembly position, pass through the BLUE Area, and will seize the RED Area (KANSAS CROSS) inclusive to 1/4th R.Lanc.R - POMMER FARM inclusive to 1/8th L'pool R.) and consolidate the general line A - B.
   At least one strong point will be constructed in advance of the line AB on each Battalion front.
   The 1/5th R.Lanc.R (166 Bde) will move forward at ZERO plus 1½ hrs to the neighbourhood of Cross tracks 250 yards W. of Cross Cotts. This Battalion will be available to assist in the repulse of hostile counter attacks on the Brigade front or flanks.
   The attack will be made behind a creeping barrage which will advance as laid down in barrage map. The barrage will finally halt to cover consolidation and will continue until this is reported to be complete.

3. **Formation and Distribution of the Battn.** (3) The Battalion will be disposed on a two Company frontage and will advance in 3 waves. The dividing line between Companies will be a general line starting from P.4.d.3.3. and passing through P.9.b.70.75. both points inclusive to Right Company.

The Battalion will advance from assembly position in Artillery formation of Platoon or sectional columns in file, and will deploy into line when necessary on approaching the BLUE line.
Waves will be as follows :-

	Left.	Right.
1st Wave.	1 Plat. B Coy.	1 Plat. A Coy.
2nd "	2 " B "	2 " A "
3rd "	D Coy.	C. Coy.

with 50/100 yards between waves.

4. <u>Objectives.</u> (4) The objectives of the 1/5th L'pool R. are:-

(1) To capture the RED Area.
(2) To establish Strong Posts forward of the general line AB which will,
   (a) Provide enfilade M.G. fire against counter attack.
   (b) Ensure observation into the valley S. of TOURNEHEM.
   (c) Ensure that all the ground in front of the line AB is swept by fire from these points.
(3) Consolidate the general line AB.
(4) Seize and occupy all concrete defences within the RED Area.

<u>Objectives of waves will be:-</u>

<u>1st Wave.</u> Secure the line AB and establish a line of shell hole posts.

<u>2nd wave.</u> Mop up all strong points en route:-
No 2 Platoon will mop up Fokker Farm.
Reinforce first wave on line AB, and provide one platoon A Coy and one platoon B Coy to construct and garrison strong points forward of this line.
Strong points on left Coy, front will be in vicinity indicated on Barrage Map (P.9.d)
If it is impossible to sweep the whole of the ground in front of line AB and to obtain the fullest observation of the valley S. of TOURNEHEM, O.C. A Coy will site and construct a strong point which will secure these objects on A Coy front.

<u>3rd wave.</u> Will ensure that 1st and 2nd waves attain their objective and will occupy all captured concrete defences in the RED AREA. O.C. D Coy will detail No 13 Platoon to garrison Supporting Point at P.3.a. when constructed by R.Es. A Machine gun will be added to this garrison. When garrisons have been established they will remain in their positions and hold them at any cost.

5. **Machine Guns.** (5) One sub-section 164 M.G.Coy will move in rear of 2nd wave. These guns will be used to cover consolidation of line AB and construction of Strong point or points. When this work has been completed these guns will become part of the garrison of the Strong points.
   One sub-section will move in rear of 3rd wave and will be under order of O.C. B Coy. They will be utilised as may be necessary and one gun will be detailed to join the garrison of supporting point at P.3.b.

6. **Communications.** (6) Communication before ZERO hour and until Battn Hdqrs moves forward will be by runner. During the advance forward communication will be by runner and visual (if possible).
   At ZERO hour plus 1 hour 10 minutes the Bde forward party will proceed to establish a forward station about P.3.b.d.3.
   A Visual station will be established near the Bde Forward Station in communication with Brigade Visual Station about J.33.d.3.7.
   As soon as possible after Bde Forward Stn has been established a telephone line will be laid by this unit to it from Batt Hqrs. As soon as the final objective has been gained a Forward Command Post will be established in the vicinity of P.3.b.90.70 and a wire will be laid to it from Batt Hqs ~~Runner Relay Posts~~ will be established at Batt Hqrs in communication with Bde Visual Station and also with Forward Command Posts. All important messages will be sent in duplicate by two different routes or means of transmission; those of special importance will be sent in triplicate by three different routes or means of transmission. Runners will carry messages in the Right hand breast pocket in which nothing else will be carried.

   A Visual Station

7. **Liaison.** (7) O.C. A Coy will be responsible for liaison with the 1/4th R.Lan.R. on the line AB. O.C. B Coy will be responsible for liaison with the 194th Inf Bde on the line AB.

8. **Dumps.** (8) Brigade Dumps will be established as follow
   Main Dump   at J.34.d.25.40.
   Advanced Dump at P.3.b.90.04.

9. **Medical.** (9) An Aid Post will be established in the vicinity of Advanced Battn Hqrs.

10. **Synchronisation of watches.** (10) Watches will be synchronised at 6 p.m. on Y day.

11. **ZERO hour.** (11) Will be at 9.55 a.m. on Z day.

Runner Relay Posts will be established at P.3.b.90.70. and P.3.a.70.40. Personnel for these posts will move forward in rear of 2nd wave.

-4-

12. **Batt. H.Qrs.** (12) Will move forward in rear of the Right flank of the Battalion and will be established in the neighbourhood of CROSS COTTS.

13. **Reports.** (13) to Batt. H.Qrs.

-o-o-o-o-o-o-o-o-o-o-o-o-

Attention is drawn to the following which have been issued :-

(1) 55th Div. Tactical Exercise - General Idea.
(2) 164th Inf Bde Order No 1001 and Notes on Strong Points and Appendix "A" attached.
(3) 1/8th (Irish) Administrative Orders No 1.
(4) 164th I.B. A/25 on Pack Transport.

A25488/22

J.P. Jones
Capt & Adjt.
1/8th (Irish) K.L.R.

Issued at 5 p.m.
By Runner.

Copies to:-

1. 164th Inf Bde.
2. C.O.
3. 2nd in Command.
4. A. Coy.
5. B. "
6. C. "
7. D. "
8. Details and Signals.
9. 2/5th Lan. Fus.
10. 1/4th S. Lanc. R.
11. 1/4th N. Lan. R.
12. 164 M.G. Coy.
13. 164 T.M. Battery.
14. Intelligence Officer.
15. T.O.
16. Q.M.
17. M.O.
18. War Diary.
19. File.
20. R.S.M.

-o-o-o-o-o-o-o-o-o-o-o-o-o-o-o-o-

List of Officer, Warrant Officer, N.C.Os. and men who received awards from the B.G.C. 164th Inf. Bde. on 9/9/17.

```
2/Lieut. J.E.FENN.        Military Cross.
305891  S.S.M. GREENWOOD.  D.C.M.
307757  Sgt. W. HOWARTH.   Military Medal.
305179  A/Sgt. E.W. ELLIOTT.   do.
305195  L/Sgt. T. FOSTER       do.
305314  L/Sgt. J. ROBINSON     do.
308296  Cpl. T. COOPER         do.
308551   "   E.P. HUGHES       do.
306276  Pte. A. MORTON         do.
308355   "   J.W. PAYNE        do.
308500   "   J. BAMFORTH.      do.
305774   "   J. BECCONSALL     do.
```

-o-o-o-o-o-o-o-o-o-o-o-o-o-o-o-oo-o-o-o-o-o-

To all concerned.

Reference 1/8th(Irish)Batt.K.L.R. Operation Order No.113.

The following alterations will be made in Map references:-

Para.3, line 4, for P.4.d.3.3. read P.4.a.7.7.
" 3 " 5 " P.9.b.70.75, read P.9.a.25.70.
" 4 " 24 " P.9.d. read P.9.a.
" 4 " 35 " P.3.a. " P.3.d.
" 5 " 13 " P.3.b. " P.3.d.
" 6 " 17 " for P.3.b.00.70. read P.3.d.00.35.

Runner relay posts will be established at P.3.d.00.35. and P.3.d.40.60. instead of P.3.b.00.70. and P.3.a.70.40.

J P Jones
Capt. & Adjt.
1/8th(Irish)Batt.K.L.R.

Issued at 11 p.m.

-o-o-o-o-o-o-o-o-o-o-o-o-

NARRATIVE OF ACTION, Sept. 19th to 23rd, 1917.

1/8th (IRISH) BATTALION "THE KING'S" (L'POOL REGIMENT).

(1) **Role of Battalion.**

(1) This Battalion had been ordered to attack on the left of the 164 Inf. Bde. thus forming the extreme left of the 55th Divisional front.
Two objectives were allotted to this unit:-
(a) The dotted RED Line - including trenches and strong points on the extreme left (about D.7.c.55.15) and SCHULER GALLERIES (Northern end).
(b) The GREEN LINE - i.e. SCHULER FARM and small portion of ground to Eastward.

(2) **Formation & Distribution.**

(2) The Battalion moved up from the concentration area on night 19/20th Sept. and in spite of extreme darkness and the difficulties brought on by thick misty rain, all were established in the position of assembly, correctly distributed, by the appointed time.

The Battalion was formed for attack in 2 waves (each of 3 platoons); distance between waves 75 yds. The 1st Wave (under Capt. R.B. HODSON) had as objective the dotted RED Line; and the mopping up of all Strong Points and trenches in the intervening area. The 2nd Wave (under Capt. A. MONKS) had as its objective the GREEN Line, and was responsible for the taking of, and garrisonin of SCHULER FARM. A third wave (2 coys. less 2 platoons) followed the 2nd at a distance of 250/300 yards. This wave was to assist either of the other two in attaining their objective.
The remaining two platoons were employed on carrying duties and formed a further reserve at disposal of O.C. Battalion.

(3) **Progress of the Fight.**

(3) On the morning of 20th Sept. the battle commenced as had been arranged, i.e. the waves moved off at ZERO at correct distances - the leading wave closely following the barrage.
The enemy put down a very heavy barrage through which the advance continued, the first losses, irrespective of those from ordinary shell fire, being caused by very severe machine gun and rifle fire from a strong point about D.7.c.20.20. on the right bank of the HaneBeek.
In addition to this a large number of the enemy had taken up a position, presumably during the early hours of the morning, in shell holes and in a shallow trench approximately about 40 yds. in front of the SCHULER GALLERY Line.
As soon as the barrage passed over this line the enemy presented heavy rifle fire and bombs from this position, which was augmented a moment later by withering machine gun and rifle fire from the concrete emplacements at the Northern end of the SCHULER GALLERIES when the barrage had passed them by. The effect of this severe fire from front and flank was to momentarily check our line, but, in a very short time it rallied and the shell hole and trench positions in front of the GALLERIES were assaulted and taken.

The barrage had now been lost and the situation became critical.

The two platoons which had been held in reserve were thrown into the fight and an attempt was made to flank the NORTHERN GALLERIES which still held out, from the left. This movement was successful and at 7.15 a.m. the positions were stormed from the front and left flank. This resulted in their capture together with the garrison which was at that time about 100 strong.

The 2nd wave now reformed and attempted to advance against SCHULER FARM without the assistance of the barrage; but was unable to proceed owing to heavy machine gun and rifle fire from SCHULER FARM and from the direction and neighbourhood of CROSS COTTS. Several further attempts were made to take the "FARM" but without success.

The position now was that the RED Dotted line was in our possession and was being held by elements of several units and consolidation was proceeding. It was decided to strengthen it by every means available before making further attempts on the FARM - which was to be kept under all available Lewis gun fire, rifle, and rifle grenade fire. It was not considered expedient to make any fresh attempt to take the "FARM" until its garrison had been further reduced by fire. On the afternoon of the 20th a white flag was shewn at the farm for a few moments but this was considered to be an enemy ruse and so was disregarded.

 The defence of the "FARM" continued to be very active throughout the night of 20/21st September.

 All available fire was kept up on the "FARM" during the 21st and as the fire from it gradually slackened and finally appeared to cease altogether it was thought that the time had come when an attempt to reach it might again be made.

 A special platoon was therefore ordered to be told off for the purpose under 2/Lt. ALLERTON and this, preceded by a patrol, advanced and captured the place at 4.30 a.m. 21/9/17.

 The "FARM" was then immediately organised for defence by Infantry and Lewis gun and a Machine gun was ordered up to form part of its defence. The gun was in position by 4.40 p.m.

The force available for the defence of the RED Dotted Line was now redistributed and this position, with the acquisition of SCHULER FARM became a very strong one.

 A good line of shell hole defences had been arranged from in front of the Northern galleries to the HANEBEEK and liaison was maintained with the Bde. of left.

 The position, both on the gallery line and at SCHULER FARM was constantly subjected to very heavy artillery fire, the most severe being that which preceded the counter attack on the evening of 21/9/17.

 After the repulse of this counter attack nothing of note, except repeated heavy bombardments occurred on this front.

(4) LIAISON. (4) At the commencement of the fight liaison on either flank was good. On the left it was lost after the SCHULER GALLERY fighting - but was regained.
On the early morning of the 21st and on the evening of the 21st a system of half hourly patrols between the 2/11th Londons and ourselves was inaugurated which completed liaison and was continued until the Battalion was relieved.
On the right the overlapping of units kept up the closest touch throughout and personal liaison between Battalion Commanders was kept up by visits to the H.Qrs. of the unit concerned.

(5) COMMUNICATION. (5) Communication with Bde. and front line by telephone was almost impossible to maintain - the former being laid across the German barrage line and the later being exposed at many points - particularly at FORT HILL Batt.H.Q. which itself was continually shelled.
Communication throughout was well maintained by runner and with front line by visual.

29/9/17.

Major
~~Lieut.Colonel.~~
Commdg. 1/8th(Irish) Batt.K.L.R.

Secret.   Copy No 6.

Amendment to IMPOSE
   Operation Order N° 118.

1) Assembly position for first wave
will be a line from C.18.b.90.55
to C.18.b.90.98.

2) A + C Coys (each less one platoon) will
form a third wave following the
second wave at a distance of 200-300
yards. They will be prepared to
act immediately if required to
assist our own troops or 2/5th Lan
Fusrs in securing capture of the
dotted Red Line. On this line
being captured these Coys will
occupy in depth the area up to
the dotted Red Line, echeloned
back by platoons from R to Left;
the Right Platoon of A Coy being
in close touch with S. Hunter
Galleries, the Left platoon of C
Coy being about the flooded
emplacements C.18.d.70.95
arranged so as to guard our left
flank from Counter Attack and
acting in concert with the Garrisons

found by the first wave.

On the barrage lifting they will continue to hold themselves in readiness to come to the aid of either Battalion in gaining its further objectives.

Every man of this third wave will carry up 50 rounds extra S.A.A. as a reserve for the first and second waves. This S.A.A. to be obtained from the dump at Fort Hill.

The remaining Platoons of these Companies will be employed as carrying parties and will carry out the following tasks:-

One Platoon A. Coy - carry water and rations from St Jean to first wave (1 Platoon D Coy, 2 Platoons B Coy) afterwards carrying 30 Boxes of Lewis Gun Drums from Dump at C/Sd 8.6 to Battalion Dump at Fort Hill.

One Platoon C Coy will remove all Stores at Battalion Dump at Rat Farm to Battalion Dump at Fort Hill.

These Platoons will afterwards take up a position in the neighbourhood of Fort Hill and will carry up Rations and Water to Schuler Farm as soon as it is taken.

L/32.   Copy No. 3.

ADDENDUM TO
1/8th (IRISH) BATTALION K.L.R.
OPERATION ORDER NO. 118.
-o-o-o-o-o-o-o-o-

In the Field.
18/9/17.

(1) ARTILLERY. The attack will be preceded by a bombardment commencing on the morning of 19th September.
The attack will be covered by a Divl. Machine Gun barrage (32 Guns) moving ahead of and in conjunction with the Artillery barrage.
When the final objective is gained, the Guns forming this barrage will lay on S.O.S. lines in case of counter attack.
Artillery barrage map will follow.

(2) MEDICAL. Regtl. Aid Post will be established at PONT GALLERIES, O.1B.b.8.1.

(3) MAPS & AEROPLANE PHOTOGRAPHS. The following will be carried by all Officers and by as many N.C.Os. as supply will permit:-

1. GRAVENSTAFEL SHEET.   1/10000 Trench Map.
2. MESSAGE FORM MAPS.   to be issued on morning of 19th on scale of 3 to all Officers & senior N.C.Os.

3. BARRAGE MAPS.   to be issued on scale of one per Officer and senior N.C.O.

4. COPY OF AEROPLANE PHOTOS.

All map references in reports will be made from GRAVENSTAFEL 1/10,000 Trench Map.

2.

4. **SYNCHRONISATION OF WATCHES.**

The Signalling Officer will take two watches to Bde. H.Q. VELTJE DUGOUT at 9 p.m. on 19th Sept.
Coy. Cdrs. will send two watches to Battle H.Q. at 11 p.m. 19th Sept.

J.F. Jones
Capt. & Adjt.
1/8th (Irish) Batt. K.L.R.

Issued at 10.20 p.m.
Copies to:-
   1. 164 Inf. Bde.
   2. War Diary.
   3. File.
   4. C.O.
   5. Signals Off.
   6. A Coy.
   7. B "
   8. C "
   9. D "
 10. M.O.

-o-o-o-o-o-o-o-o-

SECRET.   COPY NO. 10

1/8th (IRISH) BATT. K.L.R.
OPERATION ORDER NO.119.

Ref: Trench Map WYTSCHAETE 1/10,000.
           GHELUVELT 1/10,000.

                                In the Field,
                                18/9/17.

(1) This Unit will move to its assembly position
    on the night of the 19/20th Sept. Coys. will
    be in position in accordance with attached
    diagram by C.O. Movement along the line
    of assembly after that hour must be restricted
    to a minimum.

(2) Leading waves will be in a position about 150
    yards short of the line marked "B" on the
    Barrage Map.

(3) Movement from LIVERPOOL TRENCH will be in the
    order:-
        D Coy. (less one platoon).
        1 Platoon B Coy.
        Batt. H.Qrs.
        C Coy.
        A Coy.
                  via No. 6. Track, and will
    commence at 6.30 p.m. Platoons will move at
    100 yards distance.

(4) Assembly positions for Coys. will be reconnoitred
    on the night 18/19th Sept. and dividing point
    of Sectors mutually agreed upon with 2/5th Lan.
    Fus.

2.

(5) O.C. Coys. will report arrival at
Assembly positions to Batt.H.Qrs.
by runner as early as possible.

(6) Batt.H.Qrs. will close at LIVERPOOL TR.
at 8.30 p.m. and will open at FORTHILL
(approx. C.18.c.30.65) at that time.

A C K N O W L E D G E.

                                      J.F.Jones
                                  Capt. & Adjt.

Issued at 11.5 p.m.   1/8th Irish Batt. K.L.R.
Copies to:-
  1. C.O.
  2. A Coy.
  3. B "
  4. C "
  5. D "
  6. Details and Signals.
  7. 164th Bde.Hds.
  8. 2/5th Lan. Fus.
  9. 2/4th Lond.R.
10. War Diary.
11. File.

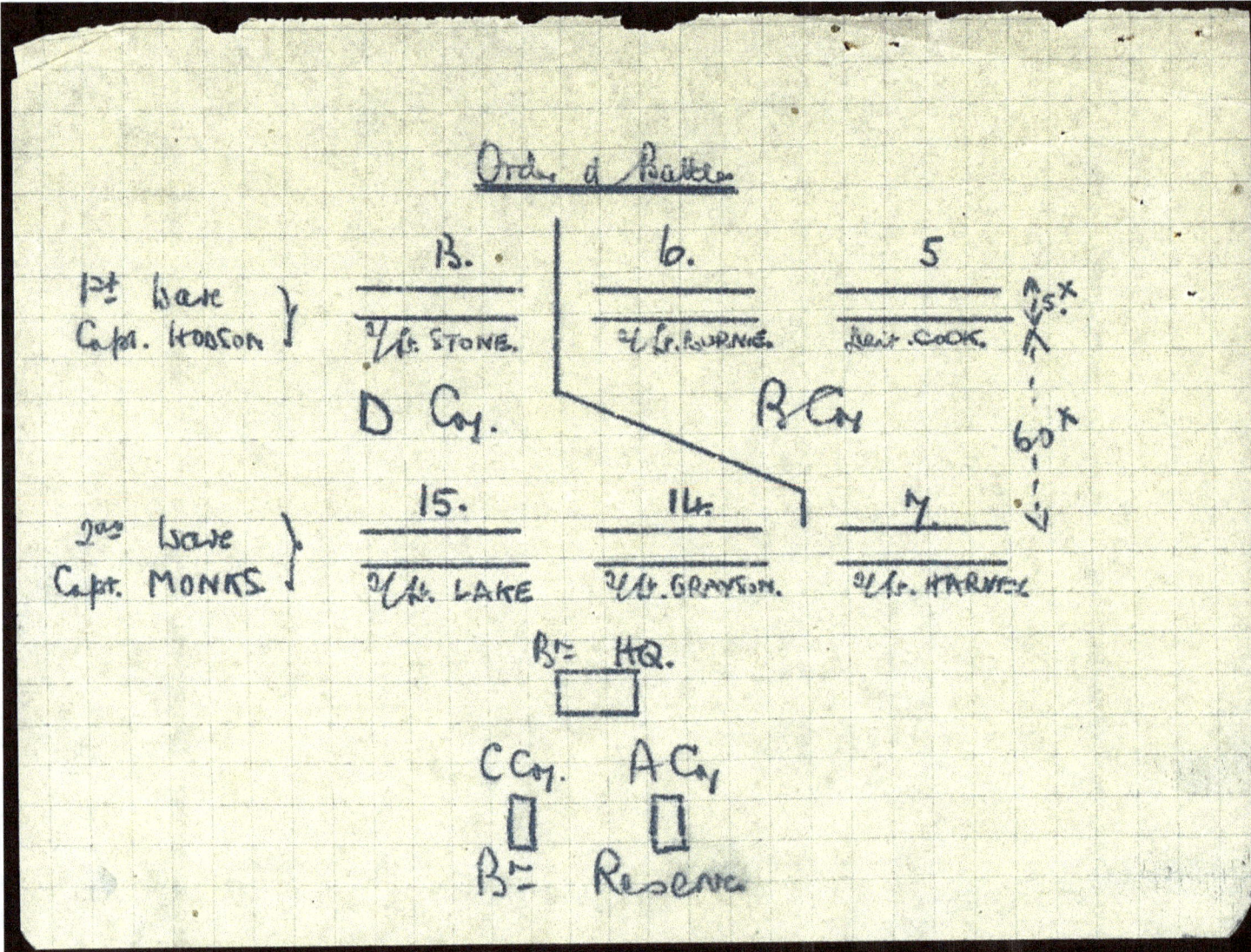

NARRATIVE OF ACTION 20/9/17 - 23/9/17.
by Cpl. CLARE, who was the only N.C.O.
who survived in "D" Company.

Our Company in conjunction with B Coy. moved off at the appointed time (5.40 a.m.). 13th platoon were on left, in touch with the 2/6th London R. They proceeded in one wave for 300 yds. when strong rifle fire was opened out on them from two trenches in front of SCHULER GALLERIES. The Company sustained many casualties from this fire and 2/Lt. STONE was sniped through the head whilst rallying his platoon. (It may be mentioned that 2/Lt. STONE had previously fallen on a German bayonet and injured his leg but he carried on). No. 13 platoon which was now led by Cpl. CLARE pressed on to the Galleries and when 30 yds. from these, were held up by heavy machine gun fire. During this fire about a dozen Bosche emerged from the Galleries and commenced to bomb our men. More casualties were incurred. As progress was impossible the whole line was reorganised and Capt. MONKS was severely wounded whilst engaged on this task. About 10 o'clock a flank attack led by Capt. HODSON and 2/Lt. ALLERTON was made upon the galleries and the remainder of the garrison surrendered. 50 germans and 2 machine guns fell into our hands. We then occupied the galleries and dug in. About 4 p.m. on Friday afternoon 2/Lt. ALLERTON who had previously reconnoitred the front made an attack upon SCHULER FARM which was taken and occupied. Subsequently Cpl. CLARE and one man made their way to the farm and found 2/Lt. ALLERTON there. They returned and reported this to 2/Lts. KELF & BURNIE, who led the remainder of the men across to the farm, and garrisoned it. The M.G.C. and one Lewis gun from C Coy. reinforced the garrison later on. The farm was then set in a state of defence and the garrison remained there until relieved at 3 a.m. on Monday morning 24th inst.

NARRATIVE OF ACTION 20/9/17 - 23/9/17.
by 325025 Cpl. JAMES, No. 10 Platoon.

On the morning of the 20th about 6 a.m. my
Company set off from the shell holes where
we had laid during the night for the attack.
We advanced in pretty good order up to about 80 yds.
from the SCHULER GALLERIES.   At this time
Capt. MONKS was leading the platoon very well
indeed but some German Bombers came out and
commenced bombing and the first wave checked,
but most of the Officers, N.C.Os., and several
men rallied and the attack advanced again.   We
then gradually worked up to about 30 or 40 yds.
of the Galleries where we were very heavily
fired on by Machine Guns, and hung on for a
time and finally charged the Galleries.   We got
something like 100 prisoners there and there were
heaps of dead Germans lying about.   Myself &
L/Cpl. KENDALL got a machine gun but it had been
put out of action.   I missed Capt. MONKS just
previously to the final assault on the Galleries
and noticed 2/Lt. ALLERTON taking charge on the
left of the line.   I also saw 2/Lt. CARBINES
when we were about 100 yards from the Galleries
and he was then coming forward and shouting
to somebody on his right.   When we arrived at
the Galleries I saw 2/Lt. ALLERTON just coming
out of a dugout.   A few minutes later I saw
2/Lieuts. BAKER, KENDRICK, & COTTIER.
2/Lt. ALLERTON attempted to carry the attack on to
the FARM and I and several others helped, but
Machine Gun Fire was bad and the advance by
the Battalion on the right had stopped.   Several
attempts were made after this to get into the
Farm but none of them were successful.   About
4.30 p.m. on the 21st 2/Lt. COTTIER told me a
message had come through that we had got to take
SCHULER FARM, and told me to get all the Irish
together and collect all bombs and rifle
grenades I could get hold of.   I went all
along the line telling the Irish to get

2.

together for the attack, but before they could be properly organised 2/Lt. ALLERTON had started. When I noticed this I just shouted "over" and followed up. 2/Lieuts. KELF & COTTIER also came over about this time. About 23 Officers, N.C.Os. and men arrived at the Farm. We found a lot of dead & wounded enemy about. 2/Lieut. CHILDS remained at the Galleries and arranged for a party to attack the strong point on the right of SCHULER FARM from the Galleries and we were placed in position to give them covering fire by 2/Lt. ALLERTON. A machine gun was sent for and 1 Officer, 1 N.C.O. and 1 man of the M.G.C. arrived with a machine gun and the N.C.O. and man stayed with us until we were relieved.

NARRATIVE OF ACTION 20/9/17 - 23/9/17.
by 2/Lt. COTTIER W.K. No.9.Platoon.

On the morning of the 20th Sept. my platoon was detailed to take up a position in shell holes adjacent to Batt.H.Q., at Fort Hill in order to act as reserve to the Battalion. About 7.45 a.m. the Commanding Officer ordered me to reinforce Capt.HODSON at SCHULER GALLERIES. I set off, immediately and reported to Capt.HODSON who was occupying some trenches about 40 yards behind the SCHULER GALLERIES, being subjected to heavy machine gun fire from the right and left fronts. On my arrival he immediately attacked the GALLERIES and after a hand-to-hand struggle with the garrison, we captured the position and took the garrison prisoners. I then got as many men as I could into shell holes in front of the GALLERIES. This took me almost two hours to accomplish. I personally garrisoned a large shell hole in front of the third "pill box" from the left, with about 20 men, comprising a good many of the King's Own.

While we were re-consolidating a counter attack was launched at us from our right front. We repulsed it, receiving 4 casualties (King's Own). During this period we were subjected to continuous heavy machine gun fire from enemy strong point at approx.D.13.b.50.30.(CROSS COTTS). and also by sniping from the same position. This enemy post embarrased our movement during the whole of the time we were attempting to take SCHULER FARM and was largely responsible for the failure of several of our attacks.

After that Capt.KEEN, King's Own came on the scene and took command of the GALLERIES. He ordered me to retire and dig trenches immediately in rear of the GALLERIES, which I did. This the evening of the 20/9/17.

2.

When 2/Lt. CHILDS took command of the whole of the IRISH I reported my Command to him. At 4.30 p.m. 2a/9/17, 2/Lt. CHILDS told me he had received orders to take SCHULER FARM. 2/Lt. ALLERTON scouted the position. I took about 20 men to the FARM, receiving support on my right from 2/Lt. KELF. The operation was again very considerably hampered by machine gun and rifle fire from CROSS COTTS but we pressed on and at 4.45 p.m. I reported to 2/Lt. CHILDS that I had occupied SCHULER FARM. I found the place surrounded by enemy dead, and a number of wounded in and about the dugouts.

I then proceeded to give covering fire to 2/Lt. KELF'S Party which was endeavouring to capture the German Strong Point at C.13.b. 30.20. This attack failed owing to casualties received from CROSS COTTS Strong Point. 2/Lt. ALLERTON and myself then placed patrols round about the farm.

About 10 p.m. 21/9/17, I was ordered by the Adjutant who was reorganising the defences to return to the SCHULER GALLERY Line, and was put in command of No.1. Strong Point (right of IRISH). I stayed there until I was relieved by the North Staffs. about 1.30 a.m. 24/9/17.

"NARRATIVE OF ACTION 20/9/17 - 23/9/17,
    by L/Cpl. BOWSER, No.7.Platoon.

After advancing on the right flank for about
250 yards we came under Machine Gun fire.
Cpl. COOPER in charge was wounded and I assumed
command of the section, and decided to work
round on the left to avoid the Machine Gun and
if possible to engage and put it out of action.
We reached a spot some 25 to 30 yards in front
of and to the left of the GALLERIES, when I
found a Lewis gun bringing fire to bear on the
enemy Machine Gun, so decided to press on,
still keeping to the extreme left sector.
About this time, enemy Bombers succeeded in
putting our L.Gun out of action, which left
my right flank exposed, so as the rest of the
Irish had established a strong line on a point
near the GALLERIES and the enemy were preparing
for a counter attack, I withdrew to a position
slightly in front of the main body. On
attempting to reorganise I found that my men
had become mixed up with other sections so took
charge of the nearest men and established my
strong point on the extreme left of the SCHULER
GALLERIES and some 20 yards in front. It was
impossible to do much work on this by day as
an enemy machine Gun in front of the Lan.
Fus. was very active. Later in the day 2/Lt.
BURNIE took charge of the left of the line and
we occupied this position under his orders until
relieved.

NARRATIVE OF ACTION 20/9/17 – 25/9/17.
by Cpl. PARRY. No.7.Platoon.

On commencement of attack we advanced in
in artillery formation under very heavy
Machine Gun fire. After advancing a good
distance the enemy counter attacked, pushing us
a few yards back; we at once pushed ahead
again, overcome the counter attack, and carried
on to the SCHULER GALLERIES. By this time
I had lost all my section, and Officer. I at
once reported myself to Capt.HODSON who detailed
me to carry on with a party of men on the left
of the position, which we were about to storm.
Meantime we waited for our right flank to close
in. On seeing them close in we dashed up and
took the SCHULER GALLERIES, also capturing
some prisoners. Capt. HODSON, while searching
prisoners for Bombs, etc. was wounded by a
sniper. Many Germans were also killed in
between our line and their own.
The Battalion on our right had also stopped at
the SCHULER GALLERIES so we began to consolidate
our position, also making positions for L.Gs.
Later on in the day we received a number of
sandbags which enabled us to strengthen our
position more.
Several attempts were made during the afternoon
to capture SCHULER FARM but the position was
strongly held by Machine Guns, and we were also
very heavily sniped from the right. We held
on to the position until the afternoon of the
21/9/17, when a very heavy barrage was put
down upon us, which lasted about three hours.
The Adjutant came up to me whilst this was
going on and ordered me to hold on to our
position in case of enemy counter attack. He
afterwards re-organised the line and put me in
command of a strong point on the right of
our line. I occupied this position until
relief.

NARRATIVE OF ACTION 20/9/o 7 - 23/9/17.
       by O.C. 6 Platoon.

On Sept.21st I was in command of No.6.Plat.
B Coy, 1/8th(Irish)Batt.K.L.R.
No.6. Platoon formed part of the 1st Wave
and were the centre platoon with No.5.Platoon
on the right and No.13 Platoon on the left, and
the objective was the RED Dotted Line in front
of SCHULER GALLERIES.   At 5.40 a.m. the attack
commenced and the first wave advanced behind the
barrage.   On reaching the ridge in front of
SCHULER GALLERIES, heavy machine gun fire was
received from the left, (approx. D.7.c.2.3.)
and from a position between the 2 & 3 galleries
from the North, which thinned the platoon out
to 6 men, and I found myself with L/Cpl.HASKEY
of the Bombers amongst the men of No.13 plat.;
the remainder of No.6 plat. had moved a slight incline to get out of the zone of enemy machine gun
fire and intermingled with No.5. platoon. I was
now mixed up with No.13 platoon who were on the
left flank, and rushed the galleries, with 2/Lt.
ALLERTON of "A" Coy.   When the galleries fell,
men were put in shell holes in front of the
galleries to repulse any immediate counter-attack,
at the same time covering a party who were
consolidating the left gallery.   After doing
this I was detailed to capture SCHULER FARM with
all available men.   This I attempted to do,
but my party of 20 men was reduced to myself and
three others, owing to withering machine gun fire
from CROSS COTTS (on the front of the Batt. on
the left) and from SCHULER FARM, and I was
obliged to return to the SCHULER GALLERY Line.
Later I constructed a strong post on the bank of
the HANEBEEK (D.7.c.5.1.) and established touch
with London R. on my left by patrol. I held this
post with one acting N.C.O. and 12 men until
relieved on the 23/9/17.

NARRATIVE OF ACTION 20/9/17 - 23/9/17,
by S t. H. CORNALL, No. 5. Platoon.

At 5.40 a.m. on the 20th inst. we commenced our advance to our objective (SCHULER GALLERIES). On going forward we met with considerable resistance in the shape of Bombing and M.G. fire from a small trench in front of our objective. At this point my platoon Officer became a casualty. I immediately placed the Bombing Section on the right flank and the Lewis Gun bringing fire to bear on enemy position. We then rushed the position from the front and left flank. On continuing our advance we came in contact with about 45 of the enemy but on pressing forward we forced them to surrender. I then sent them to the rear under escort of the Lan. Fus; then on seeing everything correct I placed a covering party 20 yards in front while the remainder of my men consolidated round SCHULER GALLERIES.

NARRATIVE OF ACTION 20/9/17 - 23/9/17.
by O.C. No. 3. Platoon.

On the 19th inst. my platoon was detailed as a carrying party during the battle. I delivered the rations at Fort Hill, fetched by my party of 20 men. Later on I was told to fetch ammunition from Wine House which I found blown up. I then tried to find another dump near by but could not. I reported this fact to the Adjutant of my Battalion, after which the Commanding Officer sent me with 13 men (all that I could find in the vicinity) to assist in the attack on SCHULER FARM. I arrived at the GALLERIES with 7 men, the remainder being knocked out as we were under heavy shell fire the whole time. Here I got my men to consolidate the newly won position. The next day the final attack on SCHULER FARM took place. 2/Lt. COTTIER and 2/Lt. ALLERTON attacked on the left, myself and 7 men attacking on the right. I ordered rapid fire whilst the party on my left advanced. I duly arrived at about 100 yds. from the German Strong Point D.13.b.30.20. with 4 men. We were then some way advanced of SCHULER FARM. I had made up my mind to try and take it but had to abandon it owing to terrific shelling and M.G. fire. When night arrived I got into SCHULER FARM and found 2/Lt. ALLERTON had been there some time, and also 2/Lt. COTTIER. We remained in ~~possession~~ possession of this until relieved by the North Staffs, having consolidated the position.

Report on Capture of SCHULER FARM,
by O.C. No. 2. Platoon.

Between 4 & 5 p.m. on 21st inst. I led a
skirmishing party of 1 N.C.O. and 4 men to
SCHULER FARM under covering fire from SCHULER
GALLERIES. I advanced from the left flank.
We rushed the farm which we found surrounded by
enemy dead and two wounded enemy were at the
entrance to the dug-out. 2/Lt. COTTIER and 15
O.Rs. reinforced me soon after my taking possession.
I immediately set to work to consolidate; During
this work heavy M.G. fire came from strong point
at D.13.b.2.7. There was one casualty caused
by a sniper. During the attacks by the troops
from the southern end of SCHULER GALLERIES we gave
covering fire with our two L.Gs. About 7 p.m.
the garrison was reinforced by 2/Lt. WILLIAMS,
1 N.C.O. and 1 man with a M.G. and later by
2/Lts. KELF & BURNIE and 7 O.Rs. About 10 p.m.
2/Lts. WILLIAMS & BURNIE returned to SCHULER
GALLERIES. At night I maintained touch with
2/11th London Regt. on my left by patrols, and
pushed out advanced posts to my front and right
flank. SCHULER FARM was frequently shelled
heavily, but the garrison showed an excellent
spirit under very trying conditions. Sgt. WOOD,
Cpl. CLARE, Cpl. SLATER and Cpl. RAWCLIFFE (2/5th
K.O.R.L.) were particularly capable and did
excellent patrol work.

NARRATIVE OF ACTION, 20/9/17 - 23/9/17,
by O.C. No.2 Platoon.

At ZERO Hour the platoon advanced in two lines.
I was in touch with No.1.Platoon on the left and
the Lan.Fus. on the right.   About 6.15 a.m. we
came under M.G. fire from a Strong Point situated
on the other side of the HANEBEEK, D.7.c.2.2.
approx.   About this time also we came under
shell fire; prior to this shells had fallen in
rear of us.   We reinforced the first two waves
which were being subjected to intense M.G. fire
from both flanks.   We took up a position in and
in rear of a shallow trench 30 or 40 yds. from
SCHULER GALLERIES from which came M.G. fire.
Several snipers were busy too.   Communication
and reorganisation were difficult.   The enemy
directed shell fire on to us by firing Very lights
which turned in the air and then burst into two
green lights.   I lit several round flares as
aeroplanes flew over.   We attempted to get
superiority of fire with L.Gs. etc. but owing
probably to bad weather conditions the L.Gs.
jambed and were of very little use.   Sometime
between 7.30 and 8 a.m. we rushed the three
concrete emplacements taking 30 prisoners and
2 M.Gs. with ammunition etc.   We immediately
set to work to consolidate and I reported to
O.C. "A" Coy.   Later I made two attempts to
advance on SCHULER FARM with a party of 7 or 8,
but owing to sniping from the direction of
strong point at D.13.b.2.7. I discovered that I
was alone when I arrived at the edge of the moat
surrounding SCHULER FARM.   From 9 to 11 I was
on patrol, endeavouring to get into touch with
an outpost of the 2/5th K.O.R.L. at D.7.c.5.2.
and then making a reconnaissance round SCHULER
FARM.   I made my report to Capt.KERN (1/5th
K.O.R.L) who was in command.

NARRATIVE OF ACTION, 20/9/17 - 23/9/17,
by L/Cpl. WOOD, No.1.Platoon.
-o-o-o-o-o-o-o-o-o-o-

Having spent the night in shell holes, somewhere round Fort Hill, I, with my section of men, and the rest of the Company marched off at the appointed time. We very soon found ourselves in the first wave. After a slight check by the enemy, he having thrown a number of bombs, I was left with only one man of my section. A few minutes later he was wounded. I carried on and was with 2/Lt. ALLERTON and party at the clearing of the Galleries. I was then detailed to assist a wounded German Officer to the Aid Post. On my way there I came across Capt. HODSON in a shell hole, being attended to by one of our men. The man went away and left me with the Captain. I had already passed on the German Officer along the line. I took off the Captain's pack and put it under him to stop the blood from choking him. (He was bleeding very freely). I then ran to the Aid Post where I found two Stretcher Bearers attending wounded prisoners. I ordered them away to the Captain in the shell hole, where they bandaged him up. I then made my way back to the Galleries. We were very much troubled by snipers and consequently could do very little digging in during daylight. At dark, I arranged parties to dig and posted sentries from the left up to Coy. H.Q. On this work I had men of the 1/8th (Irish) K.L.R., King's Own, and Lan. Fus.
After this I was attached to 2/Lt. CHILDE post from which I went with messages many times, both by day and night, also acting as guide to SCHULER FARM. We were relieved by the North Staffs.

L.35.

C.O., A, B, C, D, Signals,
File, War Diary.

The following extracts from 164th Inf. Bde. Order
No.135 are published for information;- and
communication to all concerned:-

1. Para. 4. BARRAGE.
    The advance will be regulated by the forward
    movement of the creeping barrage, as shown
    on the barrage map.
    At ZERO the leading waves of 1/4th E.Lan.R.
    2/8th Lan.Fus. and 1/8th L'Pool R. will close
    quickly up to the barrage.   Objectives:-

        1/4th E.Lan.R........ YELLOW LINE of MAIN SECTOR
        2/8th Lan.Fus........ GREEN Line of CORPS   "
        1/8th L'Pool R....... GREEN   "   " SCHULER "
        1/4th K.Lan.R........ GREEN   "   " KERR   "
    The following points about the movement of the
    Artillery barrage will be made clear to all
    assaulting troops:-
    (a) Lifts are made by 50 yards.
    (b) Exceptions to (a) are the lift of 100 yds.
    from SCHULER GALLERIES on to SCHULER FARM and
    the lift of 100 yds. to enable assaulting troop
    to rush in close behind the barrage and seize
    SCHULER GALLERIES and AISNE FARM as quickly as
    possible.
    (c) Halt of one hour & 6 mins. on the line
    marked "plus 1 hour 20 min."
    (d) Halt of one hour on the line marked "+ 2.48"

2. The following extracts from 164 Inf.Bde. Q.P.1.
    are published for information and communication
    to all concerned:-
    "During the pauses in the barrage, assaulting
    troops will:-
    (a) clean up and occupy the area up to the line
        gained.

2.

(b) Occupy all enemy concrete defences. The defence of these positions must be so arranged as to deny them to the enemy by fire. They are only to be used by men of the garrisons actually off duty at the

(c) Reorganise and be ready (less permanent garrisons) to support on their own initiative the advance of troops passing through them to further objectives. Observers and runners must be sent forward immediately behind waves passing through so as to ensure receipt of prompt news of the position in front.

(d) All messengers, prisoners' escorts, etc. despatched to the rear to bring back at least half a dozen bandoliers of S.A.A. from the forward dumps.

(e) All men of permanent garrisons not holding posts, or disposed as sentries, to solve, clean, and load rifles, British and German, collect and clean ammunition, and make dispositions to hold the defences at all cost.

(f) Enemy documents seized will be sent back to H.Q.

( ) Nameboards will be placed in positions so as to be conspicuous from our side but invisible from the enemy's.

J F Jones
Capt. & Adjt.

Issued at 10.45 p.m. 1/8th(Irish)Batt.K.L.R.
Copies to:-
1. C.O.
2. A Coy.)

A, B, C, & D Coys.　　　　　　　　　1/8 IRISH/OFFR/988.
O.C. Signals. I.O.

  Reference the 2nd edition, of the
card giving Coloured Disc and Light Code
for Tanks.

  Para.3. of the notes on the back of
the card should be amended to read as follows:-

  "3. The three following general signals
  infantry should know by heart -

  Red & Green discs - Have reached my
          objective.
  Red, Red, and Red Discs - Broken down.
  Red, White, and White discs - No enemy
          in sight."

With the above alterations, the Tank Signal
Card will not be altered.

            JG Jones
            Capt. & Adjt.
23/7/17.   1/8th(Irish)Batt.K.L.R.

A/s 11208/3/293.

L.M. & L.R Corps,
G.H.Q., B.E.F.

Reference your 29A edition, of the maps giving the coloured lines are being used for this area.

Code "A" of the words on the back of the card should be amended to read as follows:-

A. Red Apple, Yellowing Pear, and Signals - Infantry abandoning trenches.

Jet B Green Citron - East, Red Plum, afternoon.

Red, Red, and Red Peach - Enemy here. Hop, Walke, and White Plum - Relatively inactive.

Of the above signals, the Red Plum will not be altered.

Major G.S.
I/c Maps in the Field.

OPERATION ORDER.
NO.120.
BY
LIEUT.COLONEL E.C.HEATH.
COMMANDING 1/8th(IRISH) BATTALION "KING'S"(L'POOL R.

Copy for War Diary

In the Field.
23/9/17.

1. This Battalion will move to billets in the WATOU No.3. area to-morrow 24/9/17.

2. Coys. will parade in sufficient time to be at VLAMERTINGHE Station (main line) at 2.50 p.m.
All mess stores, Officers' valises and Orderly room stores etc. to be ready for loading outside orderly room by 12.30 p.m.
Water Carts, Cookers, Lewis Gun Limbers, etc. to be ready to move by 1 p.m.
Batt. Transport to be ready to move at 2.30 p.m. from present lines.

3. 2/Lieut. CURTIS and 1 N.C.O. per Coy. and one N.C.O. each from H.Qrs. and Transport will parade at Orderly Room at 7 a.m. 24/9/17. and report to Area Commandant, WATOU at 10 a.m.
All men will fill their waterbottles by 12.30 p.m.

Issued at 9 p.m.
By runner.
Copies to:-
1. 164 Inf.Bde.
2. File.
3. War Diary.   7. O.C. B Coy.   12. T.O. & Q.M.
4. C.O.   8. "   C "   13. M.O.
5. 2nd-in-Command.   9. "   D "   14. R.S.M.
6. O.C. A Coy.   10. Details.

2/Lt. & Asst. Adjt.
1/8th(Irish) Battalion K.L.R.

SECRET.   COPY NO. 8

    1/8th(IRISH) BATTALION K.L.R.
    OPERATION ORDER NO. 127.

Ref: Map Sheet 57 N.E. 1/20,000.

                                    In the Field.
                                    25/9/17.

(1) The Battalion will move to BAUPAUME WEST on the 28th September, 1917.
Movement will be by March Route to ROUPOUTRE Station, and from thence to BAUPAUME WEST by rail.

(2) The route to Entraining Station will be by road K.12.c., L.1.d., L.9.c., a, & b., L.11.b., and L.17.d.

(3) Times of arrivals at entraining station are:-

    Transport....... 14 hours 45 minutes.
    Personnel....... 15 hours 15 minutes.
for departure of No.7. train at 17 hours 45 mins
Time of arrival at BAUPAUME WEST. 3 hours 40 min 27/9/17.

(4) A loading party - 2/Lt. F. BURNIE and 50 men "A" Coy. will report to Capt. K.T. BLAMEY, 2/5th Lan. Fus. at ROUPOUTRE Station at 14 hours on 25/9/17
They will travel by 21.45 train on 26/9/17.

(5) Batt. H.Qrs. will be at head of column enroute.

    A C K N O W L E D G E.

                                                 Capt. & Adjt.
Issued at 8 p.m.
By Runner.   1/8th(Irish) Batt. K.L.R.
Copies to:-
1. 164 Inf. Bde.
2. File.
3. War Diary.
4. xxxxxxxxxx C.O.
5. xxxxxxxxxx 2nd-in-Command.
6. O.C. A Coy.

SECRET.   COPY NO. 1

1/8th (IRISH) BATTALION K.L.R.
Administrative Instructions with reference
to Operation Order No. 139.

Copy for War Diary

                                    In the Field.
                                    25/9/17.

(1) Officers' Valises, Mess Kit etc. will be
    removed by Baggage Wagon at 11 a.m. and must
    be dumped outside Orderly Room at that hour.

(2) Cook Carts, Water Carts, & Medical Cart will
    proceed with Transport at 11.30 a.m.

(3) A M.T. has been provided for conveyance of
    Q.M. and Orderly Room Stores. These will be
    dumped outside Q.M. Stores at 12.30 p.m.
    The Q.M. will detail a guide to meet the lorry
    at Bde. H.Qrs. WATOU at 1 p.m. This lorry is
    to be returned to Bde. H.Q. by 4 p.m. The Q.M.
    will give written instructions to the driver.

(4) Rations. The mid-day meat ration for 26/9/17
    and breakfast bacon ration for 27/9/17 must be
    cooked before 10 a.m. 26/9/17.
    The men will carry haversack rations for tea
    26/9/17 and breakfast ration for 27/9/17.

            A C K N O W L E D G E.

Issued at 8.35 p.m.
by Runner.
Copies to:-   Capt. & Adjt.
  1. File.   1/8th (Irish) Batt. K.L.R.
  2. War Diary.
  3. C.O.   11. M.O.
  4. 2nd-in-Command.   12. T.O.
  5. O.C. A Coy.   13. Q.M.
  6. "   B   "   14. R.S.M.
  7. "   C   "
  8. "   D   "
  9. "   Details and Signals.
 10. Intell. Off. & R.C. Chaplain.

List of casualties sustained in operations from 19th to 23 Sept.

Officers

2 Lt. A. K. Hewitt Killed 20.9.17
"   F. A. Stone   "   20.9.17
Capt A. J. Monks   wounded "
"   R. C. Hoson   "   "
2 Lt. W. Lake   "   "
"   W. J. C. Grayson "   "
"   K. Kendrick   "   "
"   C. A. Baker   "   "
Lieut F. A. Cook   "   "
2 Lt. F. A. Harvey "   "
"   F. E. Ablett   missing "

Other Ranks

26 Killed   14 Wounded   22 missing

SECRET.   COPY NO. 2.
   1/8th(IRISH) BATTALION K.L.R.
   Administrative Instructions with reference
      to Operation Order No. 124.

                                        In the Field,
                                        25/9/17.

(1) Officers' Valises, Mess Kit etc. will be
    removed by Baggage Wagon at 11 a.m. and must
    be dumped outside Orderly Room at that hour.

(2) Cook Carts, Water Carts, & Medical Cart will
    proceed with Transport at 11.30 a.m.

(3) A M.T. has been provided for conveyance of
    Q.M. and Orderly Room Stores. These will be
    dumped outside Q.M. Stores at 12.30 p.m.
    The Q.M. will detail a guide to meet the lorry
    at Bde. H. Qrs. WATOU at 1 p.m. This lorry is
    to be returned to Bde. H.Q. by 4 p.m. The Q.M.
    will give written instructions to the driver.

(4) Rations. The mid-day meat ration for 26/9/17
    and breakfast bacon ration for 27/9/17 must be
    cooked before 10 a.m. 26/9/17.
    The men will carry haversack rations for tea
    26/9/17 and breakfast ration for 27/9/17.

        A C K N O W L E D G E.

Issued at 8.35 p.m.
By Runner.
Copies to:-
                                        Capt. & Adjt,
  1. File.   1/8th(Irish) Batt. K.L.R.
  2. War Diary.
  3. C.O.   11. M.O.
  4. 2nd-in-Command.   12. T.O.
  5. O.C.   A Coy.   13. Q.M.
  6. "   B "   14. R.S.M.
  7. "   C "
  8. "   D "
  9. "   Details and Signals.
 10. Intell. Off. & R.C. Chaplain.

NARRATIVE OF ACTION.   20/9/17 - 23/9/17.

By O.C. "A" Coy.

My Company formed the right half of the third wave.

At ZERO I pushed forward, maintaining the specified distance (250 yards) from the preceding waves, and was in touch with flanks. On reaching crest of hill in front of SCHULER GALLERIES we came under very heavy machine gun fire from an apparent "Strong Point" at D.7.c.20.20. half left and on the opposite bank of the HANEBEEK. Snipers were very active at this point, and we also came under the enemy's barrage. On the reverse slope about 30 yards from the Galleries, I reinforced the leading waves which had been checked by machine gun fire from the Galleries, and left flank. I reported to Capt. MONKS, who ordered me to push round on left flank. I proceeded to do this, and when we got into position we rushed the three Northern Galleries, capturing the garrison. Under cover of enemy emplacements, I organised several small parties, which occupied 3 of the emplacements, comprising part of the SCHULER GALLERIES. I also pushed forward a small garrison who occupied a shell hole 20 yards in front of the galleries at C.13.a.65.80. I then organised several attacks upon SCHULER FARM, but we were unable to gain a foothold as exceptionally heavy fire, together with sniping from the flanks was encountered.

I sent for reinforcements, and S.A.A.; these arrived about an hour later. At night, after it was obvious that the enemy's counter attack had failed I assisted Capt. JONES who reorganised the system of defences with all available men.

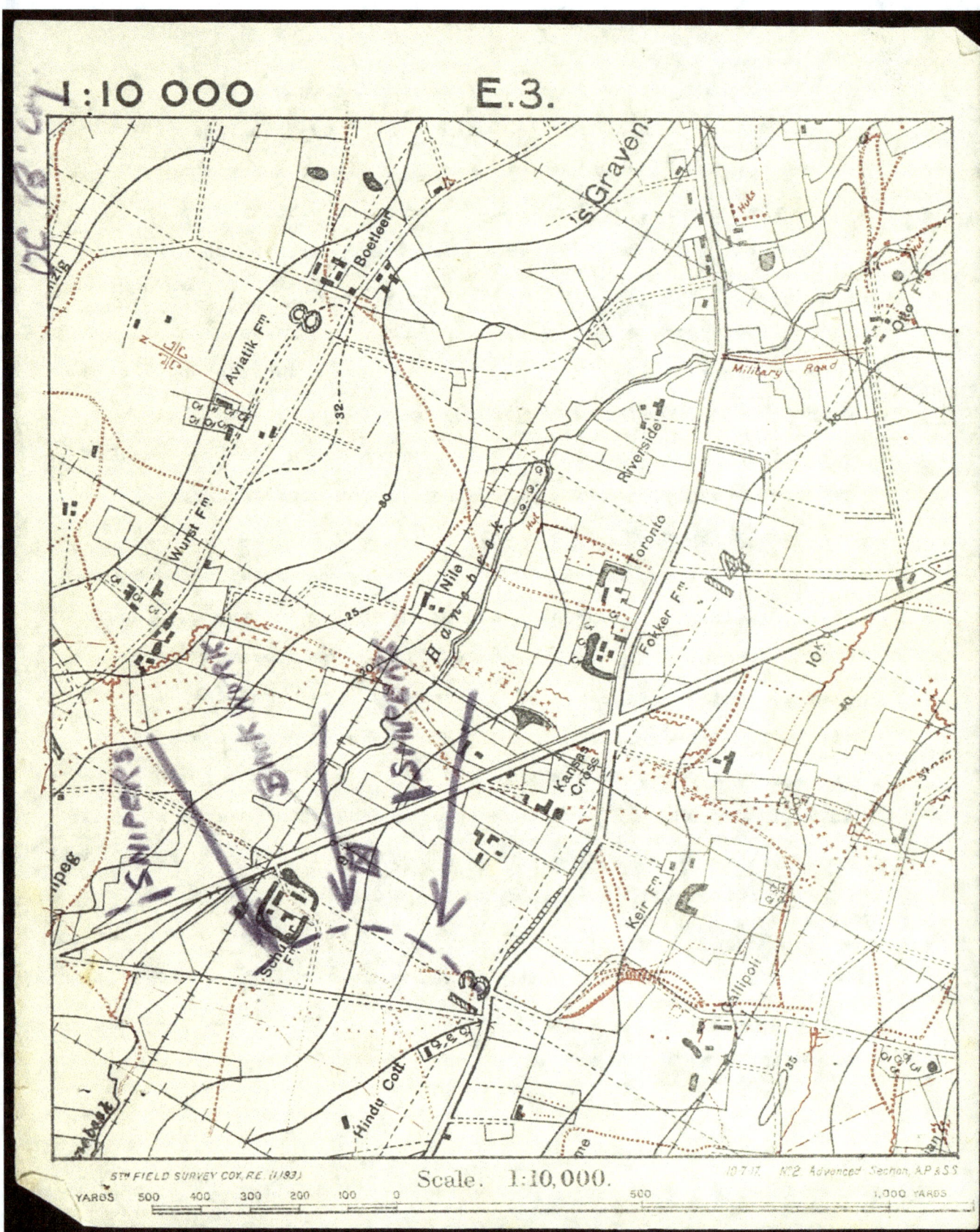

Message Form.

..............Division.

Map reference or mark own position on Map at back.

I am at..

I am at..and am consolidating.

I am at..and have consolidated.

I need :—Ammunition.
       Bombs.
       Rifle Grenades.
       Water.
       Very lights.
       Stokes shells.

Enemy forming up for counter-attack at..

I am in touch with.............................on Right / Left at............................

I am not in touch on Right. / Left.

Am being shelled from......................................

I estimate my present strength at................rifles.

Hostile { Battery / Machine Gun / Trench Mortar } active at..............................

Time   a.m. (p.m.)   Name...

Date....................................   Platoon................ Company..................

Place...   Battalion.......................................

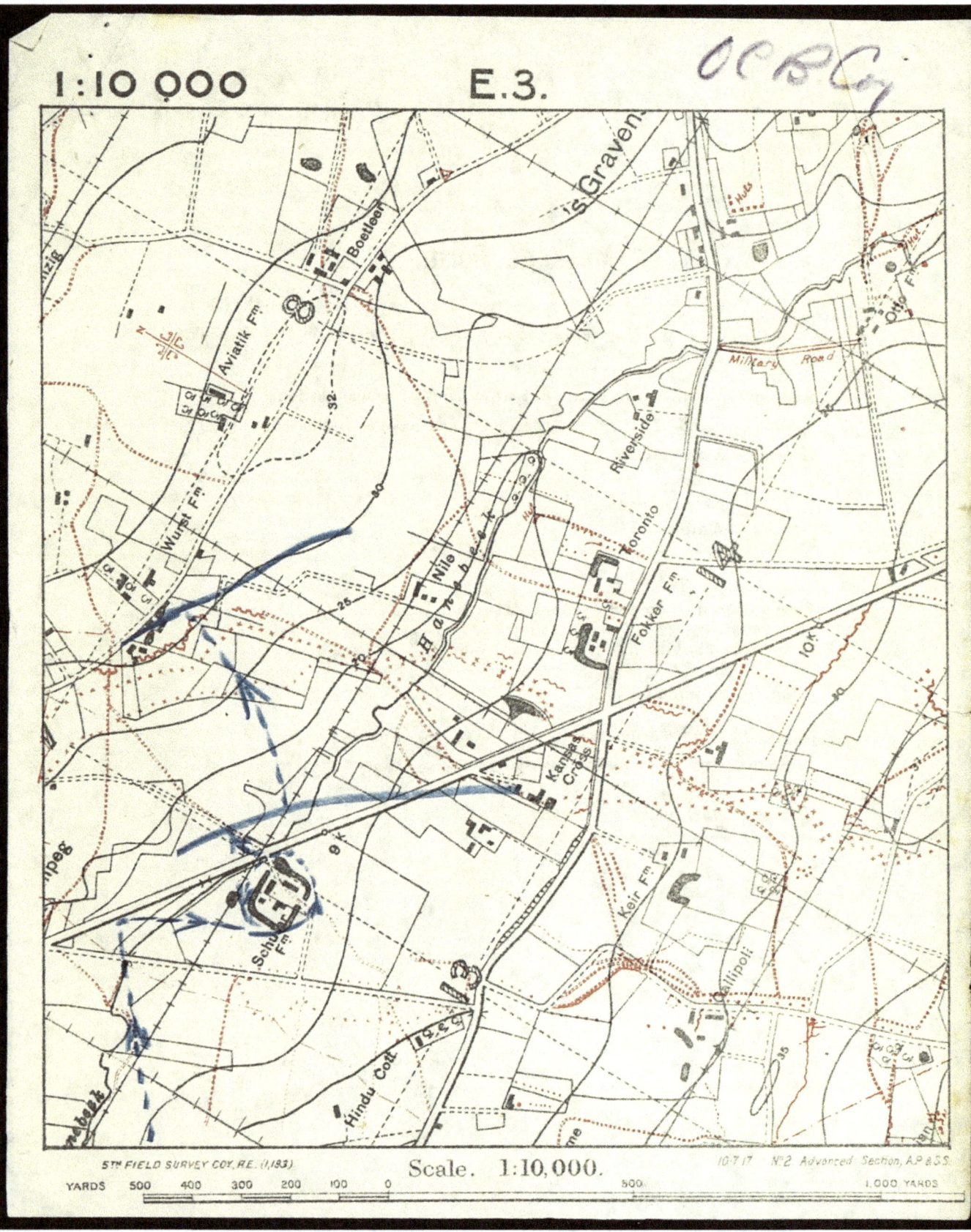

Message Form.

..............Division.

Map reference or mark own position on Map at back.

I am at...

I am at..and am consolidating.

I am at..and have consolidated.

I need :—Ammunition.
        Bombs.
        Rifle Grenades.
        Water.
        Very lights.
        Stokes shells.

Enemy forming up for counter-attack at...

I am in touch with.........................on Right / Left at............................

I am not in touch on Right / Left.

Am being shelled from..

I estimate my present strength at................rifles.

Hostile { Battery / Machine Gun / Trench Mortar } active at............................

Time   a.m. (p.m.)   Name..

Date............................   Platoon................ Company....................

Place..............................   Battalion....................................

COPY.

55th (WEST LANCASHIRE) DIVISION ORDER OF THE DAY.
@@

The following telegrams from the V Corps have been received:-

"The Commander-in-Chief visited Corps H.Qrs. this evening and expressed himself very pleased in the work of both Divisions and sends them his congratulations and thanks".

"Fifth Army wire begins aaa Please congratulate 55th Division on the gallant defence of HILL 37 yesterday and upon the energy and resource displayed by Commanders on the spot in organising counter attacks aaa Ends aaa.

         Sd/T. ROSE PRICE.

          Lieut. Colonel,
55th Division H.Q.   General Staff, 55th Division.
23rd September, 1917.

-o-o-o-o-o-o-o-o-

COPY.

55th (WEST LANCASHIRE) DIVISION ORDER OF THE DAY.

1. The following telegrams have been received :-

"Fifth Army wire begins aaa The Army Commander wishes to thank all arms and all ranks for their splendid efforts in today's battle aaa Co-operation between Infantry, Artillery and Flying Corps has been excellent and very important successes have been gained all along the front aaa Ends aaa"

"Corps Commander thanks Field and Heavy Artillery for their good work and the F.O.Os. for the very useful and timely information sent in aaa Ends aaa"

"Corps Commander congratulates 9th and 55th Divisions and thanks them for their success today aaa Ends aaa"

2. The Major General Commanding wishes to add his thanks and congratulations to all arms and ranks of the Division.

There is no doubt whatever that in addition to making a very substantial advance over difficult ground stubbornly defended, well organised, and liberally provided with strong cover, artillery, and machine guns, the Division, aided most ably by the Corps Heavy Artillery, succeeded in dealing the enemy a very heavy blow, and causing him severe losses.

Success was due to the fine determination shewn by all ranks and the hearty co-operation of Artillery, Engineers, Infantry, Machine Gun Companies, Trench Mortars and R.A.M.C. with each other, which is the sign of a united and disciplined Division.

Sd/T.ROSE PRICE.

Lieut. Colonel.
General Staff,   55th Division.

55th Division.
21st September, 1917.

-0-0-0-0-0-0-0-0-0-

55th (WEST LANCASHIRE) DIVISION.

ORDER OF THE DAY.

The following telegram has been received from Fifth Army :-

"55th Division.

Please convey to all ranks 55th Division the Army Commander's congratulations on the fine record of the Division during the hard fighting of the past two months aaa The Army Commander wishes specially to thank all ranks for their splendid efforts which have contributed greatly to the success of the last attack and to wish them all good luck and success in the future despite their long period in the line prior to commencement of operations they have well maintained and increased their high reputation.

FIFTH ARMY ".

The following telegram has been received from the West Lancashire Reserve Brigade :-

"G.O.C. 55th Division, FRANCE.

Brigadier General STUART and all ranks West Lancashire Reserve Brigade send heartiest congratulations to West Lancashire Division on their splendid success."

55th Division H.Q.,
27th September 1917.

T. Rose Price.
Lieut-Colonel,
General Staff, 55th Division.

COPY.

55th WEST LANCASHIRE DIVISION ORDER OF THE DAY.

The following telegram has been received from GENERAL SIR HERBERT PLUMER, G.C.M.G., G.C.V.O., K.C.B., commanding the 2nd Army:-

"GENERAL JEUDWINE, Commanding 55th Division.

Many congratulations to you and your
Division on your success yesterday aaa
You must have accounted for a great many.

GENERAL PLUMER ".

Sd/T. ROSE PRICE.
Lieut. Colonel.
General Staff, 55th Division.

55th Division.
22nd September 1917.

-0-0-0-0-0-0-0-0-0-0-

55th WEST LANCASHIRE DIVISION ORDER OF THE DAY.

The following telegram has been received from The Right Honourable E.G.V. Earl of DERBY, K.G., G.C.V.O., C.B., Secretary of State for War:-

"GENERAL JEUDWINE, 55th Division Hdqrs. B.E.F.

Well done 55th West Lancashire Divn. accept
my most hearty congratulations I sincerely trust
your losses are not heavy.

DERBY "

Sd/T. ROSE PRICE.
Lieut. Colonel.
General Staff, 55th Division.

55th Division H.Q.
24th September 1917.

-0-0-0-0-0-0-0-0-0-

Ref

Direction of enemy
Counter-attacks

←
←
←

1/8th(Irish)Batt.K.L.R.

From O.C.   B Coy.

To Adjutant, 1/8th(Irish)Batt.K.L.R.

Narrative of Action 31st July/1st August.1917.

Ref.Map.
ST.JULIEN
1/20,000.
&
attached
map.

----
denotes
direction
taken.

Line occupied.

       I have the honour to make the following report on recent operations 31/7/17 - 2/8/17.

B Company took up its position in the assembly trench at about 12.30 a.m. 31/7/17.

On Z day, at zero plus 4 hours 40 mins, B Coy. left its assembly trench following in rear of IMPUTE.
The disposition of the Coy. was as follows:-
No.7.Platoon on the right supported by No.6 platoon, No.5.platoon on the left, supported by No.8 platoon. Company H.Qrs. following in the centre of the two supporting platoons.
Our direction was about half right, the bearing being taken from the compass.
Very little opposition was encountered up to BOSSAERT FARM (C.2 3.b.2.3.) and here we came under heavy shell fire. This shelling was the cause of the two rear platoons losing connection.
The two leading platoons No.5 & No.7 pushed forward and reached a point of the WINNIPEG - KANSAS Road, approx (D.7.c.5.4.). At this point we found that we were too much to the left and made a right incline in the direction of SCHULER FARM (D.13.a.6.2.) and up to this point were in touch with with the 118th Brigade on our left and A Coy. of IMPOSE on the right.
I have since ascertained that the two rear platoons losing direction, bore away to the left. The surviving N.C.O. of Coy.H.Q. states that Capt.DUDER was killed at VENHEULE Fm. and from this point appears to have gone too much to the left, mixing with the 118th Brigade, who were attacking ST.JULIEN.
No.5. and No.7. Platoons combined, assisting IMPUTE took SCHULER FARM, very little resistance being offered by the enemy. This place appeared to have been used as a H.Qrs. being surrounded by water and wired, and reached by two small bridges.
It was concreted and very strongly made, and apparently undamaged by shell fire, and while we were searching the place very heavy machine gun and rifle fire was opened upon us. The machine gun fire appeared to be coming from the right flank, the result being that we suffered heavy casualties. The party then took cover behind a ridge in front of the farm and commenced digging in. At this point we were joined by Lieut.ORCHARD and a few men of "D" Coy. Here Lieuts.TOWE and ORCHARD were hit.
Having reached our objective I gave the order to dig in, and consolidated.
Whilst engaged in doing this Capt.WARD joined us. IMPUTE having apparently suffered heavy losses, Capt.WARD gave me the order to reinforce IMPUTE.

C.S.M. GREENWOOD went to the left, and I pushed forward in the direction of WURST FARM, Capt. BODEL joined my party while we were crossing the W - K road.

On reaching the final objective we found IMPUTE holding the line with 2 officers and about 25 other ranks. The total strength of the party was not 4 officers and 40 other ranks.

All this time we were being subjected to heavy machine gun and rifle fire, the result being heavy casualties.

We endeavoured to get in touch with the left Batt. and later heard that they had been pushed back, and accordingly, messages were sent back by runner and pigeon, stating our position and asking for ammunition and reinforcements. While holding this position five enemy aeroplanes, flying very low, were locating our position by dropping Very lights, the result being that we were subjected to heavy shelling.

We tried to get in touch with the right and were unable to do so. We held on to this position for about one hour and a half, and having two exposed flanks and being heavily pressed, we were compelled to retire. withdraw

We retired to the W - K road and here took up a new position in shell holes, rapid fire being opened. On this road I met an Officer and a Lewis gun team of IMPEL, and he took up a position in a shell hole on our left, and opened fire until all his ammunition was expended.

Capt. BODEL was killed at this point and the total number was now about one officer and ten other ranks.

To the best of my knowledge the only survivors of this party are myself and one N.C.O.

Just before reaching the BLACK Line we met a carrying party of about 10 other ranks, carrying up ammunition, but owing to the enemy counter attacking on the right and left I ordered them to stand to, and reported the situation to Capt. JONES who was holding CAPRICORN SUPPORT with about 25 men.

It was now about 6.30 p.m. Later in the evening Capt. JONES was wounded in the legt. His wound was bandaged and he carried on for some time afterwards but was obliged to go to the dressing station and he then placed me in charge of the Battalion.

We were relieved the following day at 12 noon by INANE and according to orders took the party back and took up a position in our original front line NORTH of LONE ST.

The men were very wet and cold and were given an issue of rum and hot tea. Hot meals came up later.

At 2 p.m. 1/8/17 Capt. MONKS arrived and I handed over to him.

About 3 p.m. the same day 2/Lt. HODSON rejoined us. Whilst holding this trench a number of men rejoined the Batt. We were relieved the following day 2/8/17.

On reaching our transport lines a roll was called.

I have the honour to be, Sir,

Your obedient Servant,

(Signed) J.E. FENN

O.C. "B" Coy.

WAR DIARY

1/8th L'POOL R

CONFIDENTIAL

OCT 1917

WAR DIARY or ~~INTELLIGENCE SUMMARY~~

(Erase heading not required.)

Army Form C. 2118

Place	Date	Hour	Summary of Events and Information	Remarks and references to Appendices
Lealvelett	1/10/17	—	Coy training and training of specialists. Drill instruction to all Junior Officers, Warrant Officers, and N.C.O.'s under Adjutant. Casualties nil.	J/C
"	2-10-17	—	Coy training. Training of specialists. Drill instruction to all Junior Officers, Warrant Officers and N.C.O.'s under Adjutant. Casualties nil.	J/C
"	3-10-17	—	Batt. march - Seven Stocking 9am. O.O. 122. Casualties nil.	J/C
Villers Faucon	4-10-17	—	Coy training and training of specialists. Reconnaissance of right and left brigade sectors by Officers and N.C.O.'s. Casualties nil.	J/C
"	5-10-17	—	Coy training and training of specialists. Reconnaissance of right and left Bent. Headquarters by Officers and N.C.O's. Casualties nil	J/C
"	6-10-17	—	Coy training and training of specialists. Reconnaissance of right and left sect. sectors by Officers & N.C.O.'s. 122 other ranks proceeded back to Divisional Depot. Batt. Casualties nil.	J/C
"	7-10-17	—	Church Parade C of E 10.30 a.m. R.C. 10.15 a.m. Nonconformists' parade ~~10.30~~ 10.45. Batts. in afternoon. Casualties nil	J/C

WAR DIARY or INTELLIGENCE SUMMARY

Army Form C. 2118

Place	Date	Hour	Summary of Events and Information	Remarks and references to Appendices
Villers-Faucon	8.10.17		The Brigadier General inspects battalion. Lecture to all officers and N.C.O.s by Adjutant. Casualties nil	
"	9.10.17		Coy training. Training of specialists. Lecture by Adjutant. 2/Lieut. L. Shields to be a/Capt. 2/Lts. R.C. Robinson, L. Curties, and R.B. Thorpe to be Lieut. Casualties nil	
"	10.10.17		Coy training. Training of specialists. Lecture by Adjutant to all officers and N.C.O.s. Casualties nil	
"	11.10.17		Inspection of Transport by Brigadier General. Coy training. Training of specialists. Lecture to officers and N.C.O.s by Adjutant. 2/Lt. W.L. Ball to be a/Capt. 2/Lt. L. Daniel's promoted Lieut. 41 O.R.s sent to 1/10 Liverpool control. 18 men join us as reinforcement. Lt. A.G. Lewis been Releaved. Casualties nil Adjutant to all officers. A.C.I.	
"	12.10.17		Coy training. Training of specialists. 2/Lt. H.S. Storry to Cookery Course. All platoon officers to reconnoitre sectors too. Casualties nil. Batt moved to Empire in support. O.O. 128.	
LEMPIRE	13.10.17		Coy training. Working parties to the Tunnels. Relieve the 9th Kings in the Tunnels. O.O. 124. Casualties nil	

WAR DIARY or INTELLIGENCE SUMMARY

Army Form C. 2118

Place	Date	Hour	Summary of Events and Information	Remarks and references to Appendices
TRENCHES LEMPIRE SECTOR (LEFT)	14/10/17		In trenches. Capt J.A. Jones arrives for duty and to vice Capt Brand on leave.	Casualties Nil
	15/10/17		In trenches. 2/Lt G Sweed to be a/Capt. 2/Lt R.E. Heath resumes command of the bn with effect from 12.10.17 Noon. Ainsworth resumes duties as 2nd in command with effect from 12.10.17.	Casualties Nil
	16/10/17		In trenches. 2/Lt Shaw from Cookery Course.	Casualties Nil
	17/10/17		In trenches. Received by 2/5 Lanc. Fus.	Casualties Nil
	18/10/17		In trenches. 2/Lt K'Oathes appointed Intelligence Officer vice 2/Lt 2/Lt Chatwick returned to D.Coy.	Casualties Nil
			O/125 at LEMPIRE.	Casualties — 2 O.R.
SUPPORT LEMPIRE	19/10/17		In support. Working parties to trenches. General training for men not on working parties. 2/Lt Cosgrave supt. pol. Lts J.G. Marsdale & W.G. Woolcock arrives to duty, any R. Posted to A.Coy. No 760,625 Pte 09 Jones from 28 Lond. R. to be 2/Lt 24 Sept 1917. Temp 2/Lt Field to be Act Capt whilst (continued)	

1875 Wt. W593/826 1,000,000 4/15 J.B.C. & A. A.D.S.S./Forms/C. 2118.

WAR DIARY or INTELLIGENCE SUMMARY

Army Form C. 2118

Place	Date	Hour	Summary of Events and Information	Remarks and references to Appendices
SUPPORT LEMPIRE (contd)	9/10/17		Coys carrying a company. 5/10/17. 2/Lt R.B. Hodson relinquishes the acting rank of captain on ceasing to command a Coy. 21.9.1917. Siat. 157.	MC
	20/10/17		Bn in support. Working parties to trenches. General training for men not on working parties.	MC Casualties Nil
	21/10/17		Bn in support. Working parties to trenches. C.O. Holy Communicants. R.C. Voluntary Mass. Pictures. 2/Lt. Chadwick and Shelling Aus. to C. Coy. B.M.G. Woolacock to D Coy. Casualties Nil.	MC
	22/10/17		Bn in support. Working parties to the trenches. Lt Col G.C. Search to 3rd Army Course for C/Os. Major J. Duckworth assumes command of Battalion. Casualties Nil	MC
	23/10/17		Bn in support. Working parties into front line, relieving 75 Lanc. Regt. O.O.126. 2/Lt Daniels returned from R.E. course 27/10/17. Casualties Nil.	MC Casualties Nil
TRENCHES LEFT SECTOR LEMPIRE	24/10/17		Bn in trenches. Casualties Nil —	MC
	25/10/17		Bn in trenches. Extract from S.O. No 859 d/ 24/10/17 — "Under authority delegated by the Field Marshal Commanding in Chief the 4th Corps Commander has	MC

1875 Wt. W593/826 1,000,000 4/15 J.B.C. & A. A.D.S.S./Forms/C. 2118.

WAR DIARY or INTELLIGENCE SUMMARY

Army Form C. 2118

Place	Date	Hour	Summary of Events and Information	Remarks and references to Appendices
TRENCHES LEFT SECTOR LEMPIRE	25/10/17		has awarded the following decorations to the N.C.O.s and men as stated below for gallantry and devotion to duty in action. "The Commanding Officer heartily congratulates these N.C.Os and men on their decorations:- MILITARY MEDAL. 305192 Sgt. SHANNON P. 307411 L.Cpl. LEROY W. 308099 L.Cpl. GATLEY F. 308534 Pte WATKINSON R. 303696 Pte BANKS G. 307875 Pte DRUMMOND H. 307924 HUGHES J.H. 307744 Pte McGUIRE G.T. 36532 Pte SIMPSON H.B. 2Lt J.B. Henn transferred to 14th/17 B. hussars struck off the strength of Bn. K.L.R. 2Lt Jones to England 23/10/17. Casualties Nil. known Trenches. Kept J.J. Jones to England 23/10/17. Casualties Nil.	
	26/10/17		Bn. in Trenches. Casualties Nil.	
	27/10/17		Bn in Trenches. Following Officers arrive as reinforcements 28/10/17 and are posted to Companies as follows:- 2Lt E.H.N. CLAYDON A.Coy. 2Lt P.A. SEDDON. B.Coy. 2Lt A. HAYES D.Coy. 2Lt C.W. VICK. C.Coy. Casualty 1 O.R (accidentally wounded)	
	28/10/17			

WAR DIARY
or
INTELLIGENCE SUMMARY
(Erase heading not required.)

Army Form C. 2118

Place	Date	Hour	Summary of Events and Information	Remarks and references to Appendices
TRENCHES LEFT SECTOR LEMPIRE	29/10/17		Bn. in trenches.	Casualties Nil.
			(The 1/4 Royal North Lancs having taken over the "BIRDCAGE" on night 29/30 Oct. 1917, this sector now became the Centre Sector of the right Brigade.)	
CENTRE SECTOR	30/10/17		Bn in trenches. Capt. H.E. Evans M.O. returns from leave, Capt. LaFeur R.A.M.C. returns to 1/3 West Lancs Field Amb.	Casualties Nil.
	31/10/17		Bn. in trenches	Casualties Nil.

E. J. Toah
Lieut-Colonel.
Comdg 1/8 (Irish) K.L.R.
16 w. Infy Brigade

SECRET.   COPY NO.

1/8th (IRISH) BATT. "THE KING'S" (L'POOL R.)

OPERATION ORDER NO 182.

In the Field.
12/10/17.

Reference: Map of C. N.E. 1/20,000
Trench Sheets, T.1.77s.

(1)   The Battalion will relieve the 1/5th L'pool Regt at LEMPIRE as Support Battalion, Right Brigade Sector, on the night 12/13th October/17. These Billets will be taken over by 1/4th N.Lancs.R on the night of October 12th/17.

(2)   Companies will parade at 5.0 p.m. 12th October, and will move off by platoons in the order - Headquarters, A, B, C, D, Coys. Leading Platoon will pass Road junction N.24.A.95.35. at 5.30 pm Distance between Platoons, 100 yards.
        Corresponding Companies will be relieved.

(3)   1/5th L'pools have arranged for Platoon guides to be at junction of Road and Track N.19.b.40.95. at 5.30 p.m.

(4)   Advanced parties of Intelligence Officer and one N.C.O for Headquarters, and one Officer and one N.C.O. per Company will proceed to LEMPIRE at 2.0 p.m. October 12th to take over Billets and Trench stores.
        Defence schemes, Maps, Secret documents, and details of all Working parties will be taken over by the Intelligence Officer.
        Lists of Trench or Area stores will be forwarded to Battalion Headquarters immediately after relief.

(5)   (a) Completion of reliefs will be reported to Battalion Headquarters by the Code word ZIP.
        (b) Exact dispositions will be forwarded to Battalion Headquarters as early as possible after relief has been completed.

(6)   Battalion Headquarters will close at VILLERS FAUCON at 5.0 p.m. and will open at LEMPIRE (N.15.a.85.40) at that hour.

(7)   Administrative instructions have been issued to all concerned.

        ACKNOWLEDGE.

Issued at 9.0 a.m.   1/8th (Irish) Bn K.L.R.

        Copies to:-
1. 164 Infantry Brigade.   9. B. Coy.
2. 1/5th L'pool Regt.   10. C. "
3. 1/4th N.Lancs.R.   11. D. "
4. C.O.   12. O. i/c Details & Signals.
5. 2nd in Command.   13. M.O.
6. Adjutant.   14. T.O.
7. Intelligence Officer.   15. Q.M.
8. A. Coy.   16. R.C. Chaplain.
                                 17. War Diary.
                                 18. File.
                                 19. R.S.M.
                                 20.

SECRET.   COPY NO....
         1/8th(IRISH)BATT."THE KING'S"(L'POOL REGT).

                    OPERATION ORDER NO.124.

Ref.Map. 62c. N.E. 1/20,000.
         Trench Sheets W.L.77a.   In the Field.
                                                 12/10/17.

(1) (a) This Battalion will be relieved on the night of
        Oct. 13/14th by the 1/4th N.Lan.R.   Relief will
        commence about 6.30 p.m.
    (b) On relief, this Battalion will move into Front Line
        Left Subsector, relieving 1/9th L'Pool R.

(2) Companies will take over as follows:-

                 Headquarters at LEMPIRE F.16.a.7.6.

        "A" Coy. to relieve "B" Coy. 1/9th L'Pool R. in
        support at SART LANE.
        "B" Coy. to relieve "D" Coy. 1/9th L'Pool R. at
        GRAFTON POST.
        "C" Coy. to relieve "C" Coy. 1/9th L'Pool R. at
        FLEECEALL POST.
        "D" Coy. to relieve "A" Coy. 1/9th L'Pool R. at
        EGO POST.

(3) Platoon Guides will be furnished by 1/9th L'Pool R. and will
    report to O.C. Coys. at 6 p.m. October 13th.

(4) The positions to be taken over have been reconnoitred
    by Company Commanders.   Platoon Commanders and Platoon
    Sergeants will reconnoitre their Company Frontage on the
    morning October 13th.   O.C. Coys. will detail one Officer
    and one N.C.O. to remain to take over trenches and trench
    stores.   Lists of trench stores to be taken over will be
    forwarded to Battalion H.Qrs. as early as possible.

(5) (a) Details of all work on defences, in progress and proposed
        will be most carefully taken over in detail, and arrangements
        made for work to be continued without interruption.
    (b) All Defence schemes, Maps, and Secret documents, will
        be taken over.

(6) Reports are required as soon as possible after relief:-
    (a) Detailed disposition by platoons - shewing location and
        strength.
    (b) That touch has been definitely established with Companies
        on their flanks.

        ~~The Battalion on the right is 11th ROYAL SUSSEX (Very Ins. Etc.)~~

(7) Completion of relief will be reported by wire by the
    word RAT.

(8) Batt.H.Qrs. will close at LEMPIRE (F.15.a.85.40.) at
    7.30 p.m. and will open at LEMPIRE (F.16.a.7.6.) at that
    time.

(9) Administrative instructions have been issued to all
    concerned.

        ACKNOWLEDGE.

                                            Sd/J.F.JONES.
                                              Capt. & Adjt.
                                        1/8th(Irish)Batt.K.L.R.
Issued at 12 p.m.
Copies to:-
1. 166 Inf. Bde.
2. 1/4th N.Lan.R.
3. 1/9th L'Pool R.

4. C.O.
5. 2nd-in-Command.
6. Adjutant.
7. Intell.Off.
8. A Coy.
9. B "
10. C "
11. D "
12. Details.
13. M.O.
14. T.O.
15. Q.M.
16. R.C.Chaplain.
17. R.S.M.
18. File.
19. War Diary.
20.

SECRET.   COPY NO 17

1/8th (IRISH) BATT. "THE KING'S" (L'POOL REGT).

Ref Map. 62. C. N.E. 1/20,000.
Trench sheets, W.L.77.a.

OPERATION ORDER NO 125.

In the Field,
18/10/17.

1. (a) This Battalion will be relieved on the night Oct 18/19th by 2/5th Lan Fus Regt. Relief will commence about 6.30 p.m.
   (b) On relief, this Battalion will move into Brigade Support in LEMPIRE, relieving the 1/4th N.LAN.REGT.

2. (a) Companies will be relieved by 2/5th Lan Fus as follows :-

   A Coy in Support at SART LANE by 2/5th L.Fus A Coy.
   B " at GRAFTON POST by 2/5th L.Fus D Coy.
   C " at FLEECEALL POST by 2/5th L.Fus C Coy.
   D " at EGG POST by 2/5th L.Fus B Coy.

   (b) Corresponding Companies of 1/4th N.Lan.Regt will be relieved by this Unit.

   The Garrisons of LEMPIRE CENTRAL, LEMPIRE EAST, YAK and ZEBRA POSTS will be provided by C Coy.

3. Guides will be provided for 2/5th Lan. Fus as hereunder, and will rendezvous at /F.15.d.70.85 at times stated. *Road Junction*/

   For Lewis Gun and Signalling Posts at 2.30 p.m.
   Platoon Guides at 5.45 p.m.

   All movement to and from the Front Line on day of relief must be reduced to a minimum; not more than two men must move together, and they must be at a distance of 150x.

   Lewis Guns must be slung and not carried under the arm.

4. Particulars of all work on defences, in progress and proposed, must be carefully handed over to incoming Unit in detail. A copy of this will be forwarded to Battalion Headquarters by 3.0 p.m. 18/10/17.
   All Defence schemes, Maps, and Secret documents will be handed over.

5. O.C. Companies will detail one Officer and one N.C.O to report to 1/4th N.Lan.Regt for the purpose of taking over Posts, Billets, and Area Stores, at 3.0 p.m. The Assistant Adjutant will take over for Headquarters.

   Lists of stores handed over to 2/5th Lan. Fus will be forwarded to Battalion Headquarters as soon as signed.

   Lists of trench stores taken over from 1/4th N.Lan.R. will be forwarded to Battalion Headquarters as early as possible after relief.

6. Completion of reliefs will be reported by wire by code.

7. Battalion Headquarters will close at LEMPIRE (F.16.a.7.6.) at 9.0 p.m. and will open at LEMPIRE (F.15.a.8.5.) at that time.

   Administrative instructions have been issued to all concerned.

   A C K N O W L E D G E.

W. Hornby 2/Lt
Capt & Adjt.
1/8th (Irish) Bn. K.L.

Issued at 10.0 a.m.

COPIES TO :-

1. 164 Infantry Brigade.
2. 2/5th Lan. Fus.
3. 1/4th N. Lan. R.
4. C.O.
5. 2nd in Command.
6. Adjutant.
7. Intelligence Officer.
8. A Coy.
9. B Coy.
10. C Coy.
11. D Coy.
12. Details.
13. M.O.
14. T.O.
15. Q.M.
16. R.S.M.
17. War Diary.
18. File.
19.
20.

SECRET.   COPY NO.....
        1/8th(IRISH)BATT."THE KING'S"(L'POOL REGT).

                    OPERATION ORDER NO.126.

Ref.Map: 62s. N.E. 1/20,000.   In the Field,
         Trench Sheets W.L.77a.   22/10/17.

(1) This Battalion will move into the Front Line, Left Subsector
    on the night of Oct.23/24th, relieving the 2/5th Lan. Fus.
    Relief will commence about 6.30 p.m.

(2) Companies will take over as follows:-

        H.Qrs. to LEMPIRE (Lancaster House) F.16.a.7.6.
        A Coy. to relieve D Coy. 2/5th Lan. Fus. at GRAFTON POST.
        B "   "   "   C "   "   "   " " FLEECEALL POST.
        C "   "   "   A "   "   "   " in SART LANE.
        D "   "   "   B "   "   "   " " EGG POST.

    Platoon Guides will be furnished by 2/5th Lan. Fus. for
    A & B Coys. and will rendezvous at Batt. H.Q. F.16.a.7.6. at
    6 p.m. Guides for C Coy. will be provided as under:-

        ZEBRA POST.)
        YAK POST.   ) Road Junction F.16.a.90.75. 6 p.m.
        LEMPIRE CENTRAL.)
          "   EAST.   ) Report to Garrison at 6 p.m.

    Company Lewis Gun Teams will rendezvous outside Batt. H.Q.
    F.16.a.7.6. as under, where guides will conduct them to their
    respective positions:-
        "A" Company....... 2 p.m.
        "B"   "   .... 2.10 p.m.

    O.C. "C" Coy. will provide 1 guide for each post who will
    report to O.C. "C" Coy. 2/5th Lan. Fus. at FLEECEALL POST at
    6 p.m. On arrival at the posts these guides will hand over
    any stores etc. to incoming garrisons and rejoin their Coy. in
    SART LANE. One N.C.O. per Company of 2/5th Lan. Fus. will
    report to Coy. H.Q. in SANDBAG ALLEY at 10.15 a.m. to take
    over stores, billets etc. Provost Sergeant 2/5th Lan. Fus.
    will report at Bn. H.Q. F.15.a.8.5. and will take over H.Q.
    stores and billets from R.S.M.
    Sgt.WAINWRIGHT will report to H.Q. Lancaster House at 2 p.m.
    to take over dumps at GRAFTON POST and FLEECEALL LANE.
    Sgt.BIGGS will report to H.Q. Lancaster House to take over
    H.Q. stores.

(3) (a) Details of all work on defences, in progress and proposed
        will be most carefully taken over in detail, and arrangements
        made for work to be continued without interruption.
    (b) All Defence Schemes, Maps, and Secret Documents, will be
        taken over.

(4) A report is required as soon as possible after relief that
    touch has been definitely established with Companies on the
    flanks.
    Batt. on right - 1/4th R.Lan.R.   Batt. on Left. -1/5th S.Lan.R.

(5) Completion of relief will be reported by wire by the word PROG.

(6) Battalion H.Q. will close at LEMPIRE (F.15.a.8.5.) at 6.30 p.m.
    and will open at LEMPIRE (F.16.a.7.6.) at the same hour.

(9) Administrative Instructions have been issued to all concerned.

    A C K N O W L E D G E.
                                            W. Tornley.
                                           2/Lieut. & A/Adjt.
                                         1/8th(Irish)Battalion K.L.R.

Issued at 9.15 p.m.
By Runner.
Copies to:- see over.

1. O.C. 164 Inf Bde.
2. 2/5th Lan. Fus.
3. O.C.
4. O.C.   A Coy.
5. "   B "
6. "   C "
7. "   D "
8. "   Details & Signals.
9. M.G.
10. A.M.
11. T.C.
12. R.S.M.
13. File.
14. War Diary.

Confidential

War Diary

1/8th Spool. R.

for

November

1917.

WAR DIARY or INTELLIGENCE SUMMARY

Army Form C. 2118

Place	Date	Hour	Summary of Events and Information	Remarks and references to Appendices
TRENCHES CENTRE SECTOR LEMPIRE.	1/11/17		Bn in trenches. Lt-Col E.C. HEATH having returned from the Course for Commanding Officers, resumes command of the Battalion. 1/11/17. Major L. DUCKWORTH resumes the position of 2nd-in-command 5/11/17. 2Lts F.J. CHADWICK and F. BURNIE to 7th Corps. Infy. School 1/11/17. Lt & QM. H.G. CLARKE is struck off the strength of this Battn. 31/9/17 (Auth:- W.O. list No (A.G.4.a.) 13/10/17 and DAL 1536/2348 B. 30/10/17). 2 Lt. H.G. RAYMENT and 741 O.R. returns from 180 Tunnelling Coy. 1/11/17. Casualties NIL	
	2/11/17		Bn in trenches. Relieved by 1/7 K.L.R. O.O. 128. Bn from Stokes mortar Course Travelled. NIL FAUCON. 2 Lt. A.H.C. RAE	
VILLERS FAUCON	3/11/17		Bn in Divisional Reserve. Working parties to Divl Baths, Divl HQ. and R.E. Dumps:- Baths, Rif inspection, cleaning of equipment, foot inspections &c. Casualties Nil	
"	4/11/17		R.C., C of E. Three non Conformist Church Parades. Working parties to Hutting Dump, Divl. Baths - 2 parties to R.E. & 2 to Area Comm. dump at "Linden". allegedly by H.M. Hellering the field	

WAR DIARY
or
INTELLIGENCE SUMMARY.
(Erase heading not required.)

Army Form C. 2118.

Place	Date	Hour	Summary of Events and Information	Remarks and references to Appendices
VILLERS FAUCON	1917 4/11/17		Marshal Commanding in Chief has awarded the following decorations to the officers and NCO for gallantry and devotion to duty in action. D.S.O. Lt Col E.C. HEATH M.C. Capt J.F. JONES Capt G. SURTEES 2Lt Mr. H. EXTON D.C.M. #30546 a/R.S.M. Capn. W. 30735 Cpl E. CLARE. Casualties NIL	WCL
"	5/11/17		A Coy. 25 yds range. All Coys Lewis gun range. Specialist training. Working parties from Cross 2 to RE 21 to Girl Bath. Casualties NIL	WCL
"	6/11/17		O.C. 178 Coy. reports to discipline, accoutrements dress & equipment of all details. B Coy 25th range. All Coys Lewis gun range. Specialist training. Working parties as for 5/11/17. 21 OR as reinforcements. 14/11/17 Casualties NIL	WCL
"	7/11/17		Specialist training. Area Comdt. Regimental L.G. course under C. Coy on 25 range. D. Coy and 2Lt Mc Macklin G. Commenced. Casualties NIL	WCL
"	8/11/17		Specialist training by all coys. 1 hour continuous wearing of Systems L.G. range. Trench digging by all coys. small box respirator. Casualties NIL	WCL

Army Form C. 2118.

WAR DIARY
or
INTELLIGENCE SUMMARY.
(Erase heading not required.)

Instructions regarding War Diaries and Intelligence Summaries are contained in F.S. Regs., Part II. and the Staff Manual respectively. Title pages will be prepared in manuscript.

Place	Date	Hour	Summary of Events and Information	Remarks and references to Appendices
VILLERS FAUCON.	8/11/17		D Coy M. Gunners on 25ᵗ range. Coy training, trench-digging, Specialist training. Working party to Area Comdt. Casualties Nil.	WC
	9/11/17		All Companies, Practice Attack (full) + trench-digging. Working party to Area Comdt. Casualties Nil.	hBf
	10/11/17		All Coys. bathing at Divisional Baths, + completion of Battn. trench System. 2/Lt. A.H.G. TRAE returned from 3ʳᵈ Corps School. 2/Lt. A.R. ALLERTON to 3ʳᵈ Army Infantry School 2/Lt. W.K. COTTER to 3ʳᵈ Army Signals School. Working party to Area Comdt. Casualties Nil.	hBf
	11/11/17		Practice Attack (Whole Battn.) Casualties Nil.	hBf
	12/11/17		Practice Attack. (Whole Battn.) Trench digging + Bombing. Casualties Nil.	hBf

Army Form C. 2118.

WAR DIARY
or
INTELLIGENCE SUMMARY.
(Erase heading not required.)

Instructions regarding War Diaries and Intelligence Summaries are contained in F. S. Regs., Part II. and the Staff Manual respectively. Title pages will be prepared in manuscript.

Place	Date	Hour	Summary of Events and Information	Remarks and references to Appendices
Villers Faucon	13/10/17		A and B Coys. Bombing and firing on 25 yds Range. C and D Coys. Specialist Training + Trench Digging. Casualties Nil.	HBJ
	14/10/17		Battn. Attack Drill in conjunction with 2/5 Lan. Fus. Specialist Training. Casualties Two (accidentally wounded whilst bombing)	HBJ
	15/10/17		Battn. Specialist Training. Bombing, Bayonet Fighting, Musketry. Lewis Gun Course, 25 yds Range. Casualties Nil	HBJ
	16/10/17		2/Lt. H.G. SPARY to be acting Quartermaster with effect from 21/9/17 + Specialist Training. Bombing, Bayonet Fighting, Musketry. Inspection and preparations for the Trenches. Casualties One. (accidentally wounded by Lewis Gun firing on Range)	HBJ
TRENCHES CENTRE SECTOR. LEMPIRE.	17/10/17		Battn. in Trenches. Casualties Nil.	
	18/10/17		Battn. in Trenches. 2/Lt. A.W. HICKLING to 3rd Army Musketry Camp. Casualties Nil.	HBJ

Army Form C. 2118.

WAR DIARY
or
INTELLIGENCE SUMMARY.
(Erase heading not required.)

Instructions regarding War Diaries and Intelligence Summaries are contained in F.S. Regs., Part II. and the Staff Manual respectively. Title pages will be prepared in manuscript.

Place	Date	Hour	Summary of Events and Information	Remarks and references to Appendices
TRENCHES CENTRE SECTOR LEMPIRE.	19/11/17		Battn in Trenches. Casualties Nil. 2/Lt. A.H.G. RAE to 164 T.M.Bty.	WBJ
	20/11/17	6.20 a.m. 6.40 a.m.	Battalion attacked enemy defences in the Knoll Area but on account of wire being uncut was forced to retire. Officers Cases attd. Casualties 9 O.R. and 119 O.R.	WBJ
	21/11/17		Battn in Trenches. Casualties Nil.	WBJ
	22/11/17		Battn in Trenches. Casualties Nil. Relieved by 1/5 Battn. K.L.R. Bn. proceeded to HAMEL	WBJ
HAMEL	23/11/17		Batt. Cleaning up. (Baths. to A, B, + H.2. Companies) Casualties Nil.	WBJ
	28/11/17		All Companies Inspection + reorganising. Coy. (C + D Coys. Baths) Regimental Lewis Gun Course assembled under ex H.G. PAYMENT. 2/Lt. HAYES assumed Command and Payment of C. Coy. with effect from 23 Lh h/17. Capt. C.S.I. NORTHCOTE (Wachtell) Casualties Nil 2/Lt. R.E.L.F.H. to R.F.C.	WBJ

Army Form C. 2118.

WAR DIARY
or
INTELLIGENCE SUMMARY.
(Erase heading not required.)

Place	Date	Hour	Summary of Events and Information	Remarks and references to Appendices
HAMEL	25/11/17		C.E., R.C. + Nonconformist Church Parade. Casualties Nil.	ABJ
	26/11/17		2/Lts. H.W.T. LIPSCOMBE, W.O. SKINNER, O.P. CASEY, W.E. WELSBY from Reinforcement Depot. Whole Battn. Physical Training, Bayonet fighting, musketry etc. Box Respirators tested in Gas Chamber. Casualties Nil.	ABJ
	27/11/17		2/Lt. F.H. KELF to R.F.C. 24/11/17. Stokebats. Special training. Offrs. Battn. training. Casualties Nil	ABJ
	28/11/17		Battn. training. Casualties Nil	ABJ
	29/11/17		Battn. training. Battalion ordered to be ready to move at half an hours warning. Casualties Nil	ABJ

WAR DIARY or INTELLIGENCE SUMMARY

Army Form C. 2118.

Place	Date	Hour	Summary of Events and Information	Remarks and references to Appendices
Hemel	30/11/17	8.10am	Battalion ordered to man its defensive line W. of ST. EMELIE	H/S
		11.45am	Battalion ordered from ST EMELIE to a position 4 mile S.W. of EPEHY in support of 166 Bde.	
		1.30pm	Battalion received orders to move from EPEHY to PEIZIÈRE where it took up a position in the line N.N.E. of the village. Casualties 2 killed 6 wounded	

C. A. Toall
Lieut. Colonel,
Comdg. 1/9th (Scot) Bn. K.L.R.

SECRET.   COPY NO. 14

1/8th (IRISH) BATT. "THE KING'S" (L'POOL REGT).

OPERATION ORDER NO.128.

Ref.Map : 62c. N.E. 1/20,000.
    Trench Sheets N.L.77a.   In the Field.
                                              2/11/17.

(1)(a) This Battalion will be relieved on the night Nov. 2/3rd
       by the 1/7th K.L.R.   Relief will commence about
       6.30 p.m.
   (b) On relief this Battalion will move into Divisional Reserve
       at VILLERS FAUCON to billets vacated by 1/5th K.L.R.

(2)(a) Companies will be relieved by 1/7th K.L.R. as follows:-

       B Coy. in Support at BART LANE by B Coy. 1/7th K.L.R.
       A "   "   GRAFTON POST   " D "   do.
       C "   "   FITZGERALD POST " C "   do.
       D "   "   MEO POST   " A "   do.

   (b) Guides will be provided for 1/7th K.L.R. as hereunder
       and will rendezvous at LANCASTER HOUSE F.16.a.0.6. at
       times stated:-
             Snipers' Posts........ 1.45 p.m.
             L.G. & Signallers Posts ... 2 p.m.
             Platoon Guides (4 per Coy) 5.30 p.m.

       All movement to and from the Front Line by daylight on
       day of relief must be reduced to a minimum, not more than
       two men must move together and they must be at a distance
       of 250 yds.
       Lewis Guns must be slung and not carried under the arm.
       Particulars of all work on defences, in progress and
       proposed, must be carefully handed over to the incoming
       unit in detail.   A copy of this will be forwarded to
       Batt. H.Qrs. by 12 noon 2/11/17.
       All Defence Schemes, Maps, and Secret Documents will be
       handed over.
       O.C. Coys. will detail 1 Off. and 1 N.C.O. to report to the
       Town Major, VILLERS FAUCON, at 3 p.m. 2/11/17 for the
       purpose of taking over billets.
       The Q.M. will take over for H.qrs.
       List of Stores handed over to 1/7th K.L.R. will be
       forwarded to Batt.H.Q. as soon as ~~received~~ signed.
       Completion of relief will be reported by code word "PIP".

(3)   Batt.H.Qrs. will close at EMPIRE F.16.a.3.6. at 6.30 p.m.
      and open at VILLERS FAUCON E.28.b.40.95. at that hour.

      Administrative Instructions have been issued to all
      concerned.

      ACKNOWLEDGE.

                                              W. Hornby.
                                              2/Lt. & A/Adjt.
                                              1/8th(Irish)Batt.K.L.R.
Issued at 9 a.m.
By Runner.
Copies to:-
   1. 164th Inf. Bde.
   2. 1/7th K.L.R.
   3. C.O.   12. M.O.
   4. 2nd-in-Command.   13. T.O.
   5. Adjutant.   14. Q.M.
   6. Intell. Off.   15. R.S.M.
   7. O.C. A Coy.   16. File.
   8. " B "   17. War Diary.
   9. " C "   18.
  10. " D "
  11. " Signals & Details.

SECRET.   COPY NO. 14

1/8th (IRISH) BATT. "THE KINGS'" (L'POOL REGT).

Administrative Instructions with reference to Operation Order No. 128.

In the Field.
2/11/17.

(1) Officers' Trench Kits, Small Dixies, and Company Stores will be dumped at the respective Ration Dumps by 6 p.m. 2/11/17 and will be carried by limber to Company H.Qrs. VILLERS FAUCON.

(2) Blankets will be rolled in bundles of 10, plainly labelled, and dumped at Batt. H.Q. by 6.30 p.m. They will be carried after dusk.

(3) Lewis Guns and ammunition with 2 men per Company for packing will be at Batt. H.Qrs. by 6.30 p.m.

(4) Officers' Valises, Orderly Room Stores, and Canteen Stores will be packed and dumped at H.Q. by 6 p.m. H.Qrs. Mess, 7.30 p.m.
One Officers' Servant per Company will report to Q.M. by 4 p.m. 2/11/17 for the purpose of sorting out his Company Officers' Valises and remove same to their Company Officers' billets.

(5) All Petrol tins will be handed over to incoming unit FULL.

Issued at 8 p.m.
By Runner.
Copies to:-
  1. C.O.
  2. 2nd-in-Command.
  3. Adjutant.
  4. A Coy.
  5. B "
  6. C "
  7. D "
  8. Details & Signals.
  9. Intell. Off.
10. M.O.
11. T.O.
12. Q.M.
13. R.S.M.
14. File.
15. War Diary.
16.
17.

W. Hornby
2/Lt. & A/Adjt.
1/8th (Irish) Batt. K.L.R.

SECRET.   COPY NO. 17.

1/8th (IRISH) BATTALION "THE KING'S" (L'POOL REGT).

OPERATION ORDER NO. 130.

Ref: Map. 62c, N.E. 1/20,000.
     Trench Sheets W.L.77a.

                                                In the Field.
                                                15/11/17.

(1)   This Battalion will move into the Front line, Centre
      Battalion Sub-sector, on the night Nov. 16/17th,
      relieving the 1/7th Batt. K.L.R.
      Relief will commence about 5.30 p.m.

(2)   Companies will parade at 4 p.m. 16th November and will
      move off by platoons in the order -
                  Headquarters,
                  B Company.
                  D   "
                  C   "   and
                  A   ".
      Leading Platoon will pass Road Junction E.24.a.95.35.
      at 4.30 p.m.   Distance between Platoons 100 yards.

(3)   Companies will take over as follows:-

      Headquarters : Lancaster House (F.16.a.7.6.).
      A Company to relieve 1/7th L'Pools A Coy. at SART LANE.
      B   "   "   "   "   "   D "   " GRAFTON POST
      D   "   "   "   "   "   B "   " WHITEHALL "
      C   "   "   "   "   "   C "   " EGO POST
      Platoon Guides will be furnished by 1/7th L'Pools and will
      rendezvous at Battalion H.Qrs. F.16.a.7.6. at 5 p.m.

(4)   Advance parties composed of the Intelligence Officer
      and 1 N.C.O. for Headquarters, and one Officer and one
      N.C.O. per Company will proceed at 12.30 p.m. 16th inst.,
      for the purpose of taking over.
         The two senior members of each Lewis Gun Team will
      proceed with these parties for the purpose of taking over
      Lewis Gun positions by day.   All particulars with
      reference to gaps in enemy wire and details for night
      firing will be carefully taken over.   Signal Stations
      and Sniping Posts will also be taken over by daylight.

(5)(a) Details of all work in progress and proposed must be
       taken over in detail, and arrangements made for work to
       be continued without interruption.
    (b) All Defence schemes, maps and secret documents will be
        taken over.

(6)   A report is required as soon as possible after relief that touch has been definitely established with Companies on the flanks.

The Battn. on the Right will be 1/5th K.L.R.
  "   "   "   " Left   "   " 1/8th   "

(7)   Completion of reliefs will be reported by runners only, by the Code word **SLOG**.

(8)   Battalion H.Qrs. will close at VILLERS FAUCON at 4.30 p.m. and will open at EMPIRE at that time.

(9)   Administrative Instructions have been issued to all concerned.

A C K N O W L E D G E.

                                    J.F. Jones
                                    Capt. & Adjt.
                                    1/8th (Irish) Batt. K.L.R.

Issued at 8.15 p.m.
By Runner.
Copies to:-
  1. 16th Inf. Bde.
  2. 1/7th K.L.R.
  3. C.O.
  4. 2nd-in-Command.
  5. Adjutant.
  6. Intell. Off.
  7. O.C. A Coy.
  8. " B "
  9. " C "
 10. " D "
 11. " H.Qrs. Coy.
 12. M.O.
 13. T.O.
 14. Q.M.
 15. R.S.M.
 16. File.
 17. War Diary.
 18.
 19.
 20.

SECRET.   COPY NO. 15

1/8th (IRISH) BATTALION "THE KING'S" (L'POOL REGT).

Administrative Instructions
with reference to Operation
Order No. 180.

In the Field.
15/11/17.

Officers' Valises. Will be returned to Q.M.Stores by 3 p.m.

Blankets. Will be carefully rolled in bundles of 10, labelled, and returned to Q.M.Stores by 3 p.m.

Coy. Boxes and kit not required for trenches.
Will be returned to Q.M.Stores by 3 p.m.

Officers' Trench Kits and Company Boxes.
Will be called for by Company Batmen Billets at 3.30 p.m.

Canteen Stores, Orderly Room, and H.Qrs.Mess
Will be called for at 4 p.m.

Lewis Guns.
Will be taken up by Limbers with their respective companies.

Billets.
Will be left in a clean and satisfactory condition and will be ready for inspection at 3.30 p.m.

Water.
The Medical Officer will arrange with the Transport Officer for a sufficient quantity of water to be taken to LEMPIRE.

water to be taken to

Issued at 8 p.m.
By Runner
Copies to:-
1. C.O.
2. 2nd-in-Command.   8. O.C.H.Qrs.Coy.
3. Adjutant.   9. Intell.Off.
4. O.C. A Coy.   10. M.O.
5. "   B "   11. T.O.   14. File.
6. "   C "   12. Q.M.   15. War Diary.
7. "   D "   13. R.S.M.   16.

Capt. & Adjt.

SECRET. COPY NO. 12
1/8th (IRISH) BATT. "THE KING'S" (L'POOL REGT).

Administrative Instructions
No. 1

In the Field.
17/11/17.

DRESS & EQUIPMENT.

The rules contained in S.S.135 Sections XXXI – Dress and Equipment will be adhered to with the following exceptions:-

(a) Entrenching tool and carrier will not be carried by men who carry picks or shovels.
(b) Tube helmets will not be carried.
(c) Articles carried in the haversack : The Iron Ration will not be carried. Greatcoats will not be carried.
(d) One No.23. Rifle Grenade complete with rod and cartridge will be carried in each top pocket of the jacket. These will be collected and dumped under Company arrangements when objective has been gained.
(e) Aeroplane flares: Two will be carried by 50% of N.C.Os. and men.
(f) Sandbags: 3, Under the braces of equipment.
(g) Rations and Water: On Z day every man will go forward with 24 hour's rations and filled water bottle. Solidified alcohol in proportion to be notified later.

In addition to the foregoing:-

(h) Each Bomber will carry 15 No.23 Grenades in Bomb Buckets, excepting throwers who will carry 10. Bombers will carry Cup attachments.
(i) Extra wire cutters will be issued to Companies as follows:-

A Coy....... 1.
B " .... 8.
C " .... 8.
D " .... 8.

(j) 12 S.O.S. Signals will be carried by each of the assaulting Companies. 20 will be carried at Battalion H.Q.
(k) All Rifle Grenadiers will carry 6 No.24 Grenades in Grenade Carriers. These will not be detonated until arrival in assembly positions. O.C. Coys. will ensure that this is done immediately upon arrival there.
(l) Every man will carry a pick or a shovel – proportion of 1 pick to 1 shovel will be observed.

Maps. Maps will be carried as follows:-
(a) Operations Map, 1/10,000. – 1 per Officer and Senior N.C.O.
(b) Message form maps – 2 per Officer and platoon Sergeant.
(c) Barrage Maps (to be issued later) – 1 per Officer and N.C.O. as available.

Fitting Out.

O.C. Coys. will arrange to draw picks, shovels, and sandbags from LONDON ROAD DUMP Y/Z night.
Grenades, Aeroplane Flares, S.O.S. Rockets, and VERY PISTOLS will be delivered to Coy. H.Qrs. on night 14/15th. Nov. 1917.
18/19th

-2-

100 Petrol tins will be drawn from LONDON ROAD DUMP
and placed in position in Assembly Positions -
D Coy. 30., C Coy. 20., B Coy., 20., EGG POST 30., on
night 18/19th Nov, 1917, by A Coy.
O.C. D Coy. will ensure that this water is not used until
authority is given from Battalion H.Qrs.

Surplus Kit and equipment.

All packs containing great coats and other kit will
not being taken forward will be dumped at SART LANE DUMP
before 9 p.m. Y/Z night. This will be removed by
Transport to Q.M.Stores.

A C K N O W L E D G E.

Capt. & Adjt.

Issued at 3.30 p.m.
By Runner.
Copies to:-
  1. C.O.
  2. 2nd-in-Command.
  3. Adjutant.
  4. Intell. Off.
  5. O.C. A Coy.
  6. "   B "
  7. "   C "
  8. "   D "
  9. "   H.Q. Coy.
10. Q.M.
11. T.O.
12. War Diary.
13. File.
14.
15.
16.

SECRET.   COPY NO. 14.

1/8th (IRISH) BATT. "THE KING'S" (L'POOL REGT).

Movement Table to accompany
1/8th (Irish) Batt. "The King's"
(Liverpool Regt) Operation Order
No. 131.

In the Field.
18/11/17.

(1) On Y/Z night the following movements will be made to assembly positions.

   (a) D Coy. will take up position in DANIEL TRENCH/ISLAND TRAVERSE, F.12.c.60.76. to F.12.c.60.90. inclusive.

   (b) C Coy. will move to the right along FAG TRENCH until touch is established with D Coy, occupying a frontage, F.12.c.60.90., exclus. to F.12.a.40.00. (inclus).

   1/4th N.Lan.R. will send 4 Lewis Gun detachments at 5.30 p.m. "Y" night to take over FLEECEALL POST.

   (c) B Coy. will move from GRAFTON POST on relief by company of 1/5th L'Pool R. via GRAFTON TRENCH, POMPONIUS LANE, SART LANE, and will occupy a frontage in FAG TRENCH from F.12.a.40.00. exclus. to F.12.a.27.10. inclus.

   (d) Batt. H. Qrs. will close at LANCASTER HOUSE at 9 p.m. and will reopen in mined dugout at EGO POST at that hour.

(2) Routes and assembly positions will be reconnoitred in advance by all officers, and N.C.Os. All movement will be conducted with the utmost silence and on no account are lights of any description to be used.

(3) Company Commanders will report that they have taken up assembly positions and in the case of flank Companies that they are in touch with units on the right and left flanks of the Battalion, using the Code word "SIP". This must be sent by runner only. Companies will report not later than 12 midnight that they are in position.

A C K N O W L E D G E.

Issued at 5 p.m.
By Runner.
Copies to:-
1. C.O.
2. 2nd-in-Command.
3. Adjutant.
4. Intell. Off.
5. O.C. A Coy.
6. " " B "
7. " " C "
8. " " D "
9. " " H.Qrs. Coy.
10. O.C. Batt. on Right.
11. O.C. "   " Left.
12. Medical Officer.
13. File.
14. War Diary.
15.
16.

Capt. & Adjt.
1/8th (Irish) Batt. K.L.R.

SECRET.　　　　　　　　　　　　　　　　COPY NO. 21.

1/8th (IRISH) BATT. "THE KING'S" (L'POOL REGT).
OPERATION ORDER NO. 131.

Ref: Corps Map Topa. Section "T" (S) 1/10,000.

In the Field.
18/11/17.

1. **INFORMATION.** (1)　The enemy appears to hold his line in much the same way as we hold ours.
　　KNOLL TRENCH seems to be held in some strength, WILLOW TRENCH is probably a travel trench, with a strong point in the valley about A.7.b.60.25.
　　In KNOLL C.T. and LONE TREE TRENCH are several dugouts and T.M. positions.
　　Map references of all known emplacements (T.M. & M.G.) Dugouts, Blocks etc. have been issued separately.

2. **INTENTION.** (2)　The Brigade will attack as under:-
Right Battn. 1/4th R. Lan. R. - GILLEMONT FARM.
Centre　"　1/8th L'Pools. - KNOLL TRENCH, C.T. & SUPPORT - WILLOW & LONE TREE TRENCHES.
Left　"　2/5th Lan. Fus. - THE KNOLL.
Support "..... 1/4th N. Lan. R.

The attack will be made behind a barrage of Artillery, Machine Guns, Trench Mortars, and Gas.

3. **OBJECTIVE.** (3)　The task allotted to this Battalion is the capture and consolidation of the Trench System - KNOLL, KNOLL C.T. & SUPPORT, WILLOW and LONE TREE TRENCHES - from A.7.d.65.30. to A.7.b.15.80. in FRONT LINE, and A.7.d.99.40. to A.7.b.25.90. in SUPPORT LINE.
　　The line WILLOW-KNOLL TRENCH will be organised as the main line of defence.
　　LONE TREE - KNOLL SUPPORT and KNOLL C.T. will be held as a forward line of observation with Strong Points to break up hostile counter attack.

4. **GENERAL METHOD OF ATTACK.** (4)　The attack on KNOLL TRENCH (North of A.7.b.65.35.) KNOLL C.T. and KNOLL SUPPORT will be by direct assault, aided, if and as necessary, by storming parties moving along the trenches. The attack on KNOLL TRENCH (South of A.7.b.65.35.) LONE TREE, and WILLOW TRENCHES will be made by storming parties moving along the trenches.

-2-

5. PLAN OF ATTACK & FORMATIONS. (5) The Battalion will assault on a 3 Company frontage in the order, D, C, B, from Right to Left.

D Coy. in three waves; C & B Coys. each in two waves.

The leading wave of each Company will be in 2 lines (with moppers up as required) - the rear waves in lines of section columns in single file.

Distance between lines... 15 yards.
" " waves... 50 "

6. FRONTAGES (6) The Companies will attack on the following frontages:-

"D" (Right) Coy: - from A.7.b.65.35.(junction of trenches) to point 50 yards to North, (A.7.b.60.42)(both inclus).. frontage 50 yards.

"C" (Centre) Coy: - from thence to A.7.b.25.75. (both exclus).... frontage 200 yards.

"B" (Left) Coy:- - from thence to COCHRAN AVENUE (both inclus).

7. OBJECTIVES OF WAVES. (7) Objectives are as under:-
"D"(Right)Coy, plus 2 platoons of "A" Coy.
1st Wave. KNOLL TRENCH (as in para. 6) whence No.1.Party storms along KNOLL TRENCH to the right to A.7.b.75.20. while No.2.Party assaults the "JONES" and clears it to its junction with KNOLL SUPPORT (A.7.b.70.50.)

2nd Wave. WILLOW & LONE TREE TRENCHES to PRGGINS LANE (incl). Enter KNOLL TRENCH (as in para. 6.) move to A.7.b.75.20. Here No.3.Party moves down LOW LANE to WILLOW TRENCH, storms WILLOW to its junction with PRGGINS LANE at A.7.d.55.73. No.4.Party clears LONE TRENCH to A.7.d.88.90. and PRGGINS LANE.

3rd Wave. WILLOW & LONE TREE TRENCHES from PRGGINS to Right Boundary of Battalion. Enter KNOLL TRENCH (as in para. 6), move along LONE TREE TRENCH, to A.7.d.88.90.
No.5.Party moves thence down PRGGINS LANE and clears WILLOW TRENCH to GRUB LANE. No.6.Party clears LONE TREE TRENCH to GRUB LANE. At GRUB LANE contact will be made with the Right Battalion.

"C"(Centre) Coy.:
1st Wave. KNOLL TRENCH (as in para. 6)
2nd Wave: KNOLL C.T., SWITCH, and SUPPORT from A.7.b.75.55. to A.7.b.62.80. - by direct assault & KNOLL SUPPORT from A.7.b.75.55. to A.7.b.72.30. by storming party working along trench from A.7.b.75.55.

-5-

8. OBJECTIVES OF WAVES.

(8) "D" (Left) Coy:

1st Wave. KNOLL TRENCH (as in para. 5.) and DOLAN POST from the South, in conjunction with the LEFT BATTALION.

2nd Wave: KNOLL C.T. and "DUG-OUTS" from WEST (by storming party) and from S.W. by direct assault, in conjunction with LEFT Battalion from NORTH.

9. "MOPPERS UP".

(9) "B" and "C" Coys. will detail their own "Moppers Up" as required.

O. C. "A" Coy. will detail two Platoons as "Moppers Up" to "D" Coy.

Company Commanders will detail "Moppers Up" for each known post, dug out, strong point or emplacement in their respective areas. (See "Information re Enemy Defences", and special maps that have been issued).

10. CONSOLIDATION

(10). On the objective being gained the work of consolidation will at once be taken in hand and companies will be reformed.
Strong Centres of resistance will be established about:-

(a) A.7.d.95.65............ "D" Coy.
(b) A.7.b.75.40............ "D" "
(c) A.7.b.40.82............ "C" "

The above will consist of Rifle and Lewis Gun Posts with machine guns in addition (if available).

Lewis Gun Posts will be established about:-

(a) A.8.c.00.55............ "D" Coy.
(b) A.7.b.95.15............ "D" "
(c) A.7.b.70.65............ "C" "
(d) A.7.b.55.92............ "C" "
(e) A.7.b.35.90............ "B" "
(f) A.7.d.75.85............ "B" "
(g) A.7.b.55.20............ "A" "
(h) A.7.b.60.45............ "A" "
(i) A.7.b.35.75............ "A" "

The Lewis Gun Sections from "A" Coy. will go forward with the rear waves (f) and (g) of D Coy. and (h) of C Coy.

11. CARRYING PARTIES.

(11) "A" Coy. (less 2 Platoons and Lewis Gun Sections) will be attached to Batt. H.Qrs. for carrying purposes. Immediately the enemy front line is taken they will commence carrying ammunition and material from SART LANE DUMP to the two dumps to be established in enemy line.

12. COUNTER ATTACK RESERVE.	(12)	One Company 1/5th L'Pool R. at FLEECEALL POST will be attached to the Battalion as Counter attack Reserve. An Officer of the Company will report to Battalion H.Q. at 12 midnight Y/Z night.
13. MACHINE GUNS.	(13)	164th M.G. Coy. will attach one Machine Gun and team to the Battalion. The Officer in charge of this will report to Batt. H.Q. (EGO POST) before 12 midnight Y/Z night.
14. TRENCH MORTARS.	(14)	164 T.M.B. will detail 1 gun and team for work with the Battalion. The Officer in charge will report to Batt. H.Q. (EGO POST) before 12 midnight Y/Z night.
15. ROYAL ENGINEERS.	(15)	A detachment of R.E. (12) will be attached to this Batt. This detachment will be primarily for the demolition of hostile trench mortars and subsequently to assist in consolidation. They will report to Bn. H.Q. not later than 12 midnight Y/Z night.
16. RESERVE OF LEWIS GUN.	(16)	One Lewis Gun per Company will be dumped at Batt. H.Q. (EGO POST) by 10 p.m. Y/Z night. These will be used as a reserve to replace any damaged gun.
17. CAPTURED MACHINE GUNS.	(17)	Captured Machine Guns will at once be brought into action. If they cannot be used they will at once be got back as soon as possible. If this cannot be done they must be broken up. To remove the lock only is insufficient.
18. LIAISON.	(18)	Company Commanders of assaulting Companies and Commanders of Flank Platoons must ensure that close touch is kept with Companies and Platoons on their flanks. Liaison will specially be made in our trenches two hours before ZERO; on gaining first objectives (with exception of Right flank of Right Company) and on reaching final objectives.
19. PATROLS - RECONNOITRING AND STRONG.	(19)	It is of paramount importance that information be speedily furnished with reference to the whereabouts of the enemy, after the capture of the position. Company Commanders will arrange for the closest watch to be kept for any signs of the enemy's presence and will push out reconnoitring patrols to gain and maintain touch with him. Immediate reports as to enemy's presence will be rendered to Batt. H.Q. by whom the necessary strong patrols will be ordered.

(20) COMMUNICATIONS (20). From Coy. to Bn. H.Q. Prior to ZERO.
Messages will be sent by runner. Only in cases of emergency may wires be used and then only Fullerphones.
After ZERO. During the attack. Communication with Batt. H.Q. will be maintained by runner and visual.
Fullerphones will be taken forward by assaulting Coys. for installation in Coy. H.Qrs. in captured positions. Lines will be laid during the advance. Two pigeons will be issued to each assaulting company and will be taken forward in the advance.
Communication will be maintained by,
(1) Fullerphone. Telephone will only be used in case of necessity and then only by Officers.
(2) Visual. (Lamp and shutter) Only BB messages will be sent back. No messages will be sent forward.
(3) Runner. Messages will be carried in right hand breast pocket, in which nothing else will be carried. All runners must realise the vital importance of getting their messages through quickly and at all times.
All important messages will be sent in duplicate by two different routes or means of transmission. Those of special importance will be sent in triplicate by three different routes or means of transmission.
From Batt. to Bde. H.Q. - Prior to ZERO.
(a) By Runner - excepting in case of emergency when the fullerphone may be used.
(b) A Bde. Visual Station at F.10.c.65.55. will receive messages.
After ZERO. (a) Fullerphone. Telephone only to be used in case of necessity and then by Officers only.
(b) Visual. (lamp).
(c) Power Buzzer and amplifier, will be installed at BGO POST. All messages by Power Buzzer (except S.O.S.) will be in cipher.
(d) Runner Post: will be established at F.17.a. 45.95. (SART LANE).

The B.A.B. Code Book will not be used in advance of our present front line. All B.A.B. Code Books will be returned to Batt. H.Q. on Y/Z night. The Playfair cipher will be used. All messages in PLAYFAIR will begin and end with the letter "K".
Flares and S.O.S. signals to be used will be as follows:-
Flares............WHITE.
S.O.S. SIGNALS......Rifle Grenade bursting into 3 green and 2 white.

Co-operation with aircraft - special instructions have been issued to all Companies.

21. DUMPS. (21) In our lines.

Main Brigade Dump at LEMPIRE..... F.15.b.1.5.
Adv. Bde. Dump...... LONDON ROAD, F.11.b.2.2.
Battn. Dump.................... F.16.a.8.6.
Adv. Batt. Dump..... SART LANE, F.11.c.7.3.

R.E. Dump.......... LONDON ROAD.

In Enemy Lines.

As soon as the enemy front line has been captured, dumps will be established at the following points:-

For B & C Coys... A.7.b.40.60. (approx).
For D Coy........ A.7.b.55.10. (approx)

These dumps will be filled up from Batt. and R.E. dumps and will contain 72 reserve Lewis Gun Magazines per Company.

22. MEDICAL (22) Regimental Aid Post will be at TOMBOIS FARM,
ARRANGEMENTS.   F.11.b.3.1.

23. PRISONERS & (23) See special orders which have been issued.
SEARCHING OF   Strength of fighting troops will not be depleted
PRISONERS.   unnecessarily for the purpose of bringing back
                   prisoners. Prisoners will be sent back with
                   escorts not exceeding 10% of their number,
                   excepting when party is below 20 when 2 men will
                   escort. Slightly wounded men should be used
                   for this purpose.

24. BRIGADE (24) Will open at F.10.c.4.6. at 5 p.m. on Y day.
BATTLE H.QRS.

25. BATT. BATTLE (25) Will open at EGG POST at 9 p.m. on Y day.
HEADQUARTERS.

26. SYNCHRONISATION (26) Details to be issued later.
OF WATCHES.

27. DIRECTION OF (27) The approximate bearing of the direction of the
ATTACK.   attack on KNOLL TRENCH is 55° GRID.

28. ZEROHOUR. (28) The hour of ZERO will be notified later.
             The B attalion will move off from the trenches
             at ZERO plus 24 minutes and will close up to the
             Artillery barrage which they will closely follow
             immediately it lifts.

28a Report (28a) to Battn. Battle H.Q.

-7-

Attention is directed to the following which have been issued:-

55th Divnl. No.74 I.O. Notes on enemy defences.
164 Inf. Bde. No.G.1086/C. Plan.
164 Inf. Bde. No.G.1086/55. Co-operation with aircraft (contact and counter attack aeroplanes).
164 Inf. Bde. No.AQ/5766/2 Collection and escort of prisoners.
164 Inf. Bde. No.AQ/5766/3 Medical arrangements.
1/8th(Irish) Adventure Instructions N.I.
1/8th(Irish) (to be issued later).
1/8th(Irish) N.I.
1/8th(Irish) Assembly Movement Table.

ACKNOWLEDGE.

J.F. Jones
Capt. & Adjt.
1/8th(Irish)Batt.K.L.R.

Issued at 10 p.m.
By Runner.
Copies to:-
1. 164 Inf. Bde.
2. 2/5th. Lan. Fus.
3. 1/4th R. Lan. R.
4. 1/4th N. Lan. R.
5. 1/5th K.L.R.
6. O.C.
7. 2nd-in-Command.
8. Adjutant.
9. Intell. Off.
10. O.C. H.Q. Coy.
11. " A Coy.
12. " B "
13. " C "
14. " D "
15. M.O.
16. T.O.
17. Q.M.
18. 164 M.G. Coy.
19. 164 T.M.B.
20. R.E.
21. War Diary.
22. File.
23. 276 Bde. R.F.A.
24. D.T.M.O.
25.
26.
27.
28.

SECRET.   COPY NO. 7

1/8th (IRISH) BATTALION "THE KING'S" (L'POOL REGT).

General Instructions No. 1,
with reference to Operation
Order No. 131.

In the Field.
18/11/17.

(1) Assembly.

All precautions will be taken to ensure that assembly is carried out as silently as possible. With the exception of sentries and a number of men proportionate to the normal garrison of the trench, bayonets will not be fixed until immediately before the assaulting troops leave the trenches.
Standing patrols will be maintained on each Company front to cover assembly.
Each Company will cut at least 8 gaps on its front as soon as possible after dusk.

(2) SMOKE & THERMIT. With the object of preventing enemy observation whilst our infantry are advancing on THE KNOLL, a detachment of No. 1 Special Coy. R.E. will, from positions in EAGLE TRENCH, fire SMOKE & THERMIT Shells on the area TINO - SPREE LANE - N. of TOMBOIS TRENCH from ZERO plus 20 min. to ZERO plus 35 min. If the wind is unfavourable, only THERMIT will be fired. Two mortars will be installed in DANIEL TRENCH, and will fire THERMIT on the area PROGGINS LANE - LOW LANE and front and support trenches between these two C.Ts. at intervals from ZERO plus 20 min. to ZERO plus 45 min. in accordance with detailed instructions communicated to O.C. Detachment, No. 1 Special Coy. R.E.

(3) MAPS. In addition to the maps to be carried laid down in Administrative Orders 1 of 18/11/17, Aeroplane photographs will be carried as available.

(4) COMPANY FLANKS IN ASSEMBLY TRENCHES. The Intelligence Officer will mark these with small boards on the afternoon of 19/11/17 in conjunction with Coy. Cdrs.

(5) Lewis Gun Magazines. Twenty magazines per gun will be taken forward. The remainder will be dumped at Bn. Dump at SART LANE on Y/Z night. The magazines of reserve guns sent to Bn. H.Q. will accompany the guns.

Issued at 11.30 p.m.
By Runner.
Copies to:-
 1. C.O.
 2. Adjutant.
 3. O.C. A Coy.
 4. " B "
 5. " C "
 6. " D "
 7. Intelligence Officer.
 8. War Diary.
 9. File.
10.

Capt. & Adjt.
1/8th (Irish) Batt. K.L.R.

SECRET.   COPY NO. 6.

1/8th (IRISH) BATTALION "THE KING'S" (L'POOL REGT).

OPERATION ORDER NO. 132.

Ref: Map. 62c. N.E. 1/20,000.
     Trench Sheets W.L.77a.
                                                             In the Field,
                                                             22/11/17.

(1) (a) This Battalion will be relieved on the night 22/23rd
        Nov. by the 1/5th L'Pool R. Relief will commence
        about 5.30 p.m.

    (b) On relief this Battalion will move into Divisional
        Reserve at TINCOURT.

    (c) Movement will be by march route to ST. EMILIE and from
        thence by light railway to TINCOURT. Time of train
        will be notified later.

(2) (a) Four guides each will be provided from garrisons of
        EGG and FLEECEALL POSTS for 1/5th L'Pool R. and will
        rendezvous at LANCASTER HOUSE, F.16.a.8.6. at 5 p.m.

    (b) All movement to and from the front line to LEMPIRE
        by daylight on day of relief must be reduced to a
        minimum, not more than two men must move together and
        they must be at a distance of 25 0 yards. Lewis Guns
        must be slung by daylight and not carried under the arm.

(3) Particulars of all work on defences, in progress and
    proposed, must be carefully handed over to the incoming
    unit in detail. A copy of this will be forwarded to
    Batt. H.Q. by 3 p.m. 22/11/17.

    All available information with respect to the tactical
    situation together with Defence Schemes, Maps, and secret
    documents relating to the sub-sector will be handed over.

(4) The 2nd-in-Command and one Officer per Company have
    proceeded to TINCOURT to take over billets.

(5) Lists of stores handed over to 1/5th L'Pool R. will be
    forwarded to Batt. H.Q. as soon as signed.

(6) Completion of relief will be reported by Code word FAST.

(7) Batt. H.Q. will close at LEMPIRE at 8 p.m. and will open
    at TINCOURT AT THAT HOUR. Administrative Instructions
    have been issued to all concerned.

A C K N O W L E D G E.

                                                    Capt. & Adjt.
                                                1/8th (Irish) Batt. K.L.R.

Issued at 12 noon.
By Runner.
Copies to:-
  1. 164th Inf. Bde.
  2. 1/5th L'Pool R.
  3. C.O.
  4. Adjutant.   12. T.O.
  5. Intell. Off.   13. Q.M.
  6. O.C. H.Q. Coy.   14. R.S.M.
  7. "   A   "   15. File.
  8. "   B   "   16. War Diary.
  9. "   C   "
 10. "   D   "
 11. M.O.

SECRET.   COPY NO...

1/8th (IRISH) BATT. "THE KING'S" (L'POOL REGIMENT).

Administrative Instructions
With reference to Operation
order No. 132.

In the Field.
22/11/17.

(1) Officers' Trench Kit, small dixies, and Coy. stores will be dumped, EGO POST garrison at SART LANE, and FLEECEALL POST Garrison at TOMBOIS ROAD, as soon as it is dusk.
Representatives from each Company will be left in charge until arrival of limbers, which will carry same to TINCOURT.

(2) One Lewis Gun Limber will report to SART LANE Dump and one to TOMBOIS ROAD for the purpose of carrying Lewis Guns, Magazines, and spare parts. All Lewis Guns, magazines and spare parts, damaged and undamaged will be carefully brought away.

(3) Blankets will be rolled in bundles of 10 which should be plainly labelled.

(4) Officers' Valises, Orderly Room Stores, Canteen Stores, and H.Q. Mess will be removed at 7 p.m.

(5) A receipt must be obtained for all Patrol tins handed over in the line.

Issued at 3 p.m.
By Runner.
Copies to:-
1. File.
2. War Diary.
3. C.O.
4. O.C. H.Q. Coy.
5. " EGO POST.
6. " FLEECEALL POST.
7. T.O.
8. Q.M.
9.
10.

J.F. Jones
Capt. & Adjt.
1/8th (Irish) Batt. K.L.R.

"A" Form
MESSAGES AND SIGNALS.
Army Form C. 2121 (in pads of 100).

TO: Offs. Cdg.
HO & FLEECEALL POSTS.

Sender's Number: L.10.
Day of Month: 22.
AAA

SECRET.

Our Posts will be taken over by the following Coys. of the 1/5th L'Pool R.:-

HO POST........ D Coy.
FLEECEALL POST...C "

Capt. & Adjt.
1/8th (Irish) Batt. K.L.R.

"A" Form
MESSAGES AND SIGNALS.

Army Form C. 2121
(in pads of 100).

TO	Offs. Cdg, M.O AND FLEECEALL POSTS.	

Sender's Number.	Day of Month.	In reply to Number.	
L.11.	22.		AAA

SECRET.

Please instruct your guidee to report to Battalion H.Q. at 4.30 p.m. today instead of at 5.0 p.m. as ordered in Operation Order No. 132.

Capt. & Adjt.
1/8th(Irish)Bn. K.L.R.

HEADQUARTERS,
164th INFANTRY BDE.

B.Q./4/54.

1/8th (IRISH) BATTALION "THE KING'S" (L'POOL REGIMENT).

Narrative of Operations East of
LEMPIRE -o- 20/11/17.
-------------o-----------

(1) Assembly (1).   On the night 19/20/11/17, the Battalion assembled as per Order No. 131, on the line ISLAND TRAVERSE - COCHRAN AVENUE (both inclusive), having on Right - about GILLEMONT FARM, the 1/4th R.Lan.R., and on the immediate left, from COCHRAN AVENUE to FLEECEALL POST, the 2/5th Lan.Fus.
 The assembly was effected without incident by 2.30 a.m., the enemy appearing not to have any knowledge or suspicion of the concentration of of the projected operations.
 The Battalion was reported as "In Position" at 2.37 a.m.
 Meanwhile gaps had been cut in our wire and ladders were placed in position ready for the forward movement.

(2) Period from (2)   The night paassed off very quietly and without
 Assembly to   incident, until 5 a.m. when the enemy fired a
 ZERO hour.   salvo of 5.9s, 4.2s, and 77 m.ms. on FAG TRENCH. At 6.5 a.m. the enemy fired six salvoes in rapid succession of 5.9s, 4.2s, and 77 m.ms. on FAG TRENCH, ISLAND TRAVERSE, and DANIEL TRENCH. A number of these shells dropped into the trench and caused a few casualties.

(3) ZERO till (3)   At ZERO our barrage opened on the enemy lines,
 ZERO plus 24 min. and almost simultaneously the enemy put down a heavy barrage of 5.9s, 4.2s, and 77 m.ms. on DANIEL TRENCH, FAG TRENCH, CAUSEWAY LANE, and EGO POST. Several casualties were caused before our men went over.

(4) The Advance (4).   At ZERO plus 24 mins. the advance began. The Artillery barrage on our trenches and a machine gun barrage on, and in front of our wire caused some losses, but the advance was continued, the formation being well kept. About half way across an enfilade Machine Gun Barrage from the Right, (WILLOW TRENCH) caused further losses, and by this time nearly every leading man of section columns had been picked off by snipers.
 On leading waves reaching the wire, close behind our barrage, it was found to be almost wholly uncut. Every endeavour was made by Company and Platoon Commanders, to overcome the obstacle - wire cutters, breakers, Lewis Guns all being used, while Rifle Grenadiers endeavoured to keep the enemy's heads down.
 The enemy meanwhile brought heavy machine gun and rifle fire on our troops and threw intense
                                                    (showers

-2-

(4) The Advance. (4) showers of bombs and grenades on those
    (continued)   attempting to effect a passage - in face of
                      which they had to desist. The behaviour of
                      all ranks under these exceptionally trying
                      circumstances was magnificient.

(5) The Withdrawal (5) On the order for the withdrawal - the troops
                       fell back slowly and in order to our own
                       line under cover of Lewis Gun fire.

(6) Reorganization (6) The task of reorganization was at once taken
    and subsequent   in hand, and it was intended to endeavour to
    projected   enter the hostile position in rear of the
    movements.   1/4th R.Lan.R. - about GILLEMONT FARM and to
                       work through LONE TRENCH and WILLOWTRENCH
                       from the South.
    (8.30 am)   Orders however were received from Bde
                       H.Q to enter enemy's trenches and work down
                       towards the 1/4th R.Lan.R. and further,
                       authorising the use of one Company of 1/5th
                       K.L.R. which had come up to FLEECEALL POST
                       in support. The plan was therefore altered
                       to one of endeavouring to enter the KNOLL
                       about SMISSON POST in rear of 2/5th Lan Fus.
                       and this was being prepared
    (11.15 am)   when a further order cancelled the movement -
                       it having been reported that the force
                       available was insufficient, and the 2/5th
                       Lan Fus by now also having been forced to
                       evacuate the trenches they had entered.

(7) Move and relief. (7) At 5.15 p.m. Operation Order No 149 was
                         received from Brigade, and the Battalion took
                         over the Front from ISLAND TRAVERSE - FLEECEALL
                         POST (both inclusive). Battalion Hdqrs moved
                         to LANCASTER HOUSE. This move was completed
                         by 9 p.m.
                         On the 22/23rd Nov, 1917 the Battalion was
                         relieved by the 1/5th K.L.R. Relief was
                         completed by 8.15 p.m.

In conclusion, I desire to place on record the excellent
work of Captains A.A.CARBERRY and W.T.BALL - commanding
the Left and Right Companies respectively - and Sergeant
S.FRASER who took command of the Centre Company after all
his Officers hadfallen, who, in spite of great difficulties
and in face of exceptional danger, made repeated endeavours
to overcome the obstacle caused by the enemy's wire, and
who handled their men with marked ability under the
circumstances of very great difficulty.

Further, I desire to mention the heroic conduct of
C.S.M. H.CORNALL. M.M. who, under heavy fire of rifles,
machine guns and bombs, endeavoured tocut a passage in the
wire, and failing, dragged himself across the remaining
portion of the obstacle and succeeded in reaching the
enemy's parapet, where he fell mortally wounded.

(Signed) E.C. Heath.
                                            Lieut Colonel.
27/11/17.   Commanding 1/8th (Irish) Bn. K.L.R.

Confidential

War Diary

for

December 1917.

1/8th (Irish) Bn. K.L.R.

December 1917.

WAR DIARY 1/8 K.L.R.
INTELLIGENCE SUMMARY
(Erase heading not required.)

Army Form C. 2118.

Instructions regarding War Diaries and Intelligence Summaries are contained in F. S. Regs, Part II. and the Staff Manual respectively. Title pages will be prepared in manuscript.

Place	Date	Hour	Summary of Events and Information	Remarks and references to Appendices
BN. IN TRENCHES N.E. EPEHY.	1/12/17		Bn. in Trenches N.E. of EPEHY. Casualties Nil	W3/
	2/12/17	2 am	Bn was relieved by 1st EAST YORKS + 15th D.L.I. & moved back to billets in VILLERS-FAUCON B.22.7	W3/
		10 am	Bn. relieved the 8th QUEENS R.W. SURREY REGT in defence of LEMPIRE & was attached to 16S Infantry Brigade. Casualties Nil	W3/ R29/ W3/
	3/12/17		Bn. in defences of LEMPIRE. Casualties Nil	
	4/12/17		Bn. in defences of LEMPIRE. Casualties Nil	
	5/12/17		Bn. in defences of LEMPIRE. Casualties Nil	
	6/12/17		Bn. was relieved by the 1st Royal Dublin Fus. on the night 5/6/12/17 + moved to billets at ST. EMELIE. O.O. No. A.	W3/ W3/
	7/12/17	2.30	Bn. left ST. EMELIE + moved to PERONNE. Casualties Nil	
			Capt. J.F. JONES to L.G. School. G.H.Q.	
			Bn. in Canvas Camp at PERONNE. Casualties Nil	
	8/12/17		Bn moved by rail to BEAUMETZ LES LOGES + marched from there to LATTRE ST. QUENTIN. O.O. No. 134. Casualties Nil	W3/
	9/12/17		Bn. at LATTRE ST. QUENTIN. Casualties Nil	W3/
	10/12/17		Bn. left LATTRE ST QUENTIN + started on the march to the new area and billeted at TINQUES. O.O. No. 135. Casualties Nil	W3/
	11/12/17		Bn. left TINQUES, proceeded on the march to the new area and billeted at ———. O.O. No. 136 Casualties Nil	W3/

WAR DIARY or INTELLIGENCE SUMMARY

Army Form C. 2118.

Place	Date	Hour	Summary of Events and Information	Remarks and references to Appendices
	12/12/17		Bn. left VALHUON & proceeded on the march to the new area & billeted at LIVOSSART and PALFART. OO No 137. Casualties Nil	W.3.f
	13/12/17		Bn. left LIVOSSART & PALFART & completed the march to the new area being billeted at DENNEBROEUCQ. OO No 138. Casualties Nil	W.3.f
	14/12/17		Bn. cleaning up & bathing at Bath at MATRINGHEM. Casualties Nil	W.3.f
	15/12/17		"A" Coy Commander has awarded Military Medals to 59152 Pte. E. WAITES & 53444 Pte G. KINE. O.C. Coys for inspection, Re-joining & Refitting. Games at disposal of O.C. Coys for Reinforcement Drill. 2/Lts. J.A. NICHOLSON, F. WHITEHEAD, S.J. WRIGHT, C.W. McLEAN, J.F. LOWE. Casualties Nil	W.3.f
	16/12/17		" F. BELANEY, C.F. COLE, H.F.F. MILLER, J.A. DOW, J.B. FENN. 2/Lt A.W. HICKLING from 3~ Army Musk't Camp. R.C. Non-conformed & Cafe E. Church Parades. Capt J.F. JONES from L.G. School. G.H.Q. Casualties Nil	W.3.f
	17/12/17		Regimental Lewis Gun course restarted under 2/Lt. A.W. HICKLING. Regimental Course for Junior Officers, N.C.Os & Senior Privates (likely to become N.C.Os) commenced. Bn. Training, Physical Training & Bayonet fighting, also new Drill, Musketry & Specialist Training. 2/Lt AR ALLERTON M.C. from 3y Army School. Casualties Nil	W.3.f

WAR DIARY
INTELLIGENCE SUMMARY
(Erase heading not required.)

Army Form C. 2118.

3

Instructions regarding War Diaries and Intelligence Summaries are contained in F.S. Regs., Part II. and the Staff Manual respectively. Title pages will be prepared in manuscript.

Place	Date	Hour	Summary of Events and Information	Remarks and references to Appendices
	18/12/17		Bn. Training. Close Order Drill, P.T. & B.F. making & Specialist Training. Under Authority delegated by Field Marshal Commanding-in-Chief the G.O.C. Command has awarded the following decoration to N.C.Os & men as stated below for gallantry & devotion to duty in action:— Bar to Military Medal. 6/8998 L/Cpl. DRAPER.A. The Military Medal. 308016 Sgt. C. WRIGHT. 308388 L/Cpl. MAYORS.J. 308261 L/Cpl. WOOD.A. 325093 Pte. HATTEN.G. 306174 Pte. LANCASTER J. 305379 Pte. COWIN R.H. 308935 Pte. BIRMINGHAM.D. Casualties Nil.	W.B.J.
	19.12.17		Bn. Training. Close Order Drill, Musketry, Company Drill, Physical Drill & Bayonet Fighting, Specialist Training. Command. Lieut. Col. E.C. HEATH. D.S.O. having resumed command of the 164th. Inf. Bde. the Command at this Unit devolves upon Major L. DUCKWORTH, with effect from 18.12.17. Casualties Nil.	W.B.J.
	20.12.17		Bn. Training. Close Order Drill, Armed Drill, Bayonet fighting, musketry, Specialist Training. Under authority delegated by His Majesty the King, the Field Marshal Commanding-in-Chief has awarded the following decoration to the undermentioned Officer & N.C.O. for gallantry and devotion to duty in action. The Military Cross. CAPT. W.T. BALL. The D.C.M. 305567 Sgt. S. FRASER. Casualties Nil	W.B.J.

WAR DIARY
or
INTELLIGENCE SUMMARY

Army Form C. 2118.

Place	Date	Hour	Summary of Events and Information	Remarks and references to Appendices
	21.12.17		Bn Training. Close Order Drill, Musketry, Platoon movement in Wave + Artillery formation. Specialist Training. C. Coy digging trenches for New Bayonet Course under R.E.	
DENNEBROEUCQ	22/12/17		Casualties NIL. Bn Training. Close order Drill, 30 yds range, 6th day Lewis Gun School (mechanism, drill, stripping), 5th day, Regt Musketry course - (iring?) distances (aiming, hot manipulation, rapid loading, intrication, and recognition (targets). Signallers - Special training. D Coy dragged? 20th 740OR on 500 x rifle range. 2/Lt SPERRY relinquishes appt of A/QMR. 18/12/17. - 30 5998 RQMS BECKETT. to perform duties of A/QMR. 18/12/17 vice 2Lt HE SPERRY to Bn. Casualties NIL. Bn Training. Close orta Drill, PT, PBT. musketry, 30'range 6th day LG School (care, stoppages, range) 6th day Musketry School, Lecture by Adjutant situation recognition, Final training. "Fire orders", Junior NCOs mess senior privates under capt. Communication Drill, Guard Drill. Signallers Special Training. Lt-Col E.C. HEATH. DSO. returned from HdQrs 164 INF Bde + resume cmd of Bn. MAJ L DUCKWORTH assumes duties of and in-command. 2Lt W.R. COTTIER returns from 3rd Army School. Casualties NIL	MJ Mathew MC

WAR DIARY
or
INTELLIGENCE SUMMARY
(Erase heading not required.)

Army Form C. 2118.

Place	Date	Hour	Summary of Events and Information	Remarks and references to Appendices
DEMNE-BREUCQ	23/9/17		Xmas Day. Divine services. Holy Communion. Casualties Nil	MC
	26/9/17		Bn training. Close order drill, PT, BT, 30x range. Night attacks. 7th day Musketry Course. Fire orders, fire discipline, 30x range. 8th day. L.G. School. mechanism, stoppages, 30x range, stripping. Signallers Snipers Special training. C-in-C arrived H.Q. to 2.7. H.E YES. Congratulations from ARMY, CORPS, DIV, BDE and Bn commanders. Casualties Nil	MC
	27/9/17		Bn training as usual. Musketry School 8th day. Range card. "Bullet Bayonet" assault practice. LG School 9th day. Stripping drill, range, cleaning. Junior Officers L.G. Communication Drill, filling-in to drums. Close order drill. Signallers and Snipers special training. 20 Vs 50 OR on 500x range (C Coy). Casualties Nil.	MC
	28/9/17		Bn training as usual. 10th day L.G. School. "Anti aircraft sight" drill, range, by 60x. "Tactical Employment" went by L.G.O. Competition by L/S to all officers. Snipers special training. Lecture by A/Sgt. to all officers. MCBs "Judging distance and interest on 30x range." 2 offrs 50 OR B Coy on 500x range to be at Caulas during muzzle. TEMP 2 Lts JELHOWATH & WCH 06. Cook Casualties Nil	MC

(Au[18500]) D. D. & L. Robson, E.C. M5787/1325 dr 750,000 5/17 Sch 32 Forms/C 2118/11

WAR DIARY
INTELLIGENCE SUMMARY
(Erase heading not required.)

Army Form C. 2118.

Place	Date	Hour	Summary of Events and Information	Remarks and references to Appendices
DENNE-BROEUCQ	29/12/17		(Restore attacks) Pln. training. 30ʸᵈ range, close order drill, Bayt. fighting musketry. Box resp. drill. Musketry School. revision and exam. L.G. School. revision and exam. Snipers regulates - special training. 2LT. H.E.E. MILLER to L.G. School. GHQ 27.12.17. — 2LT. IN HORNBY to ENGLAND 7/31/12/17. 2LT. F. BURNIE to ENGLAND 29/12/17 to 3/1/18. Casualties NIL	MG
	30/12/17		Divine service. Lecture by Capt. to all officers NCOs. & senior gunners. "The tactical handling of L.G's in attack". Casualties NIL	MG
	31/12/17		Pln. training. Athonal. Musketry school. Revision exam. L.G. School. 3ʳᵈ course 1st day. Athletic description, stripping mechanism aille. Snipers regulates special training. Lecture by Capt. to all officers NCOs & senior gunners "Tactical handling of L.G's in defence". 2LT. A.H.G. RAE is struck off strength of unit while serving with 164 T.M.B.(Auth. 16ᵗʰ Inf. Bde. AQ/5920 d/29/12/17. Casualties NIL	MG

J Booth
Lieut Colonel.
Comdg. 1/8 (Irish) K.L.R.

War Diary
of the
1/8th Liverpool R
for the period
1st to 31st January
1918 only

1/2 Bn (Prov) King's Liverpool Regt.

Army Form C. 2118.

WAR DIARY
or
INTELLIGENCE SUMMARY.
(Erase heading not required.)

Sheet 1.

SECRET

Place	Date	Hour	Summary of Events and Information	Remarks and references to Appendices
DENNEBROEUCQ	1/1/18		Training – Training area in and around DENNEBROEUCQ.	O/C
	2/1/18		Musketry – Firing on 30 yd range. 3rd Army (4th Bn.) Lewis Gun School commenced (course in all Lewis Gunners in the Bn.)	O/C Casualties nil –
	3/1/18		Training – Musketry – Firing on 30 yd range. Bathing of men at 30th in BOMY.	O/C Casualties nil –
	4/1/18		Training – Platoon and Company drill movements. Inspection of Bn. by Commanding Officer.	O/C Casualties nil –
	5/1/18		Training – Platoon and Company drill movements. Football and games during afternoon. Church Parade – Inspection of Men by Coy. Officers before moving.	O/C Casualties nil –
	6/1/18		Training – Musketry – Firing on range at RECKLINGHEM. Rallying of men (at COYECQUES in two coys "B" and "C").	O/C Casualties nil –
	7/1/18		Training – Musketry – Firing on range at RECKLINGHEM. Rallying of men (at COYECQUES) (for two coys "A" and "D").	O/C Casualties nil –
	8/1/18		Training – Musketry – practice in bolt manipulation, use of ground and cover. Trench to trench attack.	O/C Casualties nil –
	9/1/18		Training – Company and Platoon schemes.	O/C Casualties nil –
	10/1/18		Training – Musketry – Firing on range at RECKLINGHEM. The undermentioned NCOs and men awarded the Military Medal.	O/C Casualties nil –

305339 Corporal MARSDEN, H.
305686 Corporal WEBB, G.
308155 Private ROME, J. T.

1/8 Bn (Irish) KING'S LIVERPOOL REGT. WAR DIARY or INTELLIGENCE SUMMARY.

Army Form C. 2118.

Sheet II.

SECRET

Place	Date	Hour	Summary of Events and Information	Remarks and references to Appendices
DENNEBROUQ	11/1/18		Training - Musketry - firing on range at RECKLINGHEM ("C" Coy). Platoon and company schemes. Casualties nil.	O/C
	12/1/18		Church Parade - 2/Lt SIMPSON, Transport officer, on leave to England.	O/C
	13/1/18		Training by companies. Physical training and bayonet fighting. Recruits trained in use of gas respirators. Casualties nil.	O/C
	14/1/18		Training - Musketry - firing on range at RECKLINGHEM for "D" & "A" "B" "C" Coys, firing on 30ˣ range. Casualties nil.	O/C
	15/1/18		Training - Tactical scheme in co-operation of platoon and coy in attack and defence. Casualties nil.	O/C
	16/1/18		Training - Musketry - Rapid fire practice. "B" "C" Coys firing on range at RECKLINGHEM for "D" Coy "A" Coys, firing on range 30ˣ? training - Introduction of a Bayonet final assault course in woods. Casualties nil.	O/C
DENNEBROUQ	17/1/18		Training - Musketry - firing on 30ˣ range. Route march by companies. Casualties nil.	O/C
	18/1/18		Training - Bn paraded for inspection by the 1st Army Commander General SIR H.S. HORNE. General inspected the battalion, afterwards expressing his opinion of the very high standard of efficiency attained by 1st and 2nd Bde Army troops Bn. Casualties nil.	O/C
	19/1/18		Church Parade - Inspection by company comdrs of kit. Casualties nil. Before moving off.	O/C
	20/1/18		Training - Close order drill, platoon and coy formations. Musketry - firing on 30ˣ range, by companies. Casualties nil.	O/C

1/8th Bn (Irish) King's Liverpool Regt.

Army Form C. 2118.

Sheet III.

WAR DIARY
or
INTELLIGENCE SUMMARY

SECRET

Place	Date	Hour	Summary of Events and Information	Remarks and references to Appendices
DENNEBROUQ	21/1/18		Training – Musketry, firing on 30' range by companies. Practice movements in advance guard formation. – Casualties nil.	O.C.
	22/1/18		Training – Bn route march. Musketry firing on 30' range by companies. – Casualties nil.	O.C.
	23/1/18		Training – Bn exercise in advance guard scheme. – Casualties nil.	O.C.
	24/1/18		Capt. JONES J.F. M.C. leave to England. Training – Musketry – Bigger passing, upon fire practice, firing on 30" ranges by companies. – Casualties nil.	O.C.
	25/1/18		Training – firing on range at RECKLINGHEM to "A" Coy. Word – construction of the bayonet final assault scheme. LT. ROBINSON, Signalling Officer, to Hospital sick – Casualties nil.	O.C.
	26/1/18		Training – Musketry – firing on range at RECKLINGHEM to "B" Coy. Firing on 30" ranges for "A," "C," and "D" companies. – Casualties nil.	O.C.
	27/1/18		Training – Musketry – firing on 30' range – practice in platoon formation. – Casualties nil.	O.C.
	28/1/18		Church Parade – Inspection of coys before moving.	O.C.
	29/1/18		Move – received final intimation of Bn being amalgamated. Unit 2/5 Bn (Irish) KING'S LIVERPOOL REGT. – Casualties nil. Battalion dinner in billets at COYECQUES.	O.C.
	30/1/18		Address by Maj. General Commanding 55th Division, re departure of Bn from 55 Bn. 10 Officers, majority of Rest leave for other units, advanced troops leaving by 16.40. Bn Commander, also Officer Commanding Bn. – Casualties nil.	O.C.

1/8th Bn. (Irish) KINGS LIVERPOOL REGT. **WAR DIARY** Army Form C. 2118.

Sheet IV.

SECRET

INTELLIGENCE SUMMARY

Place	Date	Hour	Summary of Events and Information	Remarks and references to Appendices
DENNEBROUQ	31/1/18		Move:- Remainder of Bn. (200 men 12 officers) leave DENNEBROUQ by two trains for to join the 2/8th Bn. (Irish) KINGS LIVERPOOL REGT. (57th Division) at WATERLAND CAMP near PONT NIEPPE. Left DENNEBROUQ 11.30 A.M. Arrived WATERLAND CAMP 4.0 P.M. Casualties nil.	

C. J. Tooth
Lieut. Colonel,
Commanding
1/8th Bn (Irish) Kings Liverpool Regt.

A.B.C.D. Hq Coys.   B.O.O. 1
    O.C.   File
    T.O.   War Diary
   H.Q. Dep Btn.
Batt on Right
   "   on Left

    The Battalion will be
relieved tonight 1st November 1917 by
a Unit of the 64th Brigade. On relief
Coys will move to Billets at Villers
Faucon.

    The route will be via the
Peziere — Epehy, and Epehy —
St Emilie Roads.

    Platoons will march at
100 yards distance.

    Particulars of dispositions
will be handed over in detail to
relieving Unit by OC Coys and
the fullest possible information
will be given with respect to fields
of fire and observation of advanced
posts, and all Intelligence with
respect to Enemy dispositions.

    One guide per platoon
and one guide per strong post will
report to Batt Hdqrs and take them
to posts.

    Coy S.M. Syts will proceed

1/8th (Irish) Bn K.L.R.
Operation Order
No. A   6/12/17

Secret

(1) The Battalion will parade at 2.30pm today and proceed by march route to LONGAVESNES. The head of the column will be at the Cross Roads 62 c N.E. E.25.c.10.y.5. facing South and clear of the road, in parties of 25 at 10x entrance ready to entrain at 5pm.

6 Cavalry Corps buses will be provided to convey the Battalion from LONGAVESNES to road junction E. d'PERONNE.

ACKNOWLEDGE

W. Hornby.
Lt. Col.
Issued at 1.3pm 1/8th (Irish) Bn K.L.R.

at Billon Farm Corp and will report
to the Quartermaster on arrival.
They will take over Billets for
their Coys and will arrange for
the preparation of a Hot Supper
for all ranks.

Lewis Gun Limbers will
report to A Coy's Hdqrs at
11.30. till 5.30 when Coys will
arrange to bring their Guns and
magazines on relief.

O.C. Coys will ensure that
all Stores and tools which belong
to the Battn are brought out.

Receipts will be taken
for S.A.A, Bombs, S.O.S. Rockets
and Very Flares handed over
to incoming unit.

Completion of relief will
be reported as quickly as possible
by Codeword "GOOD".

Acknowledge

Capt & Adjt
1/4/17.   1/ Welsh Bn R.F.R

OPERATION ORDER No 124.

1/4th (IRISH) BATT. KING'S (L'POOL REGIMENT, T.F.)

In the Field,
-.1.19.

The Battalion will move from PONCHET to THIL CORPS area to-morrow, 8th inst. Personnel will move by rail from _____. The Battalion will parade in full marching order ready to march off by 12.15 a.m, and will entrain at PONCHET Station commencing at 11.0 a.m.

Time of Departure   12. Noon.
Time of arrival   3.20 p.m.
Destination   THIL ___.

The following transport will proceed to destination:-
3 Travelling Kitchens, 1 Mess Cart, 1 Maltese Cart, 1 Water Cart, and five Chargers.

First and Second line transport (less as above) will proceed by march Route from PONCHET to CHIPILLY-proceed passing the Cross Roads East of QUERRIEU I.13.d.O.O. (of m) at 11.0 a.m.

Unexpended portion of day's rations will be carried by the men. Rations for 9th will be carried on Travelling Kitchens.

Each man will carry the First Blanket, the second blanket will be carried in the Motor Lorry.

Kitbag valaby will be in charge of a convoy of six Motor Lorries proceeding from PONCHET to BLANGY-_____.

W Hornby.
2/Lt & A/Adjt.
1/4th (Irish) Bn. K.L.R.

Issued at 8.30 p.m.

Copies to:-
1. —
2. 164 Inf Bde.
3. 2nd in Command.
4. A Co.
5. B Co.
6. C Co.
7. D Co.
8. Hdqrs Coy.
9. Transport Officer.
10. Quartermaster.
11. File.
12. War Diary.

SECRET.
1/8th (IRISH) BATT. "THE KING'S" (LIVERPOOL REGT).   COPY NO. 14

OPERATION ORDER NO. 135.

Ref: Map LENS LL. 1/100,000.

In the Field.
10/12/17.

(1) The Battalion will move by march route to TINQUES today.

(2) Coys. will parade on the main road ready to march out at 9.15 a.m. in the order,
      H.Qrs.Coy.
      A Coy.
      B "
      C "
      D "

Head of column will be at the Church. 1st and 2nd line transport will march in rear of the Battalion.

(3) Dress - Full Marching Order, for all ranks.

(4) 2/Lt. O.P. CASEY is detailed to reconnoitre the route as Advance Officer and will report at Orderly Room at 8.30 a.m. today.

(5) The Battalion will pass the starting point, Road Junction 300 yards N. of the first E. in LATTRE ST. QUENTIN at 9.35 a.m.   Route - ABESNES LE CONTE - MANIN - TIVINCHY LE NOBLE - PENIN - TINQUES.
Distance to be maintained between Coys. will be 100 yards; between last Coy. and transport, 100 yards.

(6) 2 Lorries are allotted to this Unit for carrying stores etc.

(7) 2/Lt. M.B. JONES and Sergt. SMITH of B Coy. will report at Bde. H.Q. at 10 a.m. as Billeting Party.

A C K N O W L E D G E.

Issued at 3 p.m.
By Runner.
Copies to:-
1. 164 Inf. Bde.
2. C.O.
3. 2nd-in-Command.
4. O.C. H.Q. Coy.
5. Intell. Off.
6. O.C. A Coy.
7.   " B "
8.   " C "
9.   " D "
10. Medical Off.
11. T.O.
12. Q.M.   16.
13. R.S.M.   17.
14. File.   18.
15. War Diary. 19.
              20.

W. Hornby
2/Lt. & A/Adjt.
1/8th (Irish) Battalion K.L.R.

SECRET.   COPY NO. 15

1/8th (IRISH) BATT. "THE KING'S" (L'POOL REGIMENT).

OPERATION ORDER NO. 136.

Ref: Map LENS II. 1/100,000.   In the Field.
                                             10/12/17.

(1) The Battalion will continue the march to the new area to-morrow, 11/12/17.
Coys. will parade on road running N. and S. through TINQUES at 10 a.m. in the following order, head of column at junction of road 300 yds. N. of the Church:-

    H.Q. Coy.
    A   "
    B   "
    C   "
    D   "
    1st and 2nd Line Transport.

(2) DRESS - Full Marching order.

(3) STARTING POINT - Cross Roads ¾ mile due S. of E in MONCHY BRETON.
TIME OF PASSING STARTING POINT - 12.00 p.m. 11/12/17.

(4) ROUTE - CHELERS - STARTING POINT - to VALHUON.

Distances - will be kept as laid down in Operation Order No. 135 d/10/12/17.

(5) Lorries - Two Lorries will be placed at the disposal of this Unit.

A C K N O W L E D G E.

                          2/Lt. & A/Adjt.
                        1/8th (Irish) Batt. K.L.R.

Issued at 11 p.m.
By Runner.
Copies to :-
1. 164 Inf. Bde.
2. C.O.
3. 2nd-in-Command.
4. Adjutant.
5. O.C. H.Q. Coy.
6. "   A Coy.
7. "   B "
8. "   C "
9. "   D "
10. Medical Off.
11. Transport Officer.
12. Q.M.
13. R.S.M.
14. File.
15. War Diary.
16. Intell. Off.
17.
18.

-o-o-o-o-o-o-o-o-o-

SECRET.   COPY NO. 2.
                1/8th (IRISH) BATT. "THE KING'S" (L'POOL REGT).

                        OPERATION ORDER NO. 137.

Ref: Maps LENS 11.   }
     HAZEBROUCK 5A.   } 1/100,000.

                                                In the Field.
                                                11/12/17.

(1) The Battalion will continue the march to the new area
    to-morrow, 12/12/17.
    Coys. will parade on main ST. POL - PERNES ROAD, South of
    VALHUON, facing N.W. Head of column at junction of
    VALHUON - TANGRY ROAD, at 9 a.m.
    The Battalion will parade in the following order:-

                H.Qrs. Coy.
                A Coy.
                B "
                C "
                D "
                1st and 2nd Line Transport.

(2) DRESS - Full Marching Order.

(3) STARTING POINT.   Road junction immediately N.W. of N in
    VALHUON.
    Time of Passing Starting Point - 10 a.m.

    Route - TANGRY - FLEES to LIVOSSART & PAL-FART.

    Distance - 100 yards between Companies and between last Coy.
    and 1st and 2nd line transport.

(4) Lorries will be allotted as per Administrative Instructions.

(5) An Ambulance has been allotted to this Unit for the march.

A C K N O W L E D G E.

                                                W. Hornby.
Issued at 8 p.m.   2/Lt. & A/Adjt.
By Runner.   1/8th (Irish) Batt. K.L.R.
Copies to:-
    1. 164 Inf. Bde.
    2. C.O.
    3. 2nd-in-Command.
    4. Adjutant.
    5. Intell. Off.
    6. O.C., H.Q. Coy.
    7.   "   A   "
    8.   "   B   "
    9.   "   C   "
    10. "   D   "
    11. Medical Off.
    12. Transport Off.
    13. Quartermaster.
    14. R.S.M.
    15. File.
    16. War Diary.
    17.
    18.   -o-o-o-o-

SECRET

COPY NO -

1/8th (IRISH) BATT. "THE KING'S" (L'POOL R.F.T).

OPERATION ORDER NO 138.

Ref: Map HAZEBROUCK 5A.
1/100,000.

In the Field.
12/12/17.

(1) The Battalion will complete the march to the new area to-morrow, 13/12/17.
Coys will parade on LIVOSSART - PALFART ROADS facing S.W. Head of Column at junction of LIVOSSART-HONEN H LI ROAD at 8.45 a.m.
The Battalion will parade in the following order :-

    Headquarters Coy.
    A Coy.
    B Coy.
    C Coy.
    D Coy.
    1st & 2nd Line Transport.

(2) DRESS - Full Marching order.

(3) STARTING POINT. LIVOSSART.
Time of passing Starting point 9.20 a.m.

ROUTE:- LAIRES - BEAUMETZ LES AIRE - RECLINGHEM to DONNEBROEUCQ, and AUDINCTHUN.

Distance as laid down in Operation Order 137.

(4) Two Lorries are allotted to this Unit for the move.

(5) An Ambulance will be allotted and will proceed in rear of the Unit.

ACKNOWLEDGE.

W. Hornby.
2/Lieut & A/Adjt.
1/8th (Irish) Bn. K.L.R.

Issued at 10.0 p.m.
By Runner
Copies to :-
1. 164 Inf Bde.
2. C.O.
3. 2nd in Command.
4. Adjutant.
5. Intelligence Officer.
6. O.C. Hdqrs Coy.
7. O.C. A Coy.
8. O.C. B Coy.
9. O.C. C Coy.
10. O.C. D Coy.
11. Medical Officer.
12. Transport Officer.
13. Quartermaster.
14. R.S.M.
15. File.
16. War Diary.
17.
18.

-:-:-o-o-o-o-o-o-o-o-o-o-

SPECIAL ORDER.

TO ALL RANKS OF THE 1/8th(IRISH) BATTALION "THE KING'S"(LPOOL R).

CHRISTMAS, 1917.

In once again wishing all ranks a very Happy Christmas, I desire most heartily to congratulate the Battalion on its splendid achievements of the year which is now coming to a close.

The fact that we have passed through dangers and difficulties during the year, and have been spared to see its end, together with the knowledge that throughout we have performed our duty well, are alone sufficient to make this season a success.

That the Christmas of 1917 may indeed be a happy one, and that the New Year of 1918 may be for each one of you a Year of Victory, of Happiness, and of Peace, is my most sincere wish.

In these thoughts I desire to include all dear ones at home, particularly those who sorrow for the fallen; the sick and wounded in the Hospitals; the prisoners in the enemy's hands; may their sorrows be soothed, their pains alleviated, their burdens lightened.

[signature]

Lieut.Colonel.,
Commdg.1/8th(Irish)Battalion K.L.R.

In the Field,
24th Dec.1917.

SPECIAL ORDER OF THE DAY,

by

Lieut. Colonel E.C. HEATH, D.S.O.,
Commanding 1/8th(Irish)Batt. "The King's"(Liverpool Regiment).

-o-o-o-o-o-o-o-o-o-o-o-o-o-o-o-o-o-o-o-o-o-o-o-o-o-o-o-o-o-o-o-o-

TO ALL RANKS OF THE 1/8th KING'S LIVERPOOL IRISH.

On this, the first anniversary of my taking over the Command of the "Irish", I wish most warmly to thank all Officers, Warrant Officers, N.C.O's. and Privates, who have served under me during the past twelve months, for the magnificent spirit and the gallant devotion to duty that they have at all times shown; as well as for the generous response and loyal co-operation with which they have backed up my every endeavour to bring the Battalion into the position of pre-eminence that it now holds.

In the year that has rolled by, since the 16th of November, 1916, you have more than upheld the noble fighting traditions of your Regiment – You have added many fresh laurels to the glorious wreath that enciroles and enshrines the name and the spirit of the "Irish".

When I look back upon the work of the last twelve months I am filled with pride and confidence – pride in my "Irish" for their deeds of the past – confidence in them for the future; for I know well that that which we have accomplished together in the past we can do again together in the future.

I now enter upon my second year with you filled with a sure hope for the coming months – and a hope founded on the record of your grand achievements, and built up by a personal knowledge of your sterling worth.

E.C. Heath
Lieut. Colonel.
Comdg. 1/8th(Irish)Batt. K.L.R.

In the Field.
16th Nov: 1917.

-o-o-o-o-o-o-o-o-o-o-o-o-

www.ingramcontent.com/pod-product-compliance
Lightning Source LLC
Chambersburg PA
CBHW080829010526
44112CB00015B/2481